# The Hungarian
# National Museum

# The Hungarian National Museum

Edited by István Fodor
Beatrix Cs. Lengyel

Authors: Eszter Aczél, Piroska Biczó, Katalin Bíróné Sey,
Gizella Cennerné Wilhelmb, István Dienes, Katalin F. Dózsa,
István Fodor, Éva Garam, Eszter F. Gát, István Gedai, Edit Haider,
Vera G. Héri, Tibor Kemenczei, Judit H. Kolba, József Korek,
Tibor Kovács, Júlia Kovalovszki, Katalin Körmöczi, Zsuzsa S. Lovag,
Beatrix Cs. Lengyel, Mihály Nagy, Annamária T. Németh,
Gábor Németh, Nándor Parádi, György Rózsa, Ferenc Temesváry

CORVINA

Title of the original: A Magyar Nemzeti Múzeum, Corvina, 1992

© István Fodor, 1992

Translated by ERVIN DUNAY and ZSUZSA GÁBOR

Colour photographs by KÁROLY SZELÉNYI (Pictures 1–5)
and ANDRÁS DABASI (Pictures 6–155)

Black-and-white photographs by András Dabasi
and Judit Kardos
Photographs for the chapters
on the Museum and its collections:
András Dabasi and Károly Szelényi (p. 7, above)
Cover photograph by András Dabasi
Floor-plans by Péter Gaál

Design: János Lengyel

AUTHORS

*(The numbers refer to the colour plates.)*

Aczél, Eszter 93, 103, 113–114
Biczó, Piroska 63
Bíróné Sey, Katalin 122–126
Cennerné Wilhelmb, Gizella 137, 139, 140, 142–143, 145, 147–149, 152
Dienes, István 43, 47, 48
F. Dózsa, Katalin 81, 83, 86, 89, 94–95, 99, 120–121
Fodor, István (Foreword)
Garam, Éva 31–42
F. Gát, Eszter 87–88, 96, 98, 101
Gedai, István 127–130
Haider, Edit 105, 115, 117–118
G. Héri, Vera 131–135
Kemenczei, Tibor 6–17
H. Kolba, Judit 58–60, 68–71, 77–80
Kovács, Tibor (The Museum and Its Collections)
Korek, József (The Museum and Its Collections)
Kovalovszki, Júlia 61–62, 64–65, 75
Körmöczi, Katalin 90, 97, 100, 107, 109
Cs. Lengyel, Beatrix 116
S. Lovag, Zsuzsa 1–5, 50–52, 55–57
Nagy, Mihály 18–30
T. Németh, Annamária 91–92, 102, 108, 119
Németh, Gábor 104, 106, 112
Parádi, Nándor 53, 66–67, 72–74, 76
Rózsa, György 136, 138, 141, 144, 146, 150–151, 153–155
Temesváry, Ferenc 82, 84–85, 110–111

ISBN 963 13 3751 0

# Table of Contents

# Foreword

The Hungarian National Museum, founded in 1802 by Count Ferenc Széchényi, was the country's first cultural and academic institution in the modern sense of the term. It originated in the ideas of the Enlightenment and was a manifestation of the struggle waged by the Hungarians to revive their language, culture and scholarship. The aim of Széchényi and his associates was to collect all evidence relating to Hungarian history and to evaluate it rigorously and fully, thus enhancing the self-esteem of an awakening nation, and giving it the strength and courage to shape its own destiny. The fine museum building was completed shortly before March 15, 1848, the day the Revolution broke out in Hungary, and soon became the symbol of national sovereignty and bourgeois development. News of the foundation of the National Museum filled the entire nation with enthusiasm. Valuable items connected with Hungarian history were sent by the thousand; these were donated by people from all walks of life, from simple furriers to members of the aristocracy. The Hungarian Parliament also supported the cause, allocating large sums for construction work and new acquisitions.

By the end of the nineteenth century, however, rapid progress in many branches of sciences and scholarship necessitated the establishment of specialized museums, since one building was unable to house the continually growing collections of various kinds. It was at this time that the National Museum branched out into separate museums (for natural history, art, applied art and ethnography), which later on became completely independent institutions. It was also at this time that the collections of the National Museum were narrowed down to include mainly historical objects, although they still displayed considerable variety. The National Museum's collection, which consists of approximately 1,300,000 items, houses the most important relics relating to Hungary and the Hungarian nation. At the same time, some of its collections (for example, the archaeological and the numismatic) strive towards completeness.

Although under very different circumstances and with new goals in view, the Museum still remains faithful to the original ideas of its founders. These may be summed up as follows: the collection and the expert examination of the nation's more important historical relics; the fullest and most up-to-date presentation of Hungarian history; and the strengthening of national pride on the basis of facts. During its nearly two-hundred-year history, the Museum has demonstrated its ability to revive at difficult times. With the help of its exhibitions and printed material, it has always been able to reach its public, and has remained the museum of the nation all along. The Museum's scholarly reputation, carefully sustained through the work of eminent researchers, has lost none of its earlier prestige. In addition, the Hungarian National Museum has continued to be instrumental in shaping Hungarian museology, partly as a result of its senior status, but also because of its efforts to keep abreast with the times. Its exhibitions abroad have done much to promote Hungarian culture, while at the same time emphasizing the European, as well as the uniquely Hungarian, aspects of Hungary's cultural life. Now, as the year 2000 draws near, the Museum's traditional determination to revive after times of difficulty is matched with a task at once noble and uplifting: the depiction, without prejudice, of Hungarian history to a nation which has just recovered its sovereignty.

The selection presented here amounts only to a small part of a huge collection. Nevertheless, I hope that the book will provide a useful overview of the Museum's treasures to readers and visitors alike. No matter how expertly they are conceived, photographs and text always make much less of an impression than a visit; and it is to the intending visitor that this book is dedicated.

ISTVÁN FODOR
*Director-general*

# The Museum and Its Collections

## The Foundation of the Museum (1802–1807)

One can ascribe to the effects of the Enlightenment on society that the demand for public collections increased during the eighteenth century. The Hungarian National Museum, one of the first such public collections in the world, was established in response to such a demand. At this time public collections were established in one of two ways: either by the opening of royal collections to the public or as the result of charitable donations by wealthy middle-class citizens. Since Hungary was incorporated into the Habsburg Monarchy, there was no royal collection to be opened, and the collections belonging to members of the Hungarian aristocracy were either kept in Vienna or were in constant danger of being auctioned off (for example, the collections held by the Vitzai, Hédervári and Marczibányi families).

It was the Hungarian aristocrat Count Ferenc Széchényi (1754–1820) who set himself the goal of founding a museum for the nation. To achieve this objective, he made a conscious effort to impart a definite profile both to his archaeological collection and to his library of books and manuscripts. Széchényi's ancestors had been soldiers and clerics; the family lived in western Hungary and had been raised to the rank of counts in the late seventeenth century. After completing his studies at the Theresianum in Vienna, Széchényi became an assessor at Kőszeg's county court in 1776; he then married Countess Júlia Festetics, the sister of Count György Festetics, the founder of the Helikon Library at Keszthely. As a man involved in public affairs, Széchényi soon found himself confronted with unsolved problems relating to social progress, capitalist development, national sovereignty and independence–or rather, the lack of these. Széchényi used his talents in the service of his country; initially, he played an active role in politics, but after 1786 became involved in assembling a national collection. In the art of librarianship, he could rely on the expert assistance of József Hajnóczy and Márton Kovachich, and in numismatic and archaeological matters he was instructed by István Schönwiesner. Károly Alma advised Széchényi on

Johann Ender:
Portrait of Ferenc Széchényi.
Oil on canvaas

heraldry, and Márton György Kovachich guided him in the study of diplomas. But in the focus of Széchényi's work was the collection, preservation and public display of material related to Hungary. Széchényi's achievements were in fact the consummation of a cultural programme–first outlined by György Bessenyei and later advanced under the leadership of Ferenc Kazinczy–launched in the hope that it would spark off a national revival cultivating the Hungarian language, propagating progressive ideas, and fostering a modern culture. In March 1802 Count Széchényi requested Emperor Francis I to permit him to donate his collection of various Hungarian-related finds and docu-

ments to the nation. At this time the collection, which Széchényi had been putting together with much sacrifice and dedication since early youth, comprised 11,884 documents, 1,150 manuscripts, 142 volumes of maps and engravings and 2,029 armorial bearings. The coin collection consisted of 2,665 different specimens, including 702 gold, 1778 silver and 193 bronze pieces. Francis gave his consent on November 25, 1802–the day regarded as the birthday of the Hungarian National Museum. In the deed of foundation, Palatine Joseph–the Emperor's personal representative in Hungary–was appointed curator of the collection; the latter discharged this duty magnanimously and with meticulous care, thus earning the eternal gratitude of the nation.

The collection, which was originally housed in the Pauline monastery in Pest, opened (although not to the public) on December 10, 1803; its first director was Jakab Ferdinánd Miller (1749–1823), a professor at the Academy of Nagyvárad. During the period of the Napoleonic Wars, the exhibits were moved to safer locations: southeastwards to Temesvár in 1805, and, from there, northwards to Nagyvárad on 1809. On its return to Pest, the collection was given a new home in the central building of the old University; it was in this edifice that the collection was finally opened to the general public, visiting hours being published on July 30, 1811. The eighteen glass cabinets housing the coin collection proved to be the greatest attraction. The catalogue, which was also the first scholarly publication to describe the collection, was written by István Schönwiesner and was published in 1806 under the title *Catalogus Nummorum Hungariae ac Transsilvaniae*. When the Hungarian Diet met in 1807–its first session since the establishment of the collection–, it passed legislation de-

claring the collection a national institution. At the time of its creation, the National Museum was the second such foundation in Europe–and without any royal contribution. This was faithfully expressed in a letter written by the diet of Szabolcs county in 1808: "In our sincere Hungarian hearts we feel inner joy to have found a great patriot who was willing to make immense sacrifices in order to seek out ways of educating our nation, of cultivating our mother tongue, and of discovering the history of our country."

## The Period of Growth, 1807–1847

Palatine Joseph presented the museum's "growth programme" to the Hungarian Diet of 1807; this was described in a study entitled *The Conditions for Managing the Museum Hungaricum*–the national collections–, (Buda, 1807). The central idea of the programme was as follows: "Everything that belongs to national literature (science) should be placed in the building of the National Museum." By this was meant all historical documents, portraits of great Hungarians, archaeological finds, tools, arms, coins, and items of technical interest found on Hungarian soil. The principles laid down in the programme were not supported by the aristocracy, and important collections continued to pass out of the ownership of aristocratic families into foreign hands. The collection was mainly increased as the result of donations from the lesser nobility from the urban middle class and from the intelligentsia. The first donation came from a Pest furrier named Mátyás Kindli. By donating her collection of minerals to the museum, Countess Júlia Festetics foundedthe Natural Sciences Department in 1808.

The Numismatic and Archaeological Department–Széc-

The National Museum in 1847, by Rudolf Alt. Watercolour. Budapest,
Museum of Fine Arts, Department of Drawings, Inv. No.: K. 57. 11.

hényi's collection which actually predated the foundation–became an independent institution in 1814. According to the first catalogue, published

Anton Einsle: Portrait
of the Palatine Joseph

in 1820 under the title *Cimeliotheca Musei Nationalis*, the collection in 1818 consisted of 83 seals, 349 Hungarian archaeological finds and items of treasure, 193 weapons, and 495 Greek and Roman objects–1,100 pieces altogether.

The coin section comprised 12,000 pieces.

In addition to augmenting the collection, Palatine Joseph also set about raising a separate building for the Museum. To this end the Hungarian Diet of 1807 allocated 500,000 forints, at a time when, unfortunately, the currency was rapidly losing its value. Another difficulty was that the plans submitted by József Hild for an edifice to be raised on land donated by Count Antal Grassalkovich were refused building permission because they did not fit into the urban planning scheme. The palatine therefore sold the land, which was situated at the corner of Szép utca, and used the money to buy four acres of manorial land just outside the town wall from Count Antal Batthyány. Situated in Országút utca (today's Múzeum körút), the land was adequate for the requirements, although funds were still needed for the erection of a building. The necessary money, 500,000 forints, was voted by the Hungarian Diet on the very last day of its 1832–1836 session. In addition, a further 125,000 forints were provided

for the purchase of Miklós Jankovich's collection, in such a way that "the burden of this sum is not borne by the tax-paying commoners: it should be distributed among the nobility, with the money being collected solely from them".

When appointing an architect, the palatine's choice fell on Mihály Pollack (1773–1855), the designer of several buildings already put up in and around Pest. His architectural style–the balanced and immediately apparent proportions of Classicism–appealed to the contemporary Hungarian taste. It appears from a number of sources that both the architect and his patron appreciated the responsibility attached to the housing of a national institution possibly for centuries to come. The foundation stone was laid on June 22, 1837, and although the Great Flood of 1838 interrupted the work, by June 1847 the scaffolding had been entirely removed. The building, the largest in Pest at the time, measured 109 metres by 70 metres; its architrave stood at a height of 24 metres above the ground and the edifice boasted 157,600 cubic me-

tres of internal space. When viewed from Múzeum körút, the portico, which is supported by eight columns, is 34 metres wide; the central character on the tympanum is a female personification of Pannonia; to her right, receiving a laurel wreath from Pannonia, is a personification of scholarship and art, to her left and also receiving a laurel is a personification of history and fame. The figure in the right corner symbolizes the river Danube, while the one in the left corner represents the river Dráva.

Even when the Museum building was under construction, its collection was continually increasing. In 1823 Bishop László Pyrker donated 190 paintings, mostly works by Italian and Dutch masters, thus laying the foundations for the Museum's portrait gallery. In a way, the purchase of the Jankovich Collection can be seen as the second foundation of the Museum: the addition of another 6,000 coins, which included 978 gold, 4,897 silver and 55 bronze coins, greatly boosted the existing numismatic section. The Museum's jewelry department, which prior to the purchase of the

Interior. (Murals by Mór Than)

Jankovich Collection consisted of only a few items (for example, a clasp embellished with diamonds, an ebony virginal, a gold pendant once worn by Queen Isabella, and a crucifix which had belonged to Cardinal Tamás Bakócz), was also much augmented. The Jankovich Collection also included 174 weapons, and contained a sword once owned by King Sig-

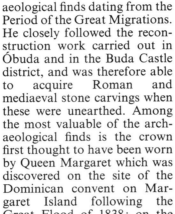

Miklós Jankovich. By Ádám Ehrenreich after a portrait by Tivadar Alkoniere. Copperplate etching. Historical Gallery

ismund, a mace which had belonged to Zsigmond Báthori, György Rákóczi II's chainmail, a sabre used by János Kemény, and an ivory saddle. In the archaeological collection, the most important pieces were those uncovered at Benepuszta. Jankovich was the first to isolate the material relating to the Hungarian conquerors of the Carpathian Basin from among the many and varied arch-

aeological finds dating from the Period of the Great Migrations. He closely followed the reconstruction work carried out in Óbuda and in the Buda Castle district, and was therefore able to acquire Roman and mediaeval stone carvings when these were unearthed. Among the most valuable of the archaeological finds is the crown first thought to have been worn by Queen Margaret which was discovered on the site of the Dominican convent on Margaret Island following the Great Flood of 1838; on the

View of the Entrance Hall

basis of Jankovich's notes and a tombstone discovered nearby, the crown was later identified as the burial crown of King Stephen V. Some of the more recent acquisitions of the gallery deserve mention; besides some foreign masterpieces, these include paintings of historical importance, such as the portrait of Palatine Miklós Esterházy from 1645 and the work showing Ferenc Rákóczi and his wife, by David Richter.

The first exhibition in the new building was opened on March 19, 1846, when the paintings donated by Pyrker were displayed. The next major event was the "Third National Handicrafts Exhibition", which opened on August 11, 1846 under the patronage of Lajos Kossuth; this showed works by 516 craftsmen.

## The Museum During the Revolution and the War of Independence, 1848–49

In the aftermath of the Hungarian revolution of 1848, the new building of the Museum acquired a prominent place in the history of the country. The Museum's ceremonial hall became the debating chamber of

the Upper Table (i.e. House) of the Parliament. Count István Széchenyi, minister of public works and the son of Count Ferenc Széchényi, entrusted the furnishing and decoration of the hall to Miklós Ybl, who was later to achieve fame as an architect. The courtyard of the Museum was used to train new recruits to the army, and it was from this parade-ground that troops were sent to the battlefront. Even in the hardest of times, the Hungarian government was able to look after the collections. At its December 19, 1848 session, the government placed the Museum under the jurisdiction of the Ministry of Education. In his capacity as minister of finance, Lajos Kossuth handed over to the Museum seventy-eight paintings which had formerly adorned the residence of the Lord Treasurer; and in his capacity as chairman of the Defence Committee he ordered the archaeological finds uncovered during the fortification of Buda to be handed over to the Museum. The minister of defence gave the Museum's experts a free hand to select what they wanted from the armoury at Óbuda. After capturing Buda Castle, the Austrian army seized most of the material collected during the War of Independence (flags, arms, seals, etc.). Because of Hungary's defeat in the conflict, nothing became of the plans submitted to the Parliament by Ágoston Kubinyi (1799–1873) concerning improvements to the building and the collections.

The skeletons of King Béla III and his wife, Anne of Antioch, were unearthed in December 1848 by János Érdy at the royal burial ground at Székesfehérvár. (These are the only royal remains to be completely preserved in Hungary.) The acquisition of the jewelry discovered there was registered in the Museum's inventory book in 1848.

During the siege of Buda Castle, the Museum building was hit by a shell, which only damaged the windows. After the Hungarian government's return from Debrecen, the Museum was placed under the supervision of Dániel Irányi, a government commissioner. It was from the courtyard of the Museum that the last contingent of volunteer National Guards left for Arad on July 11, 1849.

## The Period of Absolutism, 1849–1867

On July 19, 1849 Haynau's troops occupied the Museum and turned the building into an army barracks. Lacking all forms of financial support, the Museum was now facing bankruptcy. But eventually the military terror gave way to the Bach administration, with the result that after much petitioning the régime began to display a measure of conciliation. The first sign of this came in 1851, when permission was given for the opening of a portrait gallery in the Museum and for the exhibition there—still under the patronage of Palatine Joseph – of works by Hungarian painters. In the same year the "Exhibition of Hungarian Agricultural Produce" opened on the ground floor of the Museum. On account of the success this enjoyed, a garden pavilion was built in 1852 according to plans by János Wágner; between 1852 and 1860 several fruit and flower exhibitions were held in it. The Museum garden, which on three sides was boarded off using planks, was almost completely barren until 1855, when trees and bushes brought from every county of Hungary were planted there. Hungary's womenfolk collected money for railings to be built around the Museum garden, as well as for garden furniture; concerts were also held for the same purpose. On April 11, 1858 Franz Liszt conducted the first performance of his Esztergom Mass in the ceremonial hall of the Museum. Numerous concerts were given in the Museum by Ferenc Erkel, and Kornélia Hollós also sang in the Museum on several occasions. The railings around the garden were completed in 1862. Hungarian women paid tribute to the Museum's founder, Ferenc Széchényi, by collecting money to furnish one of the ground-floor halls in the north wing of the building with cupboards made of oak and bearing the armorial shields of all sixty-three Hungarian counties. A full-size picture of Ferenc Széchényi, painted by Ender, was hung in this hall, and the bronze statue of Dániel Berzsenyi was erected in the Museum garden in 1860, followed by the unveiling of a statue of Ferenc Kazinczy. (Both sculptures were fashioned by Miklós Vay [1828–1886]). In the meantime, the Museum's collections were growing at a very slow rate. The Archaeological Department gained through the addition of valuable finds recovered during minor excavations, such as those carried out at Hajdúböszörmény (1860) and at Nagybobróc. A unique find was the crown of Monomakhos, recovered at Nyitraivánka in 1860; it was probably made sometime around 1040 or 1050. Another outstanding find was

Detail of the fresco on the ceiling of the stairway (painted by Károly Lotz)

the gold treasure of a German prince recovered at Bakodpuszta and donated to the Museum by József Kunszt, bishop of Kalocsa. The Museum's seal collection was established by decree in 1851; this ordered the towns and the counties to hand over their seals to the Museum. The weapons collection also increased in importance. Hungarian officers who had fought in the War of Independence saved the arms and standards of their regiments by donating them to the Museum. The coin department was augmented through the acquisition of István Growe's valuable collection.

Inside, the building was a pitiful sight. Much of the continually expanding mineral collection was lying in the cellar in complete disarray. This is how the annual report of 1865 described the state of the building: "The entire Archeological Department can be regarded as a place where the nation's archaeological treasures, although being duly preserved, make no impression whatsoever on the nation's scientific development."

## The Dualist Period, 1867–1918

The political "Compromise" of 1867 between Austria and Hungary marked a turning point in the history of the Hungarian National Museum. With the active support of the subsequent ministers of education, all of whom were enlightened men with a European outlook (Baron József Eötvös, Tivadar Pauler, and Ágoston Trefort), the work of the Museum became better organized. It was during this period that the frescoes in the main stairway were completed. Furthermore, it was now that Károly Lotz em-

The National Museum at the End of the Nineteenth Century. Woodcut by Gusztáv Morelli based on a drawing by Lajos Rauscher. Historical Gallery

bellished the ceiling with representations of science, scholarship and art; Mór Than painted the murals depicting the most important events of Hungarian history.

Due to the rapid progress achieved in the different branches of science and scholarship at the end of the nineteenth century, the large all-embracing collections of the Museum no longer satisfied the public's demands; the aim now was the establishment of specialized museums. Thus began the process of the detachment from the Museum of certain departments. In 1871 the Esterházy family sold its collection of paintings to the state, and these works were displayed to the public under the description "National Gallery" in the rooms of the Hungarian Academy of Sciences. Together with the paintings of the National Museum's Department of Painting, these pictures formed the basis of the newly-founded Museum of Fine Arts. The idea to set up a Museum of Applied Arts came from Flóris Rómer (1815–1889), and was inspired by the Paris Exhibition. His plan was realized in 1872 on the initiative of the National Association for Commerce. In the same year, the Museum's ethnographical collection was turned into an independent department through the efforts of János Xantus, a participant in Mihály Zichy's Russian expedition; this event is regarded as laying the foundations for the Ethnographical Museum. With some truth József Hampel described the National Museum at this time as "an altruistic giant pelican feeding its offsprings at the expense of its own health, only to see them leave the nest".

According to a statistical report prepared for the Viennese World Fair of 1872, the Department of Numismatics and Archaeology now possessed 110,000 items, of which 90,000 were coins; the rest consisted of prehistoric finds (4038 items), Roman objects (3087 items), articles from the Period of the Great Migrations (568 items), finds from Egyptian history (378 items), arms and armour (654 items), and certain other pieces (jewelry, ceramic objects, glass objects, textiles and relics –approximately 1000 items altogether).

In 1869 Ferenc Pulszky (1814–1897) was appointed director of the Museum. Pulszky was correctly seen by contemporaries as a latter-day Renaissance man; his political activities, together with his literary and scholarly achievements, constitute an indispensable part of nineteenth-century Hungarian history. Pulszky, Flóris Rómer, and József Hampel (1849–1913) formed a team of archaeologists that contributed greatly to the development of the Department of Archaeology; in fact, archaeology was the most important area of their work. In acknowledgement of their achievements, the seventh International Palaeo-archaeological and Anthropological Congress was held in Budapest in 1876. Nearly 500 scholars and collectors participated in the congress, after which the findings of Hungarian palaeo-archaeological research were published in several volumes. In this way, the findings of Hungarian scholars were laid before the international academic community. Archaeological excavations gradually became the usual way of collecting material; at this time new acquisitions primarily came from Jenő Hillerbrand's prehistoric excavations, Lajos Márton's Bronze Age digs, Bálint Kuzsinszky's Roman Age excavations and the Great Migrations sites excavated by Géza Nagy and Béla Pósta. We should not neglect the generous donations to the Museum at this time: Ferenc Ebenhöch's collection of stone-axes, over 20,000 items; the Ráth Collection comprising Roman bronze items; and the bequest, worth over 250,000 forints, of István Delhaes, a Hungarian collector who died in Vienna in 1901. *Archaeologiai Értesítő* (Archaeological Bulletin), the first journal of archaeology in Hungary (it began publication in 1869), is still edited in the Museum.

The Department of Numismatics, previously limited to the collection of Hungarian pieces, widened its profile by adding Greek and Roman coins to its collection, as well as memorial medals. Numismatics became a separate discipline only in 1898, when László Réthy completed his work *Corpus Nummorum Hungariae*, which is still considered the definitive handbook on the coinage issued by the kings belonging to the House of Árpád dynasty. The department, which was very well financed, attemp- ted to fill the gaps: the Roman Age section was augmented through the acquisition of the Delhaes, Miles and Bitnitz collections. The Delhaes Bequest also contained an outstanding collection of weapons and musical instruments. It was at this time that the Ráth and the Szalay collections were also added to the Museum's material.

As part of the colourful programme of the Millennium Jubilee (in 1896), studies concerning the history of the Hungarian counties were published, in addition to wider-ranging works. To illustrate such publications, a Hungarian Historical Portrait Gallery was established in 1884; this used material from the Széchényi Library, as well as from other public collections: paintings, lithographs, and drawings. Originally it was intended to be an independent institution; its first exhibition was held in the Várbazár. The Hungarian Historical Portrait Gallery gained considerably through the Museum's acquisition of the Delhaes and Ráth collections. But the initial enthusiasm for the Portrait Gallery soon died away as a result of shortage of space; when the institution was merged with the Museum of Fine Arts, its collection passed out of the limelight altogether.

After the Millennium celebrations, Hungarian museology suffered a setback. Nevertheless, excavations continued on several sites, and important finds were added to the Museum's collection. Under the leadership of Elemér Varjú (1873–1944), the collection of mediaeval triptychs and furniture grew appreciably. Additions to the Museum's stock of material included Hungary's first public library, the Bártfa choirstalls, and the triptychs purchased from Upper Hungary (now Slovakia). After the abolition of the guild system, the Museum acquired the country's largest collection of objects relating to the history of guilds. At the same time, the concurrent political, social and economic crisis blocked progress more generally.

## Between the Two World Wars

The privations caused by the First World War, growing inflation, the deterioration of the fabric of its building, and the shortage of space–all conspired to hinder the Museum in its attempts to stage a "new beginning" in the early 1920s. The organizational changes planned during the brief existence of the Republic of Councils and the aim that museums should become open institutions serving to educate the public at large were realized only later, although under different circumstances and partly in a different form. In short, a small budget, a low level of service to the public, more intensive research work, additional workspace, and last but not least, far-reaching organizational changes characterized the National Museum during the interwar period.

During the course of fifteen years, three laws were passed to regulate the operation of museums; the laws passed in 1922 and 1934 respectively dealt specifically with the National Museum. As a result of these laws, the Museum became a corporate body, although its autonomy existed only on paper. The objective was to establish a broad collection looked after by a so-called Museum of Hungarian History. The Department of Archaeology, History and Numismatics–founded in 1926 along with the Historical Gallery and two formerly independent museums, the Museum of Applied Arts and the Ethnographical Museum–joined together to form the institution in 1934. The profile of the new institution was mainly cultural history. The Museum of Hungarian History also formed part of the *Gyűjteményegyetem*, the institution incorporating the most important collections, founded by Count Kunó Klebelsberg, minister of religion and education from 1922 until 1931.

The shortage of space was overcome by utilizing the area beneath the roof, in line with the plans drawn up by Ödön Lechner; these did not involve altering the outside appearance of the building. Improvements were also made with regard to the internal organization of the Museum: the establishment of specialized departments facilitated scholarly classification, storage and processing of the material using up-to-date techniques. The emphasis shifted to thoroughly documented excavation of large settlements and burial-grounds, as well as to the interpretation of the findings

# Floor-plans of the Museum

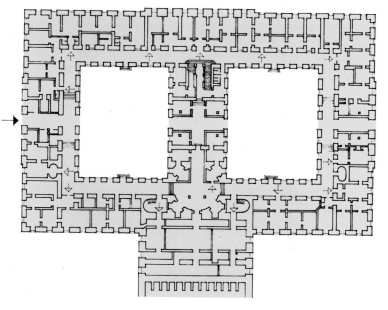

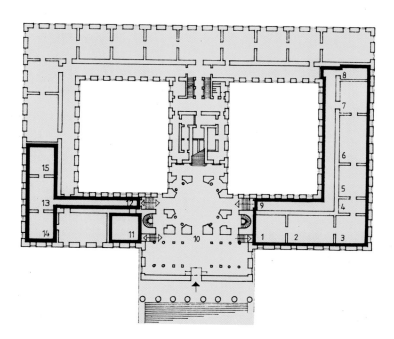

**GROUND FLOOR**

The directors' offices, the collections,
the restoration workshops, and the utility
rooms are located here.

**FIRST FLOOR**

1–9   Archaeological exhibition
10     Entrance—Rotunda
11     Coronation insignia
12–15 Temporary exhibitions

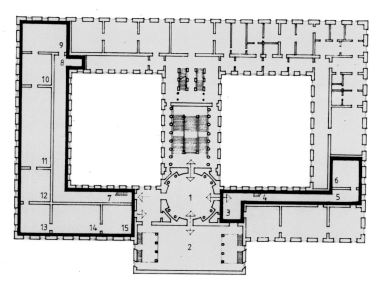

**SECOND FLOOR**

1     Dome Room
2     Banqueting Hall
3–6  Temporary exhibitions of
     the Museum of Natural History
7–15 Historical exhibition

thus gained, taking into account the economic and the social problems of the given time. With regard to approach and methods used, the appraisal of evidence in the context of the original period became more systematic. Studies were published in the Museum's two scholarly journals, *Archaeologia Hungarica* and *Bibliotheca Humanitatis Historica*, established in 1926 and 1936 respectively, with help from private sponsors.

An important episode in the history of the Hungarian National Museum occurred in the early 1930s. Following the collapse of the Austro-Hungarian Monarchy in 1918, the government of the Republic of Austria had declared the entailed collections of the Habsburg family to be the property of the Austrian nation. Paragraph 177 of the Trianon Peace Treaty (signed in 1920) opened the way to the recovery by Hungary of some of the items added to these collections over the centuries, and the Treaty of Venice, signed in 1932, arranged this. Approximately one thousand items from Hungary's national heritage were subsequently brought home, the majority of which are held in the weapons, jewelry, textile, and coin departments, and in the Historical Paintings Gallery. The objects associated with important figures from Hun-

garian history are especially valuable—for example, the medal struck in 1486 to commemorate King Matthias's campaign against Vienna; the ceremonial sword of King Ladislas II, presented to him by the Pope; the armour worn by King Louis II in his childhood; György Rákóczi II's mace, which dates from 1643; and the flag of Ferenc Rákóczi II used in the 1703–1711 War of Liberation.

During a period when in the United States and in large parts of Europe (especially in the Scandinavian countries) museums were placed more and more in the service of the public, the Hungarian National Museum assembled only three permanent exhibitions, in addition to putting on a relatively small number of temporary ones. But it was not so much this as the restrictedness of topics, the historical approach, and the abstract concepts employed that resulted in the National Museum's lagging behind world developments.

JÓZSEF KOREK

## The Recent Past, 1945–1990

The economic hardship which followed the Second World War and the introduction of a new political system in Hungary marked the beginning of a

new and trying era in the life of the National Museum.

During the siege of Budapest, the Museum building and its treasures incurred serious damage. Irreplaceable losses were suffered by the jewelry, wrought iron, and ceramics collections. The funds by which the Museum had been able to finance the acquisition of new objects lost their value during the postwar inflation and were wound up. But despite the unfavourable conditions, the reconstruction of the Museum's interior was completed between 1946 and 1948. By the centenary of the 1848–1849 Revolution and War of Independence, the National Museum had once again become a historic symbol of national progress. As compared to previous periods, the number of visitors showed a marked increase: in a ten-year period approximately ten million people saw the exhibitions, permanent and temporary, put on by the Museum. This number included the one million visitors to the high-standard centenary exhibition.

The Museums Act of 1949, which in many respects complemented previous legislation, launched the structural changes that gradually led to the present structure of the institution. A long-standing deficiency was eliminated by the setting up of a multi-purpose restoration workshop. In 1952, the year the Museum celebrated its 150th

anniversary, the Department of History was divided into two independent units: the Department of Medieval History and the Department of Modern History. (These departments, together with the Department of Archaeology, the Department of Numismatics, and the Historical Picture Gallery, still constitute the basis for the Museum's academic work.) It was also at this time that the institution's various branches assumed their present form. Through the bringing together of the specialist literature associated with the collections, the Central Archaeological Library was established; this went on to become one of the most important archaeological libraries in Central Europe, with more than 110,000 volumes. The basic tasks of the Archive, established specifically for the purpose, is to keep and to classify the documentation relating to archaeological excavations in Hungary, including custody of the collection of manuscripts, photographs and objects to do with the history of museology. In three decades, and sometimes in an atmosphere of fierce argument, the National Museum built up a network of provincial branches on various historical sites in the interest of implementing a unified concept of museology. The King Matthias Museum at Visegrád, the Rákóczi Museum at Sárospatak, and the Kossuth Museum at Monok became part of this network in 1962; the Castle Museum at Esztergom followed suit in 1985, and the Museum of Contemporary History joined in 1990. Thanks to the last addition, the scope of the "parent museum" was extended to cover the history of the peoples inhabiting the territory of modern-day Hungary from prehistoric times right up until the present age.

The progress made in museology and in the various branches of science and scholarship during the second half of the twentieth century necessitated the revision of objectives in the fields not only of acquisition, but also of cataloguing and processing. However, the implementaion of the changes became too closely dependent on the postwar political course, on the forced restructuring of society, and, last but not least, on the country's economic circumstances. The staff of the National Museum managed to avoid the dangers of the sche-

Detail of the permanent exhibition

matic approach to history, as officially encouraged over the years; they also managed to counterbalance the excessive centralization of cultural policy by preserving respect for traditions, professionalism and scientific objectivity.

The use of up-to-date techniques in the excavation and documentation of settlements, cemeteries and buildings has facilitated not only the filling in of earlier gaps, but also the addition of new finds to the Department of Archaeology–finds of intrinsic quality as well as of great scholarly interest. The following excavations have been especially important in this respect: Prehistoric times: Vértesszőlős (Prehistoric settlement); Kisköre-Gát (Stone Age settlement and cemetery); Tiszapolgár-Basatanya (Copper Age cemetery); Tiszalúc-Sarkadpuszta (Copper Age settlement); Tiszafüred-Majoroshalom (Bronze Age cemetery); Poroszló-Aponhát (Bronze Age settlement); Szalacska (Early Iron Age graves); Mátraszőllős (Late Iron Age cemetery). Roman Age: Adony and Solymár (Early Roman camps); Pusztaszabolcs-Felsőcikola (Early Roman graves); Nagytétény (Late Roman camp); Ságvár (Late Roman fortifications). Period of the Great Migrations: Szentendre-Pannónia-telep (Germanic cemetery); and Pilismarót-Basaharc and Halimba-Cseres (Avar cemeteries). The Period of the Hungarian Conquest and Middle Ages: Tiszaeszlár-Basahalom (cemetery from the period of the Hungarian Conquest); Zalavár (Early Mediaeval Slavic centre); Doboz-Hajdúirtás and Tiszalök-Rázompuszta (Early Mediaeval village); Túrkeve-Móric and Sümeg-Sarvaly (Late Mediaeval village).

Of the nationwide archaeological excavations, those investigating prehistoric surface sites, the Roman road system, the fortifications system along the river Danube (the *limes*), and the villages and the areas of jurisdiction of castles from the time of the House of Árpád dynasty are conducted under the direction of the National Museum. The National Museum also directed the excavations conducted before the building of the hydroelectric power plants on the rivers Danube and Tisza; these provided a better archaeological picture of the settlements in the Middle Tisza Region and at the Danube Bend from prehistoric times until the Late Middle Ages.

The adverse historical developments did not permit the free growth of the collections of historical and cultural interest. During the Second World War and in the years that followed, privately-owned art collections diminished greatly: some were destroyed during the siege of Budapest, some were looted by soldiers plundering mansions and manor-houses, and some were taken abroad by their owners. And since the period that followed the war did not favour the growth of private collections, proper dealing in art was unable to flourish, while the general impoverishment of the population reduced the prospects of the museums' gaining through private donations. Acquisition of articles from abroad through purchase or exchange did not occur on a large scale, especially prior to the 1970s. Accordingly, the Museum's attempts to recover some of the earlier losses, and even to complete certain collections, have not always been successful. But in spite of everything, the numismatics, the history, and the art departments of the Museum have acquired some valuable new material, either through purchase, exchange, or donation. Some of the more important of these are: gold coins of Byzantine origin from the period of the Hunnish raids, found at Szikáncs; eleventh-century silver coins, found at Nagytarcsa; a twelfth-century golden cross for wearing on the chest; the seal of Béla IV; the sword of a Bosnian potentate from the fifteenth century; a Turkish appliqué leather cloak from the sixteenth century; the sixteenth-century Renaissance gold and silver treasure found at Tolna; the so-called Odeschalchi choirstalls in the Renaissance style; a portrait of Miklós Zrínyi, the hero of the siege of Szigetvár; Transylvanian silver half-armour made at around the beginning of the seventeenth centuries; an enamelled Transylvanian saddle; a silver-gilt mace decorated with enamel; a seventeenth-century powder-horn made of antler; a fifty-ducat gold coin and backgammon board of Mihály Apafi, prince of Transylvania; the pearl-adorned kerchief of Catherine of Brandenburg; a seventeenth-century trousseau-locker; a carpet which once belonged to Ferenc Rákóczi; the portrait of Ferenc Rákóczi II by Ádám Mányoki; the portrait of Péter Pázmány by György Szelepcsényi; an eighteenth-century chest decorated with figural marquetry; the gala dress from the eighteenth century of a female member of the Kazinczy family; a set of the seventh, sixteenth and nineteenth-century golden jewelry which once belonged on an example of Hungarian gala dress; and a desk and suit of Count István Bethlen. The purchase of the Niklovits collection, with its tens of thousands of coins and medals; the Auer masonic collection; and a ninety-nine year custodianship of the Csákys' portrait gallery (which comprises fifty-one pictures) have benefited the museum greatly.

The number of articles individually registered in the inventory book of the Hungarian National Museum is 1,137,825; the great majority have undergone preservation work, and their condition is monitored continuously, using up-to-date techniques. In the approximately eighty to ninety papers published annually by the Museum's staff, the material is academically assessed. Earlier, the Museum published two yearbooks: *Folia Archaeologica* (1941-) and *Folia Historica* (1972-), as well as the periodicals *Régészeti Füzetek*, Series I. and II. (1955- and 1958). Recently, the Museum launched additional publications: *Dunai Régészeti Közlemények* (1979-); *Évezredek, évszázadok kincsei* (1984-); *A Magyar Nemzeti Múzeum Adattárának Közleményei* (1986-); *Inventaria Praehistorica Hungariae* (1988-); and *A Magyar Nemzeti Múzeum Művelődéstörténeti Kiadványai* (1990-).

In line with its own traditions, the Museum has played an important role in academic life during the past few decades. Its researchers have been involved in several national and international archaeological projects, either as organizers or as active participants. It was during these that the most important scholarly work in the fields of Hungarian numismatics and archaeological zoology was done. Also, by publishing sources, studies and monographs, the National Museum has assumed a growing role in historical and cultural research. The editing of several national journals–*Acta Historiae Hungariae*, *Archaeológiai Értesítő*, *Communicationes Archaeologicae Hungariae*, and *Numizmatikai Közlöny*–is associated with the Museum, which also helps to provide practical courses for those studying archaeology and art history. Some members of the Museum's staff also work as university lecturers, and are involved in the work of national and international academic bodies.

Perhaps the most important development of the past few decades is that the traditional relationship between the Museum and society has changed fundamentally. The continually improving permanent exhibitions, and the frequent temporary shows and associated events attract millions of people with an interest in history. Although not always and not in every respect, museums have become the institutions best suited to pass on the traditions of the Hungarian nation. The National Museum certainly fulfils an important role in this regard: it has mounted an exhibition presenting the history of the peoples who inhabited the land of Hungary before the Hungarian Conquest on three occasions (1950, 1961, and 1977), while the all-embracing exhibition introducing the history of the Hungarian people from the Hungarian Conquest to 1849 has been put on twice (1952 and 1967), renewed each time with regard to text, interpretation, and the exhibits themselves. An important development in the life of the Museum was its acquisition, in 1972, of the Holy Crown and the Coronation Regalia, which had been kept in the United States since the end of the Second World War; these were seen by more than eight million people in the twelve years following their homecoming. The Museum's functions in the field of popular education, performed by way of guided tours, lectures and creative sessions, have been especially appealing to the younger generation; these activities are primarily based on the five to six permanent exhibitions, on those temporary exhibitions taken over from foreign museums, and on the most recent research findings.

Looking back on the Museum's 150-year history, one can justly say that this fine institution has been able to perform its proper functions only when the elements of tradition and renewal could reinforce each other in its activities.

TIBOR KOVÁCS

# The Hungarian Coronation Insignia

This group of precious relics from Hungary's past include the crown and other regalia used during the coronation ceremony. They constitute some of the most important items in the entire history of such artefacts. Since their return from the United States in 1978, the regalia have been exhibited in the "Crown Room" at the Hungarian National Museum.

**1.** The *crown*, the most important symbol of royal power in Hungary, was for centuries the object of almost religious veneration; it was referred to as the "holy" crown as early as the thirteenth century. This great respect partly stemmed from the belief that it had been worn by St. Stephen, the founder of the Hungarian state. Another reason was that the crown was looked upon as the focal point of all royal power; this idea can be traced back to the beginning of the fifteenth century.

The crown was assembled from two parts. The lower part, an almost unaltered Byzantine female crown, is a circular band with pendant chains and ornamental pinnacle decorations. The splendidly balanced elegance of the cloisonné enamel plaques makes it one of the finest products of Byzantium's imperial workshop. On the front in the centre Christ is depicted as the ruler of the world, the Pantocrator enthroned, surrounded by the members of his heavenly court. The other plaques show the Archangel Michael and the Archangel Gabriel; St. George and St. Demetrius, two militant saints of Byzantium and the protectors of the Eastern Church; and Cosmas and Damian, selfless representatives of heavenly medicine. On the central enamel of the back of the crown, indicating the highest place in the hierarchy of the world, is a picture of Michael Ducas (1071–1078), the Byzantine emperor. He is flanked on his right by the emperor Constantine and on his left by Géza I, king of Hungary (1074–1077).

The lower part of the crown is almost the counterpart of the crown which King Géza I is wearing on the enamel plaque. The pendant chains and ornamental pinnacle decorations above the band are, however, different. Pendant chains were generally applied to crowns made for women, so presumably the Hungarian crown had originally belonged to Géza's Byzantine wife.

The upper hemisphere formed by two crossing bands is also decorated with cloisonné enamel plaques which, however, do not originate from Byzantium. In the square centre plaque Christ Enthroned is shown among cypress trees; on each of the four branches are the portraits of two Apostles. Their names are inscribed in Latin letters, and their features differ from those of the figures shown on the lower part. The crossing bands are decorated with rows of pearls, and around the enamel plaques there are alternating gems and filigree frames. The ends of the four branches were cut off, together with the picture of one Apostle on each end, before this piece was removed from another object and applied as a base to the Byzantine crown. Originally it probably formed part of a reliquary or some other kind of liturgical artefact. The two pieces of the crown were mounted in such a way that they could provide a place for a cross. The present cross which, owing to an accident, now leans to one side, is a later replacement of the original one. The original small cross which occupied the same position had probably come down from King Stephen, and probably contained a fragment of the True Cross.

The Byzantine crown was made during the period when all the three emperors shown on the enamel plaques ruled: in other words, between 1074 and 1077. The style of the cloisonné enamel plaques and the pattern of the filigree on the upper section's cross-bands suggest that they originated in the second half of the twelfth century. The two parts were joined after this period but before the end of the thirteenth century.

1. Crown

**2.** The *coronation mantle* was to begin with a bell-shaped, closed chasuble which was later turned into a mantle. According to the embroidered inscription, the chasuble was ordered for, and donated to, the Church of St. Mary in Székesfehérvár by King Stephen and Queen Gisella in 1031: ANNO INCARNACIONIS XPI:MX-XXI:INDICCIONE:XIIII A STEPHANO REGE ET GISLA REGINA CASULA HEC OPERATA ET DATA ECCLESIAE SANCTA MARIANE SITAE IN CIVITATE ALBA.

The chasuble is made of Byzantine rosette patterned silk, and is almost entirely covered with embroidery in golden thread. The back is ornamented with a cross, the arms of which branch upwards. Portraits of angels are embroidered along arms. On the vertical part of the Cross Christ is depicted twice in mandorlas. In the upper picture Christ, who has conquered death, is treading on the asp and basilisk, while in the other he has come enthroned to conduct the Last Judgement. The rest of the decoration is organized into sections. In the upper field below the branching arms of the Cross are the Old Testament Prophets; in the fields below them the Apostles are sitting enthroned beneath ornate arcades. The fields containing the Prophets and the Apostles are separated by a thin band bearing an inscription referring to the above. In the outermost fields are depictions of the early martyrs of the Church on medallions separated from each other by birds. Among the martyrs and on either side of the base of the Cross are pictures of the royal donors: King Stephen is portrayed wearing a crown decorated with precious stones; he has a lance in his right hand and the orb in his left. Gizella is shown presenting a tower-shaped reliquary. Between them, on the Cross itself, is a portrait, in a small frame, of a youth. This is probably the royal couple's son, Imre.

A broad strip has been cut off around the neck of the chasuble, and today only small details can be seen of the scenes framed by squares and mandorlas. On the chasuble the names of the figures and on the frames Latin hexameters are embroidered profusely.

The *Te Deum*, a well-known mediaeval thanksgiving hymn, provided the iconographical inspiration for the mantle: the angels, prophets, apostles and saints are all taken from it.

The chasuble underwent alteration probably around the turn of the twelfth and thirteenth centuries. This was the period when the sleeveless, long, bell-shaped chasuble came into fashion. At around this time a neck-piece was added to the mantle which was made of Byzantine silk embroidered with golden thread. The animal figures and arcading were decorated with pearls. The neck-piece, like the mantle itself, was originally one of the vestments worn by a member of the Church, and was embroidered in the twelfth century.

The first document in which the chasuble is mentioned refers to the coronation ceremony of Andrew III, and reveals that "the king was wearing clothes which used to belong to St. Stephen".

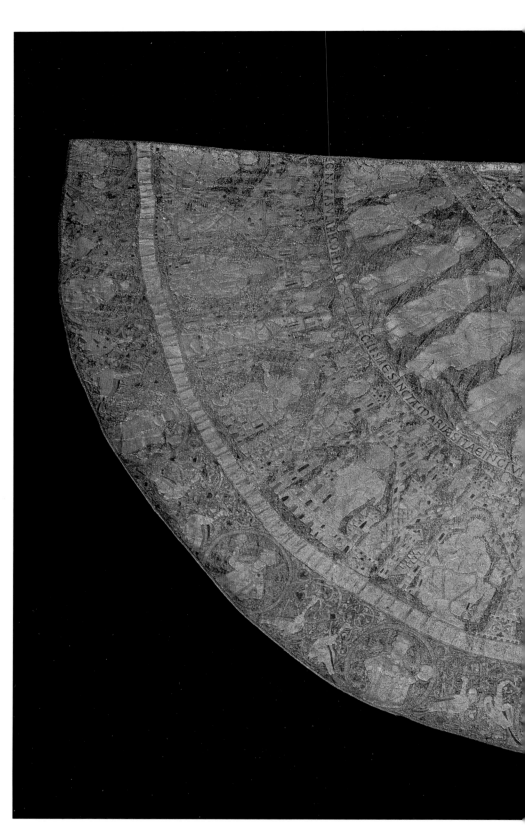

2. Coronation mantle

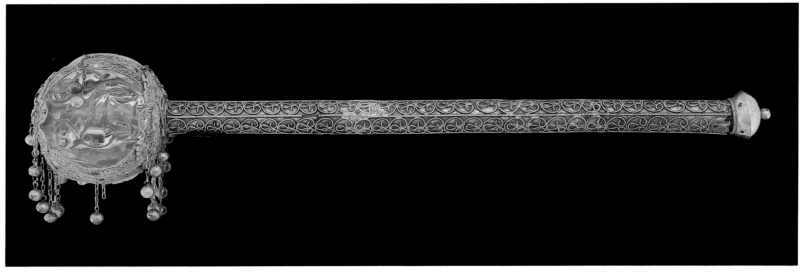

3. Sceptre

**3.** The mace-like shape of the Hungarian sceptre is unusual among European coronation regalia. Its head is a pierced rock-crystal sphere decorated with three lions engraved on one side. The crystal sphere is of Islamic origin; it was made in Egypt at the time of the Fatimid dynasty in the tenth century. Two flower-shaped gold plates covered with extremely fine filigree ornamentation flank the sceptre-head. A magic knot consisting of much-twisted plate-work appears in the centre of the upper rosette. Tiny gold spheres on short, fine chains hang from the edges of the flower-shaped rosettes. The handle of the sceptre is made of wood, and is adorned with gilded silver overlay with filigree ornamentation much simpler and coarser than that decorating the head.

The setting of the crystal sphere, which was originally intended for the end of a cane or a sceptre, was made in Hungary during the last quarter of the twelfth century. The silversmith's workshop which procured it worked in the court of Béla III (1172–1196), and applied filigree work as its most frequent or even sole means of decoration. Other works manufactured in this workshop have also been discovered. Items found in the area of the Basilica at Székesfehérvár, fragments discovered in the tomb of the child-king Ladislas III (d.1205), and an ear-clip unearthed in the Esztergom Royal Palace, which dates from the time of Béla III, are the objects most closely related to the sceptre.

On the basis of ornamentation and the materials used, a close link is discernible between the Hungarian sceptre and a filigree-adorned patriarchal cross standing on a crystal sphere held in the Treasury of Salzburg Cathedral. This cross, which contains a fragment of the True Cross, is ornamented with precious stones, among them a Byzantine gem bearing a portrait of St. Demetrius. The cross was taken to Salzburg by an archbishop who fled from Esztergom at the end of the fifteenth century. According to József Deér's monograph on the Hungarian crown, this cross was formerly the pledge-cross of Hungary's kings.

**4.** The *orb* is a very simple gilded silver sphere with a patriarchal cross cut from a sheet of gold on the top. It has a small shield-shaped enamel blazon plaque on its side depicting the arms of of the House of Árpád (*fascé argent sur gueules*) and of the House of Anjou (*fleur-de-lys-sees*). Accordingly, the orb was presumably made during the reign of the Anjou king Charles I (1308–1342), also known as Charles Robert. It probably substituted for an earlier globe since, according to a document from 1304, the orb was missing from the coronation regalia, which at that time were in the possession of Charles I's rival, Wenceslas.

The peculiarity of the orb is the patriarchal cross. It is very likely that Charles I wanted to refer to the emblem of the House of Árpád, thus emphasizing his right to the Hungarian throne. The fragment from the True Cross was probably first added to the coronation regalia by Béla III, and a patriarchal cross was very often used to contain this kind of relic. On his seal, Béla's son Imre I (1196–1204) is holding an orb surmounted by a patriarchal cross. The patriarchal cross appeared on coins and seals throughout the thirteenth century. Charles I, whose claim to the Hungarian throne was based on his family ties with the Árpad dynasty, wished to continue this tradition by using the orb with the patriarchal cross.

**5.** The *sword*, a Venetian item dating from the sixteenth century, is the most recent piece preserved among the regalia. At the base of the blade and at the rounded top of the hilt the engraved ornamentation consists of plant motifs and male masks. The poor state of the engraving and the fact that sharpening has made the blade shorter indicate that it was used as a weapon and not just as a ceremonial piece. The scabbard was made in the nineteenth century. Unfortunately, we have no information as to why and when this simple sword was included among the coronation regalia. Very probably, it replaced one which had been lost. From the very beginning, a sword had played an important role in the coronation ceremony, and in the twelfth-century tomb of Béla III—the only Hungarian royal tomb to survive intact into modern times—a sword was found among the regalia.

Two weapons are thought to be related to the present coronation sword, and may even have been their predecessors in the role. One is a gold-mounted sabre, the so-called "Charlemagne Sword", held in the Treasury in Vienna. This royal weapon, which dates from the time of the Hungarian Conquest, was kept in the Hungarian royal treasury in the eleventh century, until Salamon's mother gave "Attila the Hun's Sword" to Bavaria's Prince Ottokar (1061–1067), in order to win his support for her son's claim to the throne. The other sword is Norman and dates from the tenth century; the hilt of this second sword is made of carved bone. The fourteenth-century inventory of the treasury of Prague's St. Vitus's Cathedral, where it is kept today, mentions that it belonged to King Stephen.

4. Orb

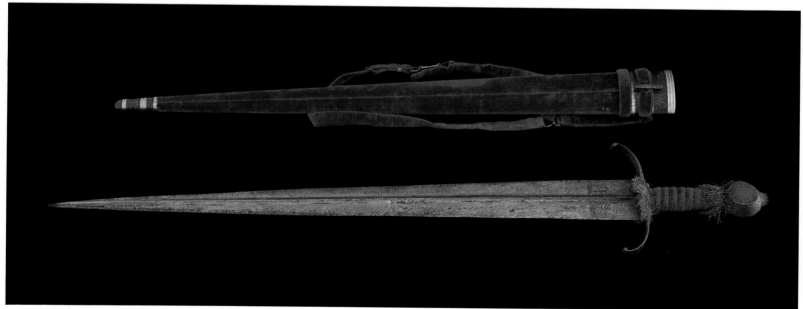

5. Sword

# Department of Archaeology

6. Bowl with pedestal

**7.** Two fine pieces of Copper Age craftsmanship were found in 1952 in Zalaszentgrót-Csáford (Zala county). Fragments of vessels were unearthed which indicate that the golden disk-shaped pectoral dates from the Middle Copper Age (the third millennium B.C.). They may have been hidden in the ground as offerings to a god.

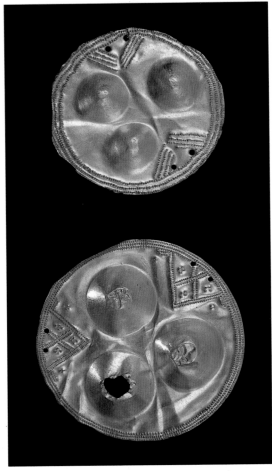

7. Disk-shaped pectoral

**6.** Thousands of years ago, in the Neolithic Age, potters developed a high standard of craftsmanship, as shown by the embossed, painted or plastically ornamented clay vessels of the period. The pottery of Neolithic people living in the river Tisza region—the so-called "Tisza Culture"—represented the best of this tradition. The embossed and engraved ornamentation of the vessels from the fourth millennium follows the patterns used on spun and woven textiles. One of the most beautiful examples, a bowl with a pedestal, was found in Lebő-Alsóhalom, a village near Szeged (Csongrád county), in 1950, during the excavation of a neolithic settlement. It is covered by a pattern of carefully constructed groups of engraved lines which create meander- and spike-shapes and rows of embossed dots. The proportions of the bowl and the high and hollow pedestal together constitute a harmonious and beautiful whole.

The round plates apparently symbolize the female body. The major decorative motifs are the three cone-shaped protrusions. Besides the protrusions the disks are ornamented with engraved geometrical patterns and rows of punched dots running along the edges. They can be hung up using the two holes on each side. On the basis of their ornamentation, we may conclude that they were worn by someone playing an important cultic role during the Copper Age.

20

8. Antropomorphic urns

**8.** Unprecedented evidence of prehistoric art and belief was uncovered during the excavation of a Late Copper Age (second half of the third century B.C.) urn cemetery at Center, adjacent to Ózd (Borsod-Abaúj-Zemplén county). In one of the graves three urns were found which resembled the shape of the human face. One of the urns is open at the top; the other two have covers which recall ornamental head-dress. Ashes had been put into these two urns through an oval opening at the back.

Despite their naiveté, these human-shaped clay urns reflect their function very powerfully: they were made to hold the ashes of human beings, serving as sepulchral statues or monuments.

9. Bell-beaker

**9.** The fine clay bell-beaker was found at Tököl (Pest county) in 1877, when an urn cemetery of a settlement in the vicinity of the Danube Bend at the beginning of the second millennium B.C. was uncovered. These people were named after the product typical of them, bell-shaped clay vessels. The decoration of these clay objects consists of bands which have been left blank which alternate with bands with embossed ornamentation. The pattern on the beaker from Tököl is constructed very harmoniously: in the centre embossed in weaving lines, clusters of vertical lines alternate with clusters of horizontal lines. After the inclusion of the blank lines, the decorated ones are followed on the top and the bottom of the vessel by bands decorated with a motif consisting of diagonal lines. The clay vessels fashioned by the "people of the bell-shaped vessels" are among the most beautiful examples of surviving Bronze Age pottery.

21

10. Bracelet

**10.** The people inhabiting the Hungarian *Alföld* (Great Plain) created a very sophisticated culture during the Middle Copper Age, in the middle of the second millennium B.C. Their craftsmen have bequeathed us many masterpieces, among them this bracelet from the sixteenth century B.C. which was uncovered at Dunavecse (Bács-Kiskun county) in 1972. It is cut from a gold sheet, and its surface is abundantly embellished. The decoration—formed by the combination of encircling ribs hammered into relief from the inside, engraved straight lines, zigzag patterns, star-shaped patterns, and dots punched inward—testifies to the aesthetic sensitivity of the goldsmith who made it. Some elements of these patterns can be traced on other jewelry found in the region of the Tisza river and in Transylvania, proving that goldsmiths achieved a high level of craftsmanship in this area during the Middle Copper Age. The Dunavecse bracelet symbolized the power and wealth of a person playing an important role in the society of the time.

11. Battle axes

**11.** In 1959 the National Museum acquired several masterpieces of the Hungarian Middle Copper Age; these were unearthed at Károlyderék dűlő in Szeghalom (Békés county). These bronze axes were made during the sixteenth century B.C., and they are decorated with finely engraved intertwining spiral lines; triangles constructed of short slashes, curved lines; and rows of dots. The spiral ornamentation is typical of the bronze and gold jewels and weapons found in the mastabas at Mycenae, which during the Middle Copper Age influenced the art of the goldsmiths' workshops in the Carpathian Basin. These workshops were among the most important ones in Europe at the time. Using copper mined in Transylvania and in the region which later became Upper Hungary, they cast splendid bronze weapons and jewelry. The decorated bronze axes from Szeghalom obviously used to belong to a high-born and affluent clan. They were not only weapons but also symbolized the power of their owners.

12. Jewelry

**12.** The treasure uncovered at Besenyszög-Fokorú-puszta (Jász-Nagykun-Szolnok county) in 1877 consists of a diadem made from a gold sheet, four bracelets ending in spiral-disks, two fibulas decorated with pearls, eighteen twirled necklets, four ornamented sheet-disks, four big and five small beads, and fragments of needles and wires. The total weight of the gold objects was 2.5 kilograms. The treasure testifies to the wealth and sophistication of the culture enjoyed by the people living in the *Alföld* (Great Plain) in the eighth century B.C., as well as to their extensive trade with other regions. The repoussé decoration of the golden diadem is typical of the art of the Kimmer People who lived on the steppes north of the Black Sea. The four sheet-disks, which served as ornamentation on reins, and the bracelets also bear traces of the Kimmers' style.

Besides those originating from the eastern steppes, there are some objects in the Fokorú treasure which show the influence of peoples in the Balkans. The sand-clock-shaped needle settings of the fibulas recall the art of the Illyrian-Trachian goldsmiths in the northern part of the Balkan peninsula. The twirled necklets are golden replicas of the bronze necklaces which were in fashion at that time in all regions bordering Eastern Europe. Presumably, the treasure had belonged to one of the leaders of a tribe that had come from the East to live on the *Alföld,* and it was presumably buried in the ground as a result of a war.

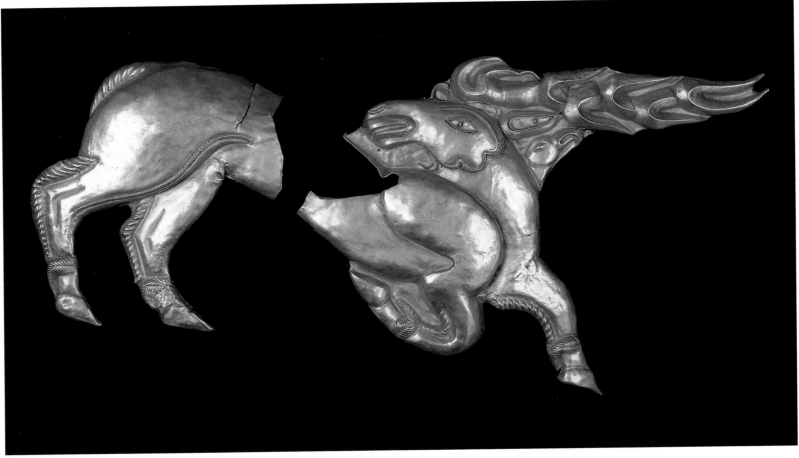

13. Golden stag

**13.** The treasure found at Zöldhalompuszta (Mezőkeresztes, Borsod-Abaúj-Zemplén county) in 1928 consists of a golden stag, a golden chain with lion decorations, 136 hemispherical golden buttons, and a pendant. The excavations revealed that the gold, together with ashes, had been buried in a tumulus.

The embossed figure of the fallen stag is made of gold. Between the horns and the neck the engraved head of a hook-billed bird can be seen. The eyes and the ears consist of small cells filled with light-blue glass paste. Small rings are soldered onto the reverse side, enabling the figure to be suspended. The stag was cut into two by someone who found it, and a triangle-shaped middle segment is missing.

The golden stag from Zöldhalompuszta dates from the sixth century B.C. It originally served as a shield ornament which may have been used by a princely chieftain as a symbol of power; its shape contours reflect the characteristic style of Scythian goldsmiths, who employed stone and bone carving techniques. Similar finds have been made among the remains of the tumuli of Scythian princes in the steppes of southern Russia.

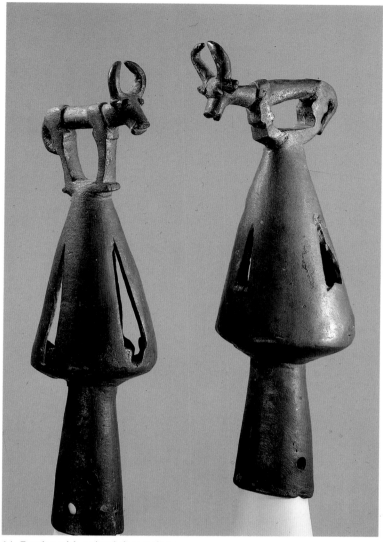

14. Rattles with animal decorations

15. Ornamental plates

**15.** The ornamental silver plates found in Titel along the banks of the Danube were acquired by the National Museum at the end of the last century (today Titel is in Serbia). Since that time, they have been the only objects in the Museum's collection depicting the art of the Early Iron Age goldsmiths in the northwest Balkans. During the fifth and fourth centuries B.C., the Illyrian people developed a kind of geometrical style of decoration on their metal objects. Silver fibulas, pendants, bracelets, and metal plates designed to ornament leather belts were made in this style. On the Titel belt ornaments the repoussé round bosses and finely engraved geometrical patterns create a harmonious impression. Goldsmiths' work of this scale and quality was very rare in the Illyric regions; accordingly, these items must have been worn by a prince or some other high-ranking person in Illyric society.

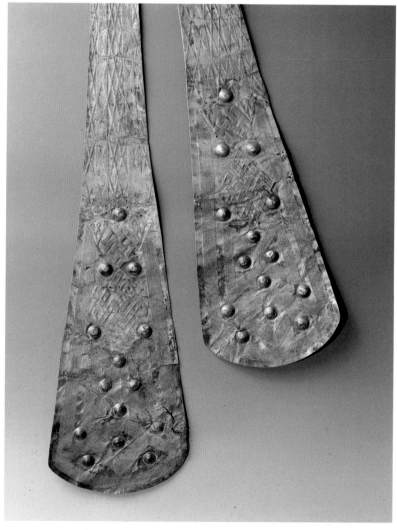

**14.** The inhabitants of the great plains and the mountains east of the river Danube had close ties with the Scythians living to the north of the Black Sea. The eastern origins and links of these inhabitants were manifest in their art and cultic beliefs. The two cast-bronze rattles decorated with animal figures which were found in Nagytarcsa (Pest county) are fine examples of the art of these people. The conical bodies are pierced through with triangular holes, on the top of each is a statue of an ox. The tubular lower part was designed to hold a wooden handle. Small iron balls inside create the appropriate noise when the rattles are shaken.

Bronze rattles decorated with animal figures are characteristic of Eastern Scythian Culture. These animal decorations had spread to East-Central Europe in the course of the Scythian campaigns during the sixth century B.C.

Four iron bits and eight bronze cattle-bells were discovered together with the rattles. When shaken together, the rattles and cattle-bells produce a musical harmony. They were probably used in ceremonies, and were concealed in the ground as offerings to gods or spirits.

16. **Celtic** people migrating from the region of the river Rhone inhabited the Danube Basin during the fourth century B.C. One of the finest examples of the artwork they bequeathed to us is the bronze statuette of a boar uncovered in 1893 at Báta (Tolna county). The figurine is not realistic in its depiction, yet it perfectly expresses the characteristic features of the animal. The strong head, the tusks and protruding ears, the wide expanse along the backbone which symbolizes the bristles, and the animated posture of the body faithfully portray an alert boar which is just about to attack. The figurine is decorated with motifs frequently used in Celtic art: spirals, circles, and semi-circles. On the basis of its style, the find can be dated from the second century B.C. Besides its artistic value, the statuette is also very important in that it recalls one of the Celts' cultic beliefs: for the Celts the boar symbolized death. It was depicted in the form of small bronze sculptures, which were often placed in graves as offerings. Because of its suggestive features, the boar discovered in Báta is one of the most significant pieces of Celtic figurative art known to us.

16. Statuette of a boar

17. Gold spheres decorated with masks

17. At the end of the nineteenth century, the National Museum purchased a unique jewelry find; this came to light in 1890, in the swampy flats of the river Kapos, between Szárazd and Regöly (Tolna county). Among the items of jewelry there were gold spheres hammered out of gold foil, and cone-frustum and wheel-shaped pendants. Artistically, the spheres decorated with masks are artistically the most precious pieces in the treasure; the goldsmith had done an excellent job: he had hammered four human faces and four conical bosses into relief from hemispherically shaped sheet gold. Wires twisted into spirals, small spheres, and braided wires were applied to the surfaces between the masks. The two hemispheres are joined together by a ribbed band. The filigree work and the granulation were techniques learned from Greek, Illyrian and Etruscan goldsmiths. The human masks on the spheres are again characteristic features of Celtic art. This jewelry was made by the Celtic workshop operating in southern Transdanubia, and was buried in the first century B.C.

18. Pitcher and patera

**18.** The bronze pitcher and patera form part of the so-called "Egyed Treasure", which was discovered on the Sopron county estate of Count Vince Festetics in 1831. The pitcher was donated to the National Museum by Count Festetics, and the patera was given to the collection by Veszprém county. The handle of the pitcher is missing. The rim of the opening is decorated with a band bearing a pattern of oval shapes. Golden bunches of grapes, silver vines and grape-leaves are inlaid around the pitcher's neck. Below the neck are sixteen Egyptian head-dresses; below these is a band bearing double spiral ornamentation. On the sides of the pitcher figures of eight Egyptian gods are depicted. Below these portraits is a row of bay-leaves and alternating lotus and palmette patterns. At the bottom the pitcher is decorated with a line of palmette bunches.

The rim of the patera is also embellished with a line of oval shapes. Below the inner rim a band consisting of bay-leaf wreathes and a wider band can be seen depicting foliage and bunches of flowers. On the middle of the patera, encircled by a wreath of oak leaves, is an engraved scene of the river Nile: a hippopotamus fighting with crocodiles. The handle of the patera is decorated with a pattern of densely woven leaves.

The two vessels bear the characteristic marks of the Alexandrian Hellenistic style of goldsmiths' work during the early years of the Roman empire. These pieces of the "Egyed Treasure" must have belonged among the cultic objects of a shrine to Isis in northwestern Pannonia.

27

**19.** These two objects were used in the ceremonies connected to the cult of Jupiter Dolichenus, a mystic religion popular mainly among soldiers. They were found in 1815 at Bottyánsánc in Kömlőd (Tolna county). The triangle consists of two embossed triangular bronze sheets plated with gilded silver. They were carried around on tall poles during the ceremony. The inscribed triangle contains four zones. At the top the ornamentation consists of foliage; below Sol, the god of the Sun; and Luna, the goddess of the Moon are depicted. In the main zone, Jupiter Dolichenus is represented wearing a breast plate and standing on the back of a bull; he holds thunderbolts in his left hand and a double-headed axe in his right hand. To the right of Jupiter, Victoria has just descended; she is offering the king of the gods a wreath symbolizing victory. In front of the bull stands a round altar which is ablaze. The half-length portrait of Minerva is in the right-hand corner; in the left-hand corner is another such portrait of Hercules holding his club. The bull stands on a low base which bears an inscription revealing that the cultic objects were donated by P. Aelius Lucilius, a centurion serving with the 1st Mounted Alpine Cohort.

On the reverse plate, five zones are to be found. These contain a foliage motif, half-length portraits of Sol and Luna, Jupiter Dolichenus standing on the back of a bull, and Juno standing on a goat on the two sides of a blazing round altar, and, on the bottom, Jupiter Dolichenus standing in the sanctuary.

Similar cultic accessories have been found elsewhere in regions which used to be border provinces of the Roman empire, regions where a great number of soldiers were stationed. These objects were probably made during the second half of the second century A.D. and during the third century A.D.

**20.** The fired clay model of a gateway was discovered at Dunapentele, the ancient Intercisa in Fejér county. Many examples of clay towers with reticulated doors and windows are known in Pannonia and in other former provinces of the Roman empire: they were used as "lighting towers" placed over light sources. With the help of this gateway model, which was made at around the beginning of the third century, we can obtain some idea of the kind of gateways Roman towns and fortresses had. The triple-arched gateway stands between two towers; above it is an engraved inscription. The third storey has four windows beneath rounded arches, above which there remains a fragment of the helm roof. The inscription says: (H)ILARUS FEC(IT) PORTA(M) FEL(ICITER), which means, Hilarus made this gateway with pleasure.

20. Model of a gateway

21. Veriuca's tombstone

The body of the child Bacchus is covered only with an animal skin knotted above his right shoulder. The attire consists of a of dog's skin instead of the usual deerskin. The child's thick curly locks are held down by a wreath woven from grapevine. With his left hand, the child Bacchus has raised part of the dogskin, and is carrying, five apples in it. In his right hand, which is now missing he was probably holding a bunch of grapes. The weight of the body is on the right leg; the left heel is raised a little—as if though the figure is about to take a step forward. This statue has many features in common with Roman triumphal personifications of autumn. This masterpiece was produced a workshop in one of the Eastern provinces at around the end of the second century or beginning of the third century; it was brought to Pannonia by traders.

22. Ivory statuette

**21.** This tombstone was found by chance during the excavations in Dunapentele at the beginning of the twentieth century; it was discovered in János Szórád's vineyard. The top of the original pinnacle was removed when the stone was used for the second time over. The mason framed the relief with pillars; within the field of the relief a half-length image of the deceased was placed in an arched niche. Rosettes and acanthus leaves fill the space between the niche and the pillars. The deceased woman is depicted in native attire; she holds a spindle in her right hand and a type of distaff in her left. Her loose dress is fastened at the shoulders with two winged fibulas; her long kerchief falls down freely below her shoulders and she wears a bulla on her neck. Originally, the representation was probably painted. Framed by a plain lath, the inscription reads as follows: "Here rests Veriuca, aged thirty, daughter of Danuvius. The tombstone was erected in memory of the most pious wife of Florus, son of Egretarius."

Based on the comparison with the tombstones of Aquincum and Intercisa, we may safely conclude that Veriuca's tomb was erected around the beginning of the second century A.D.

**22.** This relatively large, finely carved ivory statue is an outstanding example of Pannonian ivory sculpture. It was discovered during the reconstruction of Szombathely's Savaria Restaurant at the end of the nineteenth century.

23. Cultic insignia

**24.** This fragment of clothing was found in the fourth- and fifth-century cemetery at Moesia superior provincia Viminacium (today called Kosztolác). Small golden ear-rings, a ring and a jasper intaglio were also discovered in the Late Roman grave. The finds were purchased by the National Museum at the end of the nineteenth century. Against a floral background, Victoria can be seen holding a palm branch in her left hand. The figure of the goddess is framed by a mandorla. The material is woven of a thin thread entwined with gold.

24. Gold textile

**23.** All that is certain about this much-discussed small, flat, silver shaft—initially considered to have belonged to an augur, but later regarded as having been used by a bishop–is that it possessed some cultic function. It was discovered in a tomb in the small graveyard between the camp and the soldiers' settlement at Szőny, known as Brigeto in Roman times.

The cross-section of the shaft is rectangular. Its tapered end coils inwards to form a spiral shape. Two of its sides are decorated: on one, between two gold-plated, four-lobe rosettes, niello and gold-plated meandering ivy is engraved in a variegated niello surround. On the other side, also set in a variegated niello surround, are three equidistant four-leaf, gold-plated rosettes; palm-leaf motifs and trailing ivy fill the space between the rosettes. Seen in cross-section, the handle is rectangular; it ends in a hemisphere. Based on parallel finds and on the other objects in the grave, it may be concluded that the shaft was made either at the end of the third century A.D. or at the beginning of the fourth.

**25.** This small, gilded bronze bust was acquired by the National Museum from a private collector in Pécs in the early years of the twentieth century.

The bust is framed by a laurel wreath. A thick cloak covers the torso, leaving exposed only the right upper arm and a part of the neck. The cloak is fastened by a large, square fibula decorated in the corners with spheres. This type of fibula is well-known from Late Roman depictions of emperors. At the front, the carefully combed hair of the man almost reaches his eye-brows; it leaves the ears free and covers the back of the head. A diadem on his head consists of a double row of beading embellished with a jewel set in a square mounting and worn in the middle of the forehead.

The original purpose for which the bust was intended has not yet been established. Presumably, it would have been fastened onto a large metal object—for example, an ornate dish, a military standard, or an engraved bronze tablet proclaiming an imperial exploit or grant. Experts had earlier identified the bust as depicting the emperor Constans (337–350); later it was thought to have shown Valentinian II (375–392). The bust was probably made in the middle or the second half of the fourth century.

25. Bust of an emperor

26. Fragment of a table top

**26.** This remnant of a table-top was discovered at Kőkoporsó dűlő in Csopak, where another similar fragment of a table had earlier been found. Both belong to a style of find rarely seen. On the edge a detail of an event is visible: a naked archer dressed in khalamys is chasing a lion. The table-top deepens like a bowl; a band of astragalos runs along the inside edge. According to Edith B. Thomas, an expert on early Christian archaeology, carved bowl-like marble tables played an important part in the ceremonies of Eastern Christianity. Their appearance in Pannonia was certainly connected with Arianism, the most significant heresy of the period.

**27.** In the middle of the nineteenth century, Henrik Drasche, owner of the brickworks at Dunaújlak, bequeathed to the Museum the finds discovered in a Late Roman grave on the site of the factory. The set of silver belt ornaments was also unearthed there. The mounts are decorated with geometrical patterns made with gold plating and niello. The Greek cross enclosed in a circle and set against a golden background appears on three of these objects: the set of ornaments, therefore, is classified among the finds relating to early Christianity in Pannonia.

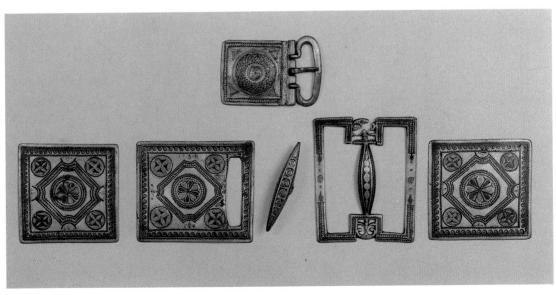

27. Belt ornaments

**28.** Gold foil decoration (*fondo d'oro*) sealed into double bottomed glass bowls is a rare find in archaeology. Such a bowl was discovered in a Late Roman grave at Dunaszekcső (Baranya county) and now is in the possession of the National Museum: a portrait of an elegantly dressed couple has been cut from golden foil and placed between the two bottoms of the glass goblet. The woman on the left is wearing a kerchief on her head which allows her curled hair to be seen. She is wearing a string of small beads on her neck, and a tunic with a wide, elaborate collar underneath a palla. The shaven face of the man, whose hair is short, has a powerful expression. Above his embroidered, long-sleeved tunic his paludament is held together at his right shoulder with a fibula shaped like an onion. Judging from his clothing, the man was probably a high-ranking soldier or an official at the imperial court. Above the heads of the couple there is an inscription: SEMPER GAUDEAT(IS) IN NOMINE DEI, indicating that St Paul's Epistle to the Philippians was known to the creator of the *fondo d'oro*. It may be presumed that this glass bowl or plate, which was probably commissioned to mark a wedding or wedding anniversary, was made in Rome at the end of the fourth century A.D.

28. Fondo d'oro

29. Cage cup

**29.** This glass goblet, together with other finds, was uncovered at Szekszárd in the middle of the nineteenth century. The sarcophagus in which it was found had been used for a second time at the beginning of the fourth century A.D. (The sarcophagus can be seen on black-and-white photograph No. 63.) The goblet is semi-spherical in shape; its rim juts out slightly. The Greek inscription on the side says: "Offer sacrifice to the Shepherd, drink, you shall live!" The inscription stands above small supports; underneath these there is a reticulated collar. Three fishes and three snails are represented on the bottom of the goblet. Many of lattice ornamented and reticulated glass goblets and iron diatrets were made using a special technique in the Late Roman period in what is now Cologne. The delicate, reticulated inscriptions and lattice ornamentation were ground or pierced into the surface. In other cases the decorations were prepared first, and were then attached to the surface of the goblet. The fishes and snails were made by blowing and were welded onto the bottom using melted glass.

The iron diatret discovered at Szekszárd was probably made at the beginning of the fourth century A.D. by an as-yet-unidentified, but technically very advanced, workshop.

30. Helmet

**30.** This commanding officer's helmet was unearthed in July 1898 at Eskü (today Március 15) tér in Budapest when the foundations for the Elizabeth Bridge were being prepared. This site is very close to the place where the Late Roman fort of Contra Aquincum was located.

The surface of the iron helmet was covered with a sheet of gold-plated silver, onto which small embossed motifs, together with square and oval glass-paste ornaments imitating semiprecious stones, were fastened. The top of the helmet was surmounted by a crest, which is now missing. One of the face-protecting plates is also missing, and the nose-protector (which originally would have been pointed) has broken off. The face-protecting plate on the right is fastened to the edge of the helmet by hinges. The section above the edge divides into two horizontal zones. In the top zone glass-paste ornamentations can be seen, together with the embossed lions and god, on the bottom a few letters of a longer inscription are visible.

Beside the decorative motifs known from Roman art, some ornamental elements of the helmet recall the goldsmiths' art of the free Germans. In various border provinces of the Roman empire analogous helmets have been found. The helmet from Eskü tér was probably made in one of the large weapons manufacturing workshops in Pannonia.

34

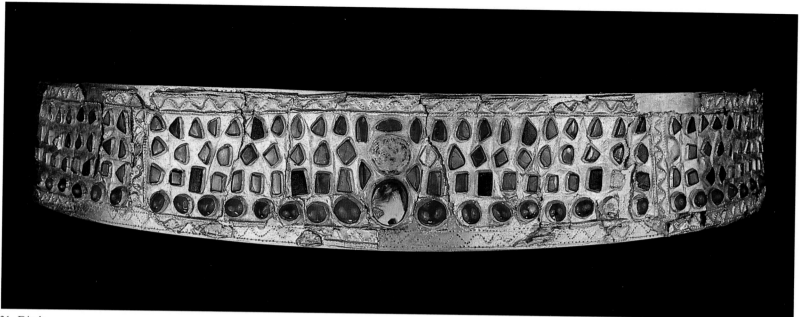

31. Diadem

**31.** The least damaged diadem from the age of the Huns known in the Carpathian Basin was discovered in a grave at Csorna (Győr-Moson-Sopron county) in 1887. It was acquired by the National Museum in 1950. (The other finds in the grave have been lost.) The long, thin, rectangular gold plate, which narrows slightly towards the ends, was originally attached to a piece of bronze sheeting. On the top and bottom edges pressed waving lines run along. One hundred and fifty-eight jewels arranged in four rows decorate its surface, which is divided into three zones (carnelian, granite, amber, green and clear glass). The largest oval-shaped carnelian is in the centre; in each row the shape of the other stones is different.

The Csorna diadem, which would have belonged to an upper-class woman, is characteristic of the Hunnish style which spread from the Caucasian Mountains to southwest Poland. Similar pieces were found in Budapest and Csatár. The last-mentioned can be reconstructed only on the basis of a description, but we know that the Budapest example, after being cut up, was re-used for some purpose before being put into the grave.

On the basis of its style and the technique employed, the Csorna diadem is related to the objects unearthed from the Carpathian Basin's burial places for the most wealthy. The diadem was probably put into the grave during the first third or in the middle part of the fifth century A.D.

32. Pair of bracelets

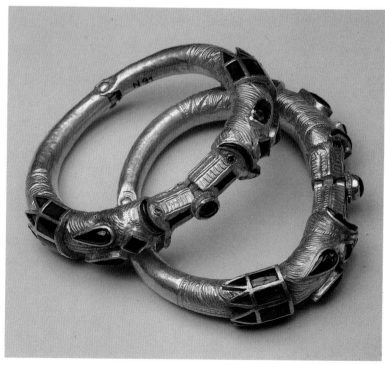

**32.** In 1859 magnificent gold and silver jewelry was discovered in the graves of three women at Bakodpuszta (Bács-Kiskun county), not far from Dunapataj, on the estate of the archbishop of Kalocsa. The archbishop donated the objects to the National Museum in 1860. These included earrings, a buckle, rings, flitters, necklets, fibulas and a pair of bracelets.

The bracelets are decorated with lions' heads facing each other. They open on pivots and lock with screws which turn anti-clockwise. On each of the lions' heads the nose, eyes, eyebrows, ears and mane are outlined in dark red, highly polished almandines set in raised mountings. The bracelets are masterpieces of the goldsmiths's art in the Black Sea region, which preserved Hellenistic traditions. These items are among the most splendid gold masterpieces of their time.

The jewelry found in the Bakodpuszta graves belonged to Germanic women, possibly members of the family of the prince of the Scyrri tribe. On the basis of shape and stylistic features, it may be concluded that the bracelets were made in the first half of the fifth century A.D., but were afterwards in use for a long period of time.

35

33. Buckle

34. Fibula

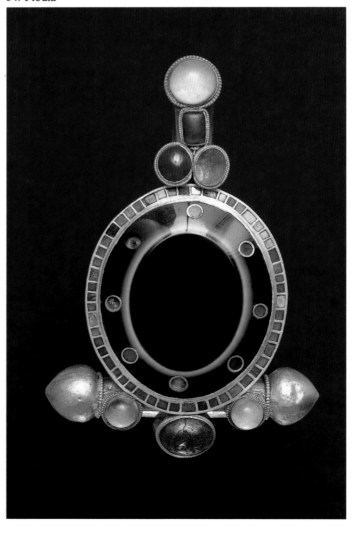

**33.** This large, partly gilded ornate buckle was fashioned from two almost perfectly circular pieces of silver sheeting which were riveted together. The top of the body is framed with stamped and niello decoration. In the centre field, against a hammered background, a grape-leaf motif consisting of four sections is visible. A thick, solid silver oval ring and a solid fastener with embossed and incised triangular decoration are attached to the circular body of the buckle. The reverse side of the buckle is a plain silver sheet; in the centre the name MARING is engraved in runic letters.

The ornate silver buckle, which was probably discovered at Szabadbattyán (Fejér county), was purchased by the National Museum in the early part of the twentieth century. This masterpiece of goldsmiths' work was made in the fifth century A.D.; it was probably in the possession of Eastern Goths. The name MARING is of South Germanic origin.

**34.** This large onyx fibula is a masterpiece of Late Roman goldsmith's art. The oval onyx has three layers; the top layer is of a blackish colour. The onyx is fixed to a massive gold base. On the slanting, chiselled edge of the onyx, rounded and square fragments of granite are set in golden cloisonné work. The fibula imitates the Late Roman onionhead-shaped type. The "head" attached to the oval body of the fibula is elongated; it consists of rock-crystal, green glass and carnelian stones set in deep cloisonné work showing round, oval and rectangular shapes and holding the pin-structure fixed onto the last section. The "leg" which is ornamented with rock-crystal and amber, ends in onion-shaped bulbs. The three ringlets fixed onto the "leg" formerly held the pendants which are now missing.

The onyx fibula belonged among the possessions of a man—a very high-ranking one, maybe even the emperor himself. He may have given it as a gift to one of the princes or kings of the Gepids, who, around the 420s, hid their royal treasury from the attacking Huns. Part of this treasure was discovered in Szilágysomlyó in 1797, and a splendid gold chain, gold medallions and other jewelry are now kept in Vienna's Kunsthistorisches Museum. The other part of the treasure was unearthed in 1889. Besides this Roman onyx fibula, the find contained a Germanic golden pledge-ring, three gold cups, three pairs of pure gold fibulas, and three pairs of gold and silver fibulas ornamented with cloisonné and precious stones. Today, these are among the most valued treasures held in the Hungarian National Museum.

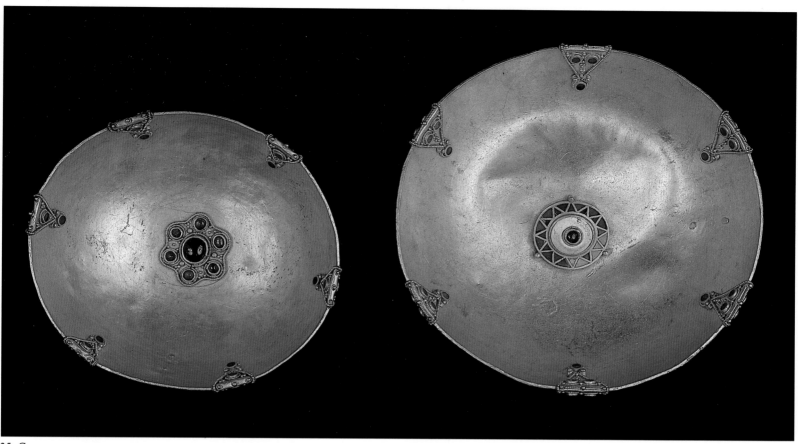

35. Cups

**35.** The semi-spherical pure gold cups are part of the so-called Second Szilágysomlyó Treasure discovered–along with the onyx fibula shown on the previous picture–in 1889. Each cup is ornamented in the centre with a six-lobe rosette and appliqué with almandine and white limestone inlays. Around the rim there are six triangular, granulated ornaments inlaid with almandine. Similar mountings embellished the cups of the period, which are often reconstructed on the basis of such small triangular appliqué additions. The cups could be hung from belts by means of their solid gold handles. The decoration of the two larger cups is similar, but the third cup has decoration of a different type.

36. Vessels

**36.** These vessels, typical products of Gepid pottery in the sixth century A.D., were made from well-sluiced clay using a hand-driven wheel; they were and fired to greyish-black colour. The imperfect vessels—which are sphere-, truncated cone- or pear-shaped—are not very tall. The necks of this type of vessel are usually short and straight; the rims jut out a little, and the bottoms are round. They do not have handles. The decoration consists of strokes and other patterns, or lattice, and various forms and imaginative ensembles of stamped-on motifs. The intact clay vessels are from the Gepid burial sites in the *Alföld* (Great Plain). They were placed next to the dead to hold food and drink because, according to Gepid belief, these were needed in the afterlife. However, it is hard to determine whether these graves contained Christians or followers of ancient Germanic belief, since both placed vessels in their graves.

37. Jug and beaker

**37.** This silver beaker with its cornet-shaped neck and round body, and the silver pitcher with its cornet-shaped neck and oval body belong to the splendid early Avar find uncovered in Kunágota (Békés county). Oblique ribs run around the neck of the beaker and zig-zag ribs embellish its body. The small pitcher is not ornamented, but has a ribbed band running around its mouth; its handle is round.

The noble owner of the above items was buried, together with his horse, on his estate. The two were interred in a single grave around the beginning of the seventh century. His clothing was held together by a belt embellished with golden mountings. The handle and scabbard of his straight double-edged sword

are embellished with Byzantine mountings made of gold. A Byzantine chain with an opal pendant hung around his neck. He wore rings on his fingers; the harness of his horse was decorated with items of pressed silver.

The silver beaker and pitcher belonged among tableware which originated in Central Asia. The two runic marks on the inside of the pitcher's rim either denoted the name of the owner or conveyed information concerning the contents of the vessel. Besides the gold and silver finds, a Byzantine solidus, a coin minted around 565 by the Byzantine emperor Justinianus I (527–565), makes this group of finds really outstanding.

38. Pair of earrings

**38.** Large spherical golden earrings were worn by members of the upper class during the early Avar age; they have been discovered in the graves of both men and women. This fine example of such an earring was, according to the reference data, unearthed in Debrecen; it consists of a round golden ring and a sphere joined to it. This sphere is followed by three smaller ones–with another very large sphere on the end (all component parts are fashioned from gold). The spheres are joined together by small granules, and granules organized into rhomboid shapes embellish the surface of the largest sphere.

Pendants made from gold and silver and incorporating spheres pyramids belong among finds of Asian origin relating to the earliest period of Avar settlement in the territory of present-day Hungary. Wall paintings in Central Asia dating from the period between A.D. 500 to 800 often depict men in caftans wearing spherical earrings. Most golden earrings from the early period of Avar settlement were made in the Carpathian Basin; Byzantine gold solidi procured by way of taxes provided the raw material for these. Byzantine goldsmiths also took part in making these earrings.

**39.** The finest example of goldsmiths' work from the early Avar age is the golden pseudo belt buckle which was discovered at Tépe (Hajdú-Bihar county). This buckle-shaped mounting was fastened to a belt in an upright position; the arched frame was joined to the body of the buckle by means of hinges, which enable it to be moved freely. The pin of the pseudo buckle, however, could not be moved—hence the name pseudo belt buckle.

The use of pseudo buckles as belt mountings first occurred in Asia. The earliest silver pseudo belt buckles were brought into the Carpathian Basin by the Avars, but those made of gold were produced in the Carpathian Basin. Since they symbolized power in society, they were placed in the graves of princes and chieftains. The Tépe pseudo belt buckle was found in the grave, which had already been robbed, of an Avar chieftain from the early seventh century: the robbery must have occurred in the Avar period. The pseudo belt buckle, a gold sword hilt, the quarter part of a Byzantine silver bowl, and the silver goblet testify to the wealth of objects which typically characterized the grave of a prince or chieftain.

The Tépe pseudo belt buckle is an excellent example of the goldsmith's art. "Its multifarious structure, so to speak, is a synthesis of the goldsmiths' craft throughout the whole Avar period. Constructing such a pseudo buckle, if the goldsmith had all the material at his disposal, would require twenty-seven to thirty elements," wrote Professor Gyula László in 1940 in his analysis of the Tépe find.

39. Pseudo buckle

40. Buckle, strap end, belt and saddle accessories

**40.** In 1832 the National Museum purchased the gold ornaments found in the grave of an early Avar prince from Miklós Jankovich (1773–1846). Since then these objects have been known to archaeologists as the "Jankovich gold". The set consists of a buckle with an oval ring and a shield-shaped pin, a rounded strap-end, a rhomboid belt mount and saddle furniture with a boar's head and bird's body embellished with gems. The stylized birds which embellish the trappings (buckle, strap-end, mount) bite into themselves or twist back onto their own bodies. They are typical of the so-called second serrated style of Germanic animal ornamentation. The serrated version of this particular Germanic style is only found in the territory formerly occupied by the Avars. It is not known where exactly the Jankovich objects were made, although it is certain that they were made for a high-born Avar and in line with the Avar taste. They were produced and used at around the end of the sixth century A.D., but not later than the beginning of the seventh. These dates can be established on the basis of similar graves found in the Carpathian Basin or in territories inhabited by Germanic peoples.

**41.** These gold belt ornaments are rarities among the work of goldsmiths of the late Avar age. One of the finest pieces preserved in the National Museum is a golden belt loop from Tab (Somogy county); this was purchased by the Museum at the end of the nineteenth century. The cover part of the curved gold sheet was cast in a shape imitating a small strap-end; it is framed with a wire-type structure consisting of small beads. Its surface is divided into sections, and wavy ribs are decorated by means of punching. A small ring-shaped pendant on the bottom and the two little loops on the back were attached for fastening.

The cast bronze belt mounts decorated with griffons, plants, and, sometimes, geometrical motifs recall the goldsmiths' work from the late Avar age. A set of belt mountings usually consisted of a large strap-end, a small strap-end, a buckle, ornaments, hole-protectors and loops. Griffon representations were more popular in the first half of the eighth century on both the large rectangular mountings and on the long strap-ends. The loops on this type of belt were similar to those found at Tab. Graves of princes or chieftains from the late Avar age have not yet been found in the Carpathian Basin: the belt loop found at Tab was discovered in the plundered grave of a high-ranking person who lived in the eighth century. It is the only memento of the wealth belonging to a member of the Avar élite.

**42.** This pair of large, square, box-like clasps were used to fasten garments—for example, cloaks or capes. They are reputed to have been discovered in the vicinity of Dunapataj, and were purchased by the National Museum. Each square sheet is embellished with a row of bosses and fourteen loops which were originally used to thread beads through. The stones are missing from the curved mounting in the centre. On the side sheets male and female faces confront each other in an embossed frieze; in the row of male heads a hand holding a cross can be seen.

This pair of clasps is of Byzantine origin: the components of the decoration, the rows of bosses, the loops to hold the beads, and the heads which are familiar from the portraits of emperors on coins are characteristic of Byzantine goldsmiths' art in the sixth and seventh centuries A.D. Another box-clasp made from sheet gold is known from the vicinity of the former Sirmium, now Mitrovics, Yugoslavia. However, square-shaped gold box-clasps—and, later, oval-shaped gold plated bronze box-clasps—have been found throughout the territory inhabited by the Avars. The earliest examples uncovered in graves from the mid Avar age date back to the end of the seventh century and the early eighth century, whereas the oval-shaped box-clasps are typical of those dating from the eighth century. The two clasps from Dunaboglár were probably made at around the beginning of the eighth century for a high-born Avar lady: they are of the style favoured by the Avars at this time.

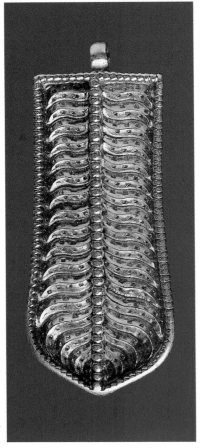

41. Belt loop

42. Pair of clasps

42

# Mediaeval Department

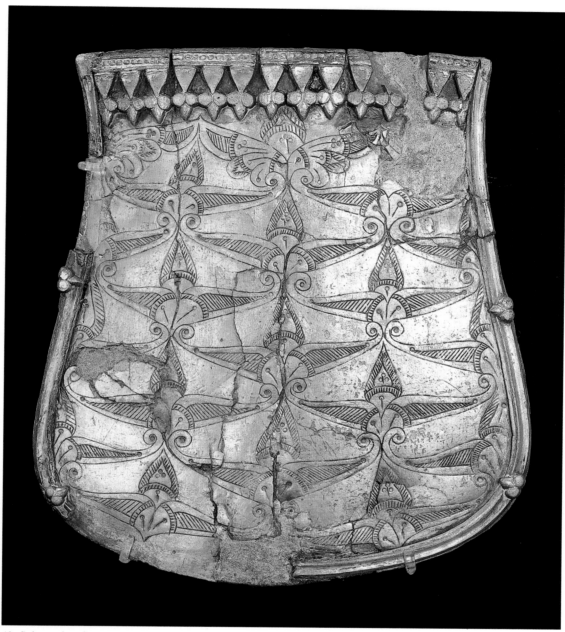

43. Sabretache plate

**43.** The palmette bunches on the sabretache plate make up a continuous pattern which was designed to be two-dimensional. The sense of plasticity is produced by the glittering of the silver leaves standing out against the lavishly gilded background. The upper border is decorated with a row of tassel-shaped mountings.

High-ranking members of clans, and leaders of their military retinues, wore such ornamental belts designed to carry their sabres as symbols of their status. A leather bag, either inlaid or embellished with tooled patterns, held the flint and steel and whetstone. First, the area around the fastening of the strap was covered with metal mounts and then the strap itself. Following this procedure, cast ornaments were fitted along the border of the flap and onto the bag. Competing with each other in magnificence, the owners of the sabretaches applied more and larger mountings, until these decorations lost their original function and structure, and covered the entire surface. By this time, the covering the sabretache with a single silver plate became more practical. These plates could be elaborately ornamented with goldsmiths' work before being attached to the leather bag.

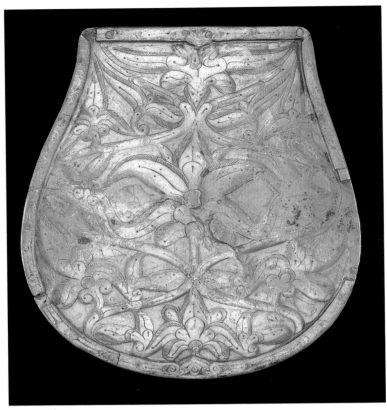

44. Sabretache plate

**44.** One of the several graves discovered in 1894 in Tarcal (Borsod-Abaúj-Zemplén county) contained a wealth of auxiliary finds, which were donated to the National Museum by the owner of the land, Dávid Tarczaly. This artistic *sabretache plate* belonged to this group of finds. It is made up of two plates, which are riveted together in a way which facilitated the application of a narrow, ornamented silver band along the edge of the ornate plate. Using this method, three layers were fastened together with silver rivets. After the pattern had been engraved with a pointed tool, all the lines, including the hatching of the outside surface of the leaves, were deepened by the punching of tiny dots very close to one another. The low-relief-like plasticity of the floral pattern was achieved by the hammering of the background after the design had been outlined completely. The lavish clusters of leaves on coiling tendrils were typical motifs used during the age of the Hungarian Conquest.

**45.** This find, consisting of a sabretache plate, a pair of silver earrings, a silver necklace and a silver coin, was discovered in 1868, and was donated to the National Museum by Ferenc Erdődy in 1871. The pattern of the silver *sabretache plate* was first outlined using a pointed tool, then embossed by the hammering of the background of the braid and palmettes inwards. Finally, the design was enhanced by punching dense lines of dots along the motifs. During this operation, the plate was fastened onto tar or some other substance so tightly that the pattern went through onto this material as well. A silver band was nailed onto the edge of the plate; this silver band and the background of the plate are gilded. Coiling foliation divides the surface of the sabretache plate into smaller zones. These zones are lavishly filled out using short-stemmed palmette bunches. The continuous pattern of these palmettes evokes woven and embroidered designs.

45. Sabretache plate

46. Sabretache plate

**46.** This *sabretache plate,* which was found at Tiszabezdéd (Szabolcs-Szatmár-Bereg county) in 1896, is made of copper. The patterns were outlined on the gilded surface of the plate by means of a tool, probably a chisel. The background was densely filled out with small rings made with a punch. This piece stands out among the sabretache plates, which were all individually designed and very different from each other. The owner of the plate, or the artist whom he commissioned to produce the work, was familiar with the symbols of both pagan and Christian mythology: this is shown by Jesse's Tree and the Crucifix motifs. Two animals rearing up flank the Tree of Life and the Cross. One is a peacock-dragon with dog's or wolf's head, two-clawed paws, huge wings and a spread peacock's tail. Similar dragons can be seen on the brilliant Sasanida silk-brocades and on Byzantine textiles. The other mythical animal is a four-legged, winged unicorn with its tail held high.

47. Apex of a tall fur cap

**47.** The sheet silver of the apex of a tall fur cap was patterned before being moulded into its present cone shape. After the two serrated edges had been soldered together, the knob on the top, made up of two half-spheres, was soldered on separately. The pattern begins, close to the bottom rim, with four double palmettes. Foliation starting out from these palmettes fills out the whole tapering surface of the cone. In the spaces encompassed by the tendrils, the motif of palmettes, which grow out of each other, is repeated three times. The pattern is broken by a braided band encircling the base of the knob which is decorated with rows of dots and little circles. Double-twisted wires are soldered onto the base and onto the top of the cone. Twelve tiny holes are punched into the silver plate: two at the base of the four palmettes around the lower edge and one at each point where the palmette leaves meet.

This silver cone from Beregszász adorned the tall fur-trimmed leather or felt hat of a member of the Hungarian élite.

46

**48.** It is an Eastern tradition which survives even today that women embellish their hair with beads, jewels, or pierced coins. Such items have also been discovered in women's graves from the time of the Hungarian Conquest: women braided in their hair simple metal rings or shells or beads that had been polished. The most striking among these accessories, which are probably of Finno-Ugric origin, were the pairs of large *plait-disks*. This kind of ornament could be made in countless variations, mostly by casting different shapes or by making thin round silver plates which then were worked on by silversmiths. There are refined, artistically decorated pieces among the cast ones, too, just as there are simple ones among the thin silver plates ornamented with nothing but plain stylized leaves, rows of dots or just a groove running along the edge. Sometimes similar motifs—trees of life, palmette bunches, or mythical animals—were produced using different techniques.

On this cast disk from Sárospatak, the tree-of-life motif was drawn in exactly the same way as on another disk from Anarcs made of a silver plate. The abundant foliage of the tree of life is inserted in a masterful way into the circular space. The bottom branches hang down heavily, as though weighed down by an abundance of fruit. Following Iranian traditions, the trunk forks at the bottom, and through this division the life-giving fluid of the tree bursts forth.

48. Plait disc

**49.** A woman's grave from the age of the Hungarian Conquest was discovered near Heves village. The finds were donated to the National Museum by Eger's Cistercian School in 1938. This *bracelet* is the most important among the pieces of the acquisition; its bronze band is covered with thin gold plate. Cut red stones (granite) in serrated mountings are set into the two ends of the bracelet, as well as in its centre. The three sets were soldered onto the band and then enclosed with thin, twisted gold wires. The ends of these wires were then bent back. Bracelets made of strips of metal sheet not joined at the two ends are frequently found in graves dating from the time of the Hungarian Conquest. They are typical of the period between the settling of their Hungarians in the Carpathian Basin (the late ninth century) and the conversion to Christianity (the late tenth and eleventh centuries). Produced by Hunnish goldsmiths, similar objects manufactured from cheap metal and plated with gold can be found in southern Russia. The shape and the use of the twisted wire presents the possibility of even more ancient origin: the analogy with Scythian necklaces and bracelets which were developed under Greek and Persian influence.

49. Band-shaped bracelet

50. The Monomachos Crown

**50.** The Byzantine crown—consisting of seven curved, cloisonné enamelled gold plaques with arched tops—was uncovered in 1890 at Nyirvánka during ploughing; the pieces were purchased by the Hungarian National Museum one by one.

Standing figures are represented on the plaques, among them Byzantine emperor Constantinos Monomachos, his wife Zoé, and his sister-in-law, Theodora. On the basis of the coincidence of these portraits, it can be determined when the coronet was made: the emperor and the two empresses ruled together between 1042 and 1050, meaning that the diadem was produced during this period. The largest, central, plaque represents the emperor in imperial robes, with a crown and glory around his head. In his right hand he holds a labarum, the emblem of his power, and in his left hand there is a scroll. His name is inscribed in the space above his shoulders, underneath the letters foliage and birds fill out the background. The empresses, holding long sceptre-like canes in their right hands, are shown in somewhat smaller plaques on each side of the central one. They are identifiable only through their insignia and their names inscribed in the background. The reticulated tops of their coronets are very typical of female crowns. A dancer holds a ribbon high above her head in each of the next two, even smaller, plaques; these plaques are not inscribed but, as in the

case of the other three, foliage and birds fill out the background. Female figures standing between cypress-trees are depicted in each of the two smallest plaques, and the writing behind them reveals that they are personifications of Truth and Humility. Allegories of the Virtues usually accompany the emperors in Byzantine representations. The strange presence of the dancers refers to King David in the Old Testament; the daughters of Israel dancing in honour of David are depicted in many mediaeval Byzantine representations.

The tiny holes in the gold frames soldered onto the backs of the plaques would suggest that the plaques were originally sewn onto a textile cap.

The coronet was assembled on the basis of the size of the plaques, the symmetricality of the figures, and with reference to a diadem from Kiev.

An empty gem mounting and two small, round cloisonné enamelled plaques depicting St Peter and St Andrew were also found in the same place at Nyírvánka. These do not belong to the coronet, since round plaques were made only after the twelfth century. The co-existence of these finds makes it likely that this gold treasure was buried by returning Crusaders following the sack of Byzantium in 1204.

**51.** Placing the Crucifix upon the altar became generally accepted practice in the Western Church during the twelfth century. Smaller churches possessed only one cross designed to be set on the top of a staff; this was carried around during the processions which were held very frequently during this time. During Church ceremonies, they were placed on a stand and set upon the altar. Therefore, these crosses—most of which were of gold-plated cast bronze—had either a socket or a spike on the bottom. Many such crucifixes have been found in Hungary among the remains of churches destroyed during the Tatar invasion. The cross shown here was discovered in the village of Szerecseny (Győr-Sopron-Moson county), and was donated to the Museum by the bishop. The cross is made from a piece of sheet metal which is a little wider at the bottom. It stands on a sphere symbolizing the Earth; underneath the sphere there is a funnel-shaped socket. The eyes of the Christ figure are closed, and the knees slightly bent. The reticulated glory behind the finely-shaped bearded head has been almost completely broken off. In line with the traditions of the previous century, the pectoral muscles were moulded to seem as though a kerchief was originally worn over the shoulders. The lion's head under his feet symbolizes Satan, the evil power conquered by the death of Christ on the Cross.

The cross was made in the middle of the twelfth century. The King Stephen Museum at Székesfehérvár has a very similar one; the two were probably made in the same workshop of a Transdanubian monastery.

51. Processional Crucifix

52. Finds from the royal tomb of Székesfehérvár

**52.** Several small golden objects were discovered during construction work in the courtyard of the Bishop's Palace at Székesfehérvár in 1839. Those who found these sold them, had them altered, or had them melted down. Some were acquired by the National Museum only after a long period of time. The characteristics of these objects make it probable that, when digging a ditch through the courtyard, the workmen destroyed one of the graves of the eleventh-century cathedral founded by St Stephen; this served as the site for coronation ceremonies and as a royal burial-place.

The most important piece of the ensemble is a small golden coronet with a curved triangular pinnacle ornamented with filigree work. The two small strap-ends and a quadrangular plate, which belonged to a miniature belt, are decorated with similar filigree wire. A golden ring with garnet bezel, which would fit a man's hand; many tiny buttons and beads; a button decorated with granulation; and the fragment of a trefoil jewel decorated with filigree also belong to the same find. The last piece was purchased by the Museum in 1885, more than forty years after the discovery. It is a bracelet made by the alteration

of objects of unknown function. The round-shaped, flower-patterned cloisonné enamel piece framed by a row of pearls may have been a part of an item of jewellry probably worn as a decoration pinned to the chest and found in the grave of King Béla III. The filigree adornment on the plates attached together by chains is very similar to that found on the sceptre. Except for the Byzantine cloisonné enamelled round plaque, the objects found in the grave were made around the beginning of the thirteenth century in the same royal workshop that adorned the sceptre.

These objects were probably put into the grave of King Ladislas III (1204–1205), who died at the age of five. His father, Imre, had Ladislas crowned in his stead, but after Imre's death the child-king and his mother had to flee from Andrew II (1205–1235) to Vienna, where the child died. Nevertheless, he was buried in Székesfehérvár, as sources say, "regio more", in the royal manner—that is, together with royal insignia. The small belt and the golden buttons belonged to the attire of the child-king, and the miniature crown was a symbolic royal insignis.

**53.** Four earthenware vessels, one of which was decorated with brownish-red painting, were donated to the Hungarian National Museum in 1892. They were discovered at Hatvan during the construction of a factory at a place where there had probably once been a well. Judging by the ornamentation and the shape of the vessels, during the period of the Árpád Dynasty there was a settlement on the site of the find.

The earthenware bottles were made on a potter's wheel from clay mixed down with sand and fine-grained grit. Their yellowish-white surfaces are a little rough. The rounded rims and the tall, slender necks are separated by sharp ribs. The oval bodies are decorated with ten horizontal brownish-red bands on the outside, and one stripe on the inside.

Earthenware vessels made during the period of the House of Árpád kings are generally simple and quite similar in shape. They are often decorated with indented patterns, for example, straight, serrated, or undulating lines, but there are also those which are merely embellished with horizontal red bands. The red painting is especially decorative on those yellowish-white earthenware vessels which were in use after the latter part of the thirteenth century.

**54.** This gilded bronze mould for making large double-sided seals is one of the earliest such pieces held at the National Museum. On one side, the picture of a town surrounded by walls is engraved very finely and precisely. The legend says SIGILLUM LATINORUM CIVITATIS STRIGONIENSIS. The "nine-times-cut" triangular coat-of-arms of the country in the other piece is encircled by the legend SECRETUM LATINORUM CIVITATIS STRIGONIENSIS. The four perforated tabs on the edges were attached to ensure that the two pieces were properly secured together. The "Latins" mentioned in the legend as the owners of the seal were actually Walloon settlers, who—as merchants—were involved in money minting. Their stamp with the coat-of-arms of the country indicates that they were endowed with privileges.

The picture of the town shown on the die is very noteworthy. As latest research has proven, it is an authentic view of the royal town of Esztergom. In the centre of the front wall, reinforced by bastions ending in towers, is the St Lawrence Gate. Behind the walls a palace is shown with huge, twin, lancet windows. It can be ascertained from the topography of the royal town that this was the Szennye Palace, serving as the building of the Minters' Chamber, which was active during the twelfth and thirteenth centuries.

The die was engraved in the first half of the thirteenth century by a goldsmith from Esztergom—possibly by the master of the minters himself–who knew the town very well.

53. Clay bottle

54. Mould for making double-sided seal

51

55. Finger-bowl

**55.** This enamelled copper finger-bowl from Limoges is said to have been found among the ruins of the Archbishopry of Bátmonostor. The Museum acquired it from the Jankovich Collection.

The narrow, flat rim and the inside of the once gold-plated shallow bowl are decorated with enamel and are engraved with floral motifs. In a circular zone in the centre of the bowl, and set against a background of foliage, is a representation of Samson's fight with the lions. Around this field runs a broad band in which there are four medallions separated by palmettes and tendrils. Winged angels, outlined with engraving and not enamelled, appear in the medallions. Blue, green, yellow and white enamel fills out the background.

Pairs of these shallow bowls were generally used at the altar or during feasts held by aristocrats. The water was poured from one of them and collected with the other. The theme of the depictions on these bowls refers to their function. The finger-bowl shown here is probably an ecclesiastical object, whereas the falconer surrounded by joculators in the centre of another similar bowl held at the National Museum suggests that the latter was used for secular purposes.

This bowl was produced in Limoges, where enamelled objects were manufactured in large quantities as early as the thirteenth century for sale all over Europe. Many such products were brought to Hungary, where there was a big market for them because of the need to replace the ecclesiastical objects destroyed during the Tatar invasion. Bowls from Limoges were relatively cheap yet attractive; the example from Bátmonostor was made around 1240.

**56.** A tomb with an inscribed stone lid was uncovered along with the ruins of the sanctuary of the Dominican Convent on the Margaret Island during the Great Flood of 1838. A crown decorated with fleur-de-lys and a ring with a zephyr on it were discovered in the tomb. They were bequeathed to the Museum by Palatine Joseph (1776–1847), the owner of the island at that time. There was a man's skeleton in the grave, and his identity has since been much debated. Most probably he was Béla, prince of Macsó, the grandson of Béla IV who was murdered in the convent. His sister—a nun and later mother superior of the convent— placed her own crown on the prince's head at the burial.

The gilt silver crown consists of eight sections joined together by hinges. In the middle of each of these plaques stands a lily cut from sheet silver. The band is embellished with flowers, all of which have a gem in the centre and small decorative mountings holding pearls on the tips of their petals. These pearls are now missing. Both the band and the lilies are adorned with garnets and amethysts set in mountings. On the top of the pins which fasten the hinges there are three-lobed silver pinnacles.

The crown was made in High Gothic style during the last three decades of the thirteenth century; it is an example of crowns characterized by fleur-de-lys-shaped decoration, which became widespread during the fourteenth century. The crown found in the grave of King Sigismund (1387–1437) at Nagyvárad is also of this type.

56. Crown

**57.** The only information available concerning the origin of this large clasp is that it belonged to the Jankovich Collection, acquired by the Museum in the middle of the nineteenth century.

Its base is a wide, round plaque with jewel mountings and square plaques around the edge, above which there used to be pearls (only one of these pearls now remains). Above the band, the reticulated ornamentation consists of foliation and four peacocks cast from silver and plated with gold.

This mantle clasp is notable in the history of Hungarian goldsmiths' work, because it is the only example still within the borders of Hungary which was produced in a major royal workshop. The wedding crowns for the king's daughters, of which three found their way in Poland, were made during the twenty-year period between 1240 and 1260 at the court of Béla IV (1235–1270). Boleslav the Shy, prince of Poland (1226–1279), donated the crown of his wife, Kinga, to Cracow Cathedral, where a cross was later made from it. Constance, princess of Halics probably followed the example of her sister, because the large golden cross, which is still held at Cracow, is made of two crowns decorated with coiling tendrils. The third crown, that of Jolanta, was incorporated into the St Sigismund Herm, today held at Polock. The three crowns—like mantle clasp with the peacocks—were adorned not only with the gems and pearls, but also with cast tendrils and small figures jutting prominently out of their bases.

A few other smaller clasps made in the same workshop that produced the crowns and the mantle clasps are exhibited in the Hungarian National Museum and in Budapest's Museum of Applied Arts.

57. Mantle clasp

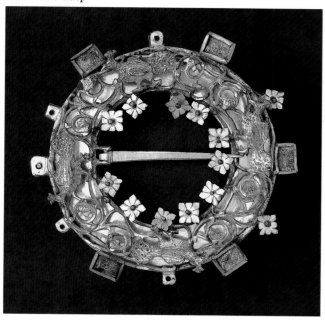

53

58. Ciborium

**59.** In the fourteenth century, the art of producing liturgical objects once again flourished. European monarchs all tried to outdo each other in founding impressive cathedrals, by this time invariably built in the Gothic style. It was customary for the founder also to donate various liturgical articles of the latest design made by master goldsmiths. Several foundations by the fourteenth-century Hungarian king Louis the Great are known, the most important being the Hungarian Chapel at Aachen (Aix-la-Chapelle), which is still open to visitors. His donations—wonderful chalices, reliquaries and candleholders—added to the splendour of the ceremonies held for pilgrims. But Louis the Great founded several churches in Hungary, too, although in most of the cases only the church buildings themselves have survived to verify this. Almost the only exception is the church at Vízakna, the foundation deed of which has recently been found. In this, the king undertook to enrich the church continuously with works of art from Italy. The Vízakna Chalice of—in the possession of the church before its acquisition by the National Museum at the beginning of the century—is a fine indication of the monarch's generosity.

The pictures of the saints and angels which adorn the base of the chalice and the radials of the node are decorated using typical Italian translucent enamel. The angels are examples of the fine decorative art of the period: the tiny half-portraits at the base of the cup show angels playing various musical instruments. In the six-lobed pictures of the node, unidentifiable saints and the coat-of-arms of the Anjou family are depicted. At the base, also set in enamel, there are the pictures of six saints.

59. Chalice from Vízakna

**58.** The ciborium originates in Old Christian art and liturgy, according to which a small portion of the Host was reserved in a small pyx for the ill. During the fourteenth century, these containers were fitted onto high poles. It was at this time that ciboriums became widely used at the places of pilgrimage where hundreds or even thousands of believers were given Holy Communion; therefore, the priests needed a container which they could easily hold in their hands. This was when the item assumed a form which has remained unchanged up to the present day. Ciboriums are usually made of gilded copper or silver. Inside, where the host touches the surface of the ciborium, gilding was obligatory.

The ciborium found at Szepeskörtvélyes is a wonderful and very typical example of fourteenth-century ecclesiastical art. It is made of copper, but is gilded beautifully. On the four-lobed foot, a nodus ornamented with red stones provides the celebrant with a good grip. The most frequently depicted scenes from the *Biblia pauperum* are engraved on the traced background of six square plaques which make up the receptacle: the Annunciation, Christ on the Mount of Olives, Christ Before Pilate, the Betrayal of Christ, the Scourging of Christ, and the Crucifixion. Pictures of S.S. Peter and Paul, and probably the four Evangelists, are engraved on the six-sided pyramid-shaped lid of the vessel. On the top there is a cross, while inside the vessel and underneath the lid we find a cup, possibly later added as a replacement.

This ciborium originally belonged to the church of Szepeskörtvélyes founded by Louis the Great (1342–1382), and it probably was donated by the king himself. It passed into the possession of the National Museum in 1914, after the outbreak of the First World War, when, in order to save it from being melted down, the church donated it to the Museum in exchange for an exact copy; the whole transaction was conducted by post.

**60.** At around the middle of the fifteenth century a technique known as filigree enamelling rapidly became popular in Hungary. Its earliest example is the St. Ladislas Herm. Filigree enamelling was made in the following way: on a plain, generally silver, plate floral motives and branches with leaves were formed from thin, twisted wire. Then, the spaces between them were filled out with various, vividly coloured enamel plaques. Peculiar heart-shaped leaves, beautiful carnations, and roses soon became widely known; this technique became known as "Hungarian enamelling" as early as the fifteenth century. Filigree enamel was used primarily in ecclesiastical art right across Europe in the decoration of chalices, crosses, reliquaries and ciboriums—although there are instances of its use in jewelry making.

The most beautiful chalice made using the filigree enamelling technique and owned by the National Museum was acquired in 1879 as a present from Ferenc Révay. The Hungarian saints Stephen, Emericus and Ladislas are shown on the base of the six-lobed chalice, together with the coat-of-arms of the Nyári family—added as replacement in the fourteenth century (complete with the words PAL NIARI). The node of the chalice is very fine: in the chamber, figures of angels playing music are standing; behind them wonderfully fine filigree enamel covers the entire stem of the chalice.

On the cup of the chalice there are half-portraits of three saints, Borbála, Dorottya and Catherine, set in round plaits and dressed according to the fashion of the fifteenth-century aristocracy. They are separated from one another by a round plait decorated with flower motifs joined together on tendrils of filigree enamel. The words on the cup read as follows:

MARIA — IHS — XPS

Of the fifteenth-century Hungarian chalices, an especially lavishly decorated type was that which featured indented nodes. Although the name of the goldsmith producing this particular chalice is not known, the filigree enamelling technique and the depiction of Hungarian saints clearly suggest a Hungarian workshop. The artist was probably a Transylvanian master of the goldsmiths' guild, possibly working in the Kolozsvár area, since the most beautiful examples of filigree enamels were produced there.

60. The Nyári Chalice

**61.** For centuries, the most important piece of furniture in people's homes was the chest. That was where the bride's trousseau and all the family's most valuable property–clothing, money, jewelry, documents and weapons–were kept. The so-called trough chests, the extremely heavy boxes made using an ancient technique and almost completely lacking in decoration, were replaced very early on in more fashionable households by timbered chests (*scrinium*s); the technique for making these was learned by the Hungarians probably only after their arrival in the Carpathian Basin. From the fourteenth century onwards, their use became widespread even among the peasant population. Coloured decoration was painted onto the chests of mediaeval origin. The timbered locker, made in Nagyszeben and given to the Museum as a donation, is an outstandingly beautiful example of this kind of piece. The planks, which were split using a hatchet, are joined horizontally and held together with vertical supports, with the top of the locker–the lid–resembling the shape of a pitched roof. The entire front panel of the piece is vividly decorated. Crowned princes wearing swords and standing in arched chambers are shown on the pillars, while the horizontal planks are decorated with fabulous animals placed in interlinking circles. The representations are set in Gothic frames, or on strips of simple but variegated elements. The painted decoration on the locker resembles murals and miniatures of the same period.

**62.** The royal borough of Bártfa was a flourishing town in the fifteenth century. The wealthier merchants and craftsmen of the town enlarged the St. Egidius Church, and provided it with new furniture in line with the taste of the period. The bookcase that once held the documents of the town and the books of the parish (this was placed in a secure room in part of the oratory above the vestry, and was made in the 1480s). The National Museum purchased the bookcase, together with the original library of seventy-five volumes and other articles, from the parish church of Bártfa in 1915.

The front panel of the huge, yet proportionate, bookcase, which is moderately decorated, is made of lime-wood. The planks of the two sides and the back, together with the planks used as shelves and inside separators, are made of larch-wood. Two upright pieces of wood divide the body of the bookcase into three equal parts, joined to the ornamental cornice by a frame of lath. A less accentuated division is produced by the middle rail, which, together with the verticals of the two posts, divides the body of the bookcase into six equal sections. Each section closes with a two-winged door. In addition to emphasizing the structural elements, the decoration is mainly concentrated on the cornice, regularly patterned using the low relief technique (*relief en creux*). Colourful painting livens up the entire piece of furniture. Iron locks and hinges make the large and smooth surface of the front panel more variegated.

The maker of the bookcase is not known. In the fifteenth century, the Szepesség–mediaeval Hungary's northern region, which was mostly populated by German colonists–was an area where important works of carpentry were produced. This particular bookcase was almost certainly made in one of the local workshops and in line with the traditions of the district.

In the literature, Hungarian as well as other, a mediaeval bookcase is something of a rarity. The value of this particular one is increased by the fact that it comes complete with the library of books it originally contained. The books were grouped according to their subject, as shown by the strips of paper glued onto the doors. The following words can still be recognized: SCHOLASTICI, MATHEMATICI, THEOLOGICI, TOMI LUTHERI. At the time of the Reformation, the library was also opened to the citizens of the town; for this reason, it can be regarded as the first public library in Hungary.

61. Trousseau chest

62. Bookcase

**63.** In 1915, along with the Bártfa bookcase, the surviving books from the library of the St. Egidius Church were also acquired by the National Museum–including a few manuscripts and a number of incunabula. Even in its incomplete state, the collection makes a precious reminder of Hungarian church libraries in the Middle Ages. The library consists of manuscripts and incunabula written in Greek and Latin. In addition to the books with a liturgical use, the library contained books on history, law, astronomy and mathematics. In 1539 the church building was passed into the possession of the Protestant congregation; after this books by Luther and his followers were added to the library.

The missal page reproduced here comes from an incunabulum known as "Missale ad usum dominorum Ultramontanorum". The incunabulum, which was produced in Verona in 1480, was the first missal ever to be made for priests celebrating Mass in Hungary. In the Late Middle Ages, when altars were set up and religious posts were created in increasing numbers, the demand for missals naturally also rose. According to an inventory taken at the St. Egidius Church in 1460, ten out of the thirty books owned by the church were missals. In 1468 the town bought another missal, while in 1488 the St. Egidius Church was presented with a printed one. It was only this last-mentioned missal that has passed into the possession of the Museum. In its outside appearance–its large size, the typesetting used, the arrangement of the text in two columns, printed in two colours–, the missal follows the model of the codices. The illuminated initials and the ornamental margins, painted by hand in the printed book, only reinforce this resemblance. When illuminating the foliage which stemmed from the initial letter, the miniaturist used fresh pastel colours, while in the ornamentation and in the tinting he applied lighter colours or pure white. His style, which shows the influence of the Czech miniature illuminators, as well as of other illuminated books found in the collection, makes it probable that the missal was illuminated at Bártfa.

63. Missal

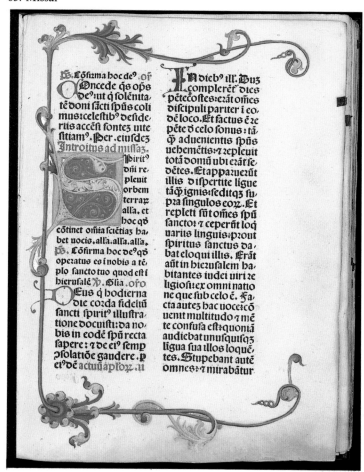

64. Gothic choir stalls

**64.** In 1915, the National Museum purchased the Gothic choir-stalls from the parish church of Bártfa, the town which guarded mediaeval Hungary's northern gate.

Originally, the stalls were placed along the southern wall of the chancel of the St. Egidius Church; later, when further stalls were added, it was taken to the western aisle of the church. The choirstalls, which have twelve seats, were rebuilt several times. The five-seat section currently on display was assembled in the Museum from the undamaged parts of the otherwise rather dilapidated whole.

The seats of the limewood stalls fold back; the arm supports between the seats are mounted on top of the partition panels and are made of thick beams shaped into a coiling form. The partition panels are divided with the help of small posts. The seats have tall back-panels joined together with a frame of lath. On both sides, the stalls end in ornate panelling. An *anse de panier* canopy is built over the seats; its gable is decorated symmetrically.

The Bártfa choirstalls go by the widely accepted name of the Matthias Choirstalls. Tradition has it that the citizens of Bártfa sent expensive gold and silver presents to King Matthias (1458–1490) and Queen Elizabeth on the occasion of their wedding–presents the king later donated to the St Egidius Church. These were subsequently sold and the money was said to have been used to finance the furnishing of the church, including the acquisition of the choirstalls. In fact, the name derives from the unique decoration: the backs of the seats are embellished with coats-of-arms carved in low relief and painted, and in the most prominent place there are the coats-of-arms of King Matthias and Queen Beatrix, flanked–on the back of each seat–by the Swedish, Norwegian, Czech, Hungarian, Spanish and English coats-of-arms on the left, and the Cypriot, Navarrean, Aragonian, Sicilian, French and Danish coats-of-arms on the right. The coats-of-arms are encircled by simple frames, or foliage made more distinct by fabulous animals. In the original configuration of the choirstalls, ornamented and plain seats alternated with each other; the unornamented ones were covered with coloured fabric.

**65.** The Renaissance magnificence of King Matthias's court motivated the Báthori family–prominent members of which occupied high positions in the state, and who were even related to the royal family–to create in Nyírbátor, the centre of their estates, an environment to accord with their social rank. To commemorate the Hungarian victory over the Turks at the Battle of Kenyérmező in 1479, the Báthori family, utilizing proceeds from the booty seized there, erected two impressive churches: one for the Franciscan Minorite Order (this had a cloister adjacent to it) and one for the Church of St George near their mansion (the latter church the Báthoris intended to use as a family burial place). Besides their splendid carved stone-work, it was the glorious altars and the valuable furniture that gave the churches their magnificence. The choirstalls, which originally consisted of fifty seats, were made for the chancel of the Franciscan Church. When the Franciscan Church was damaged at the end of the sixteenth century, the choirstalls were taken to the Church of St George. The National Museum purchased them in 1933. Following the restoration of the choir-stalls, the complete set was put on display in the National Museum; the other ones, with the missing canopy, were returned to Nyírbátor.

The structure of this monumental piece of oak furniture is basically Gothic; only the shape of the canopy is different. The canopy consists of semi-circular arches with friezes in relief and with a richly ornamented cornice.

Much artistic imagination and fine taste is revealed by the selection of the Renaissance ornaments which cover the entire structure. Some of the stalls are simply ornamented with strips of marquetry assembled from geometrical forms, but most of them have elaborate individual designs. Symbolic human and animal figures, intricate flowers in vases, arms, ornate cups and bowls, candelabra, etc. are inlaid in woods of different colours on the backs of the seats. The coat-of-arms of the Báthoris is inlaid on two panels, the shield is held up by winged putti, and the scaley body of a dragon–the symbol of the St George Order of Knights–is coiled around it. Exceptionally beautiful are the panels which show the inside of a cupboard with its doors half opened; dishes, goldsmiths' work, pomegranates, and books of Renaissance thought are lined up on the shelves. An inscription, which fills an entire panel, contains the titles and the names of the three Báthori brothers who commissioned the choirstalls: György, István and András, as well as the year when the furniture was made: 1511. The name of the master craftsman can be read in an engraving of a book visible on one of the panels: F. MARONE. The letter F stands for either "fecit" (made by) or "frater". Master Marone accomplished a work which exhibits all the merits of the joiners' and carvers' work-shops of the Via de' Servi in Florence. The joiners of the local Franciscan workshop probably also participated in executing some of the details on the choirstalls.

65. Renaissance choir stalls

66. Earthenware mug

**67.** Three decorated earthenware jugs were discovered in the well belonging to Szécsény Castle; they were probably dropped down it by accident. The one in the best condition has a tall, slender body; its upper part is glazed. From its base it rises into a bulging middle part and continues up to a high shoulder from which there stems a neck supporting a moderately wide rim with a lip. Around the base is a pattern put on using a cogwheel; above it are two closely-set incised lines. On the rim, under three incised lines, there runs a pattern also put on using a cog-wheel. Starting from just underneath the rim is a handle decorated with a row of small circles and attached to the body of the jug. Engraved lines divide the glazed area on the neck and the shoulder into three fields; these are embellished with star shapes and net-like patterns. Yellowish-brown glaze covers the handle; the outside of the upper part and the inside of the mouth, the ornaments, and the small strip immediately under the rim are light green.

Pottery during the second half of the fifteenth century achieved a high level of craftsmanship. Different clichés were in use for stamping the patterns, and glazes of various colours could be produced. The fact that the jug from Szécsény exhibits all the marks of such methods suggests that it was made in the first half of the sixteenth century. Similar earthenware vessels were found in the northern part of the country, where probably these three jugs were produced, also.

**66.** During the Late Middle Ages, special, elaborate drinking cups and dishes were imported into Hungary from all over Middle and Central Europe, sometimes even from the Near and the Far East, to meet the needs of the royal court, the households of the aristocracy, and even the wealthy townspeople. As also indicated by the written sources, the earthenware cups made in Lostice, Moravia, were especially esteemed.

Under their purplish-brown glaze these decorative mugs are covered with tiny blisters. Some of the cups are decorated under the rim with six to ten loops; some are ornamented with a cog-wheel pattern, which divides the body into fields. There are also a few which have special lids.

The cup shown in the picture belongs to the more ornate type: it has thirteen loops under the rim. The fact that its former owner had a setting made for it of gold-plated bronze shows that the mug was very valuable and held in high regard. The setting was cut out of a sheet of gilded bronze; the edge is decorated with serrated leaves. The Esterházy Treasury's cup, which was also made in Lostice, is very similar to this one.

67. Earthenware jug

68. Cruets from Nagyvárad

**68.** There were several periods in the history of Hungarian goldsmith's work when the filigree technique achieved a very high standard of craftsmanship. Undoubtedly, it showed the greatest degree of diversity around the beginning of the sixteenth century, when filigree work executed with leather pins revealed the enormous wealth of High Renaissance ornamental motifs. Sometimes the filigree technique was the only one used in the decoration of liturgical objects and jewellery, but more often it appeared together with other kinds of decoration.

There are two unparalleled cruets held in the National Museum which were used during the Mass to hold wine and water for Holy Communion. Embossed pears decorate the feet and the bulging bodies of the cruets. A network of artistic filigree embellishment covers their surfaces, with a tiny globe soldered onto each point at which the wires cross each other. Their elegantly shaped pouring spouts resemble dragons. Against a glazed background of cobalt blue, the letter "A" in one of the lids, and the letter "V" in the other, refer to the water and wine. For centuries, these cruets were in use during services in Nagyvárad Cathedral. At the beginning of the nineteenth century, Miklós Jankovich–with the help of an antiques dealer–purchased them from a member of the Bethlen family. The Museum acquired them when the Jankovich Collection passed into its possession.

69. Pendant

**70.** Usually, pendants were covered with floral and tendril motifs, precious stones and pearls. The Renaissance fashion demanded that the goldsmiths attach small cast-metal statues representing historic and mythical figures or saints to the middle of the piece of jewelry. Hungarian goldsmiths went further and placed in the middle of the pendant a tiny Madonna, enthroned and holding the child Jesus in one hand and a sceptre in the other. The inscription PATRONA HUNGARIAE revealed that the piece had been made in Hungary. (The Virgin Mary was patroness of the Apostolic Kingdom of Hungary.) The period in question was marked by the return of the cult of Mary, when the pendant worn at the neck served to invoke her protection of the Hungarian people from the Ottoman danger. Several such pendants are known, and so are copies made in the nineteenth century, complete with the inscription PATRONA HUNGARIAE.

The pendant shown here is made of gold. The coloured tendril-motifs of filigree enamel and the pearl pendant were all typical decorative elements of the Renaissance pendant. The National Museum acquired this piece of jewelry as part of the Jankovich Collection; Miklós Jankovich inherited it from Imre Lósi, the late bishop of Esztergom.

70. *Patrona Hungariae* pendant

**69.** The most exquisite example of sixteenth-century goldsmiths' work was the pendant. Whether hung from a velvet ribbon or from a necklace, or worn in the hair or attached to the dress, pendants were fashionable among ladies, young and old alike, who sometimes even wore more than one at a time. Pendants were usually made of gold, and were adorned with pearls, precious stones, stalk-motifs of coloured filigree enamel, and small cast-metal statues and flowers. The decorative elements were fastened to the pendant in several layers with the help of small screws; these elements turned it into a strikingly attractive, colourful, and lavishly ornamented piece of jewelry. Of the precious stones, it was primarily rubies, almandines and diamonds that were used, a fact that makes the Museum's only pendant adorned with opal especially interesting.

In Europe, the Felsővágás mine near the old border between Poland and Hungary was the only place in the country where opal could be obtained. The first surface finds of opal could have been recovered just shortly before this exquisite piece of jewelry was made. The regular mining of opals at Felsővágás began in the 1530s, just after the pendant was finished.

The pendant is said to have been given to the Polish-born Queen Isabella by her husband, King John Szapolyai (1526–1540). The Zamoisky family distinguished themselves through the support they gave to István Báthori's candidacy for the Polish throne (he was prince of Transylvania from 1571 until 1575). After his election as king of Poland, Báthori gave the pendant, which happened to be in his possession at that time, to the Zamoisky family in appreciation of their services. At the beginning of the nineteenth century Miklós Jankovich purchased jewelry from a Countess Zamoisky, then living in Vienna, and the pendant was in the Jankovich Collection at the time of the latter's purchase by National Museum in 1832.

**71.** To commemorate a victory, it was customary at late-sixteenth-century courts to give the military leader responsible a richly adorned cup. In 1598, when Miklós Pálffy and his small army recaptured the Castle of Győr from the Turks, thus removing the possibility of a Turkish advance on Vienna, the grateful Estates of Lower Austria presented Pálffy with a lavishly ornamented cup to mark the great occasion. Today this magnificent drinking vessel belongs to the Hungarian National Museum. The decorative motifs suggest that the cup was made by a prominent master at the court in Prague.

The beaker is made from pure gold. Standing on top of the lid and covered with translucent enamel is a depiction of Pálffy as a Roman warrior; he is shown resting a foot on the head of a dead Turk.

On the curved surface of the lid and on the vessel, arranged in several rows, there are miniature masterpieces—arms and armour, helmets and banners, musical instruments and other paraphernalia; these are all enamelled. In addition, the lid and the main body of the cup are embellished with the coat-of-arms of Lower Austria, complete with the fess and the crown. The stem and the base of the Renaissance beaker are adorned in a similar fashion. Along the rim of the lid there are finely drawn enamelled tendrils, birds and monsters.

The Pálffy Beaker has had a rather chequered history. István Pálffy, Miklós Pálffy's son, was captured at the Battle of Érsekújvár and was held as a prisoner of war by Gábor Bethlen, prince of Transylvania. The beautiful cup, as well as other treasures, was given by Miklós Pálffy's wife as ransom for her son's release. Bethlen then gave the vessel to the Turkish sultan, who in turn gave it to Ferdinand III (1637–1657) as a goodwill token. Ferdinand returned it to the Pálffy family, whose descendants donated the beaker to the Museum in 1940.

71. The Pálffy Beaker

**72.** The Ottoman-Turkish leather cloak, a masterpiece of its kind, was made at around the beginning of the sixteenth century. Tradition has it that the cloak was worn at the Battle of Mohács (1524), then taken by a member of the Almásy family to Borostyánkő, a castle in the Burgenland (today part of Austria).

When the cloak was buckled up against rain, its wide front panels lay on top of each other; when it was left open, the panels folded back and spread out like wings on the two sides allowing the appliqué decoration to be seen fully. It was cut to be worn by a horseman: the two sides are slit up to the waist, so when the rider was in the saddle, the back panel of the cloak covered the horse's croup. On the left, at the waistline, decorated with leather appliqué tulips, is a smaller slit, cut for the sabre. The sleeves covered only the shoulders and the upper part of the arms.

The two front panels of the otherwise dark-brown leather cloak are dark red; the carefully cut leather pieces are laid on pale green and yellow parchment. Strips consisting of eight longer and eight shorter sections with tendrils and flowers decorate the edges of the front panels; the corners are filled out with a lavish composition of flowers. The decoration on the back consists of a stylized lily placed in a keel-arch niche. The collar is embroidered in golden yarn.

The high level of craftsmanship shows that the leather cloak was probably made in the Constantinople workshop of the sultan for a high-ranking official of the Ottoman army.

72. Cloak

**73.** The National Museum purchased this silver writing case from the estate of Count Sámuel Teleki (1845–1916) in 1926. The superb workmanship and the finely proportioned design distinguish it from the similar artifacts made by Turkish goldsmiths of the same period.

An oblong flat case with rounded ends for the pens is soldered onto a flat, covered, tin-pot, which bulges outwards in the middle. On that end of the case which is closer to the pot the case can be opened on hinges. A ring is soldered onto the top, enabling the whole set to be hung up. Silver-gilt tendrils with leaves and flowers on an en-graved background decorate the lid and the sides of the ink-pot, as well as the top and bottom end of the case. The ornate insignia of Mehmed IV (1648–1687) are punched on both the pot and the case certifying the quality of the silver used. This helps us to determine the time when the writing set was made. Along the edge of the pen-case an inscription in Arabic reads: "made by Mehmed".

Similar portable writing cases were in use throughout the Ottoman empire for centuries. The more expensive ones were made of silver, the simpler ones of copper.

73. Writing set

74. Tent

**74.** As a result of the defeat at Mohács, most of Hungary became a theatre for continual fighting, in which the winners could secure valuable booty. Tradition has it that the ornate tent in the Hungarian National Museum was given to Louis of Baden (1655–1707) as war booty when the Christian armies relieved Vienna in 1683; Louis of Baden later gave this tent to Ferenc Rákóczi II as a gift.

The top of the elongated, hexagonal tent was held in place by two posts planted into the ground; other posts holding the side panels of the tent were joined to these. The edges of the top are trimmed with appliqué to cover the fastening of the sides; this was done with string loops and reels.

The tent was made of two layers of canvas, green and dark red. The red outside layer is luxuriously decorated with appliqué ornamentation. Twelve appliquéd pillars divide up the surface of the sides and roof of the tent. Arcades are formed between the pillars by arches, these fields are filled out with floral design: mushroom-shaped appliqué, carnations, roses, and tulips—motifs very often used in Hungarian ornamentation. The simplicity and clear construction of the decoration makes this tent very precious in comparison with other Turkish tents.

Red tents were used only by the sultans and other very high ranking people in Ottoman society—for example, viziers and beys.

75.a) Canopied bed
75.b) Bedspread

**75.** Very few pieces of furniture used in the households of the sixteenth- and seventeenth-century Hungarian aristocracy survived the devastations which accompanied the Ottoman wars and the 150-year period of the Ottoman occupation. However, in the inventories and other written sources from the period, many references are made to a great variety of carved, painted and inlaid pieces of furniture, especially in the northern and eastern regions of the country, which were not occupied by the Ottoman invaders. Influenced by Dutch furniture design, a new way of ornamenting furniture became widespread in these regions during the seventeenth century. The thin panels to be used in this ornamentation were cut to shape with a fret-saw and then glued onto the base, which was of a different colour. Sometimes this technique was used together with relief decoration.

The canopied bed donated to the National Museum by Sárospatak Castle is a very good example of the variety of effects achieved through the use of this technique. This bed was originally owned by the Vay family, and tradition has it that Ferenc Rákóczi II also slept in it while at Sárospatak Castle. The canopy stands on four lathe-turned legs. In the centre, the emblem of the Jesuits is encircled by rays. In the narrow frieze running under the sill the date 1672 is inscribed between rosettes. Three pilasters divide the surface of the end panels on the front and the back of the bed. The two arcades formed by them are filled out with stylized leaf-bunches carved in relief and surrounded by fretwork arabesques.

The pillow and the sheet on the bed in the exhibition of the Museum are fine examples of seventeenth-century domestic embroidery. The velvet bedspread was embroidered in crimson,

76. Tile stove

gold and silver thread by Zsuzsanna Lórántffy, wife of György Rákóczi I, prince of Transylvania (1630–1648) during the second quarter of the seventeenth century. The Renaissance flower pattern of this most beautiful piece of Hungarian domestic embroidery has an oriental effect. In the centre, framed by coiling tendrils, is the coat-of-arms of Transylvania, and inside is a heart-shaped shield, the coat-of-arms of the Lórántffys; both are worked in gold stitching.

**76.** This seventeenth-century Haban tile stove stood in the manor-house of the Baán family at Liptónádasd and was purchased by the National Museum after being dismantled.

The stove is made from rectangular tiles, which are decorated with a plastic white tin-glaze pattern on a cobalt-blue background. It stands on carved stone legs, the wider lower section, made up of two rows of tiles, is separated from the three-row

top by a sill. The edges of the corner-tiles are rounded off. The crest consists of a row of tiles decorated with grape-bunches crowned by yet another row of tiles. These tiles show figures of sirens between pairs of dolphins. The relatively large tiles of the stove are decorated with leaves of different sizes attached to thin coiling stems coming out of the centre and ending in tulips in the four corners. A row of leaves between two slightly slanted strips make up the sill.

Because of the design, the ideal proportions, the careful execution of the tiles, the good quality of the glaze and the harmonious colouration, we can say that this is a fine example of Haban stove manufacturing. The artistic design of the leaves and flowers on the tiles are related to the patterns employed in contemporary domestic embroidery. The stove was probably constructed during the last third of the seventeenth century in one of the Haban workshops of northwestern Hungary.

67

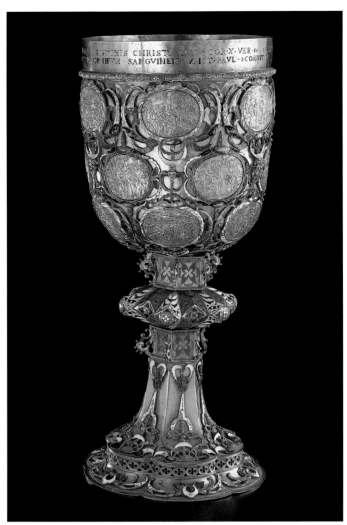

77. The Brózer Chalice

**77.** By the seventeenth century a big difference had developed between the objects used in the liturgies of the Catholic and the various Protestant Churches. The goldsmiths' works preferred by Protestants were simple and unornamented, with their beauty deriving from their classical style. In contrast, the liturgical objects in Catholic churches displayed all the grace and magnificence of High Renaissance and Baroque art. György Rákóczi I, prince of Transylvania, donated this chalice to the Farkas utca Calvinist Church in Kolozsvár on the occasion of the renovation and refurbishing of the building during the late 1630s. (The prince also supported this work.)

The golden chalice with embossed plaques and cloisonné and coloured enamel was made by István Brózer, the goldsmith of the prince's court. Brózer was a well-known and respected member of the goldsmiths' guild at Kolozsvár, and he produced many fine pieces for the Rákóczi treasury. We know that Brózer spent three years as a guest at the goldsmiths' workshop of the French court, and his impressions are reflected in some of the more unusual details of this chalice. Principal among these is the fact is that he depicted Christ's Passion from the Last Supper to the Burial in eighteen stations. No other representations on gold and silver objects are known from this period which dealt with a topic in such detail. Around the rim of the chalice are quotations from St. Paul's Epistle to the Corinthians engraved in Latin–a feature of Protestant chalices produced during this

period. Encircled by a legend relating his various titles is the coat-of-arms of Prince György Rákóczi; beneath the node on the stem of the chalice Brózer engraved his own name: "Colosvárat Brózer Istvan csinalta Anno 1640" (Made by István Brózer in Kolozsvár in the Year 1640).

**78.** The seventeenth-century nobility, tired of the goldsmiths' work of the preceding century, wanted to see new shapes and new styles on their *pohárszék*s (sideboards). This piece of furniture became widely used in royal courts and in aristocratic households during the fifteenth century. Its function was to display on its shelves the family's most treasured objects. The quest for new forms led to the employment of new materials. Ivory, coconut shell, and snail inlays in ornate silver-gilt framing became fashionable at around this time.

This seventeenth-century bowl is by Sebestyén Hann, the famous Transylvanian goldsmith from Nagyszeben. The eight-lobed bowl is fastened aslant onto its base, which is formed from coral and embellished with rows of tiny turquoises and beads. Encircled in flowers is a scene showing the Queen of Sheba paying homage to King Solomon; this is embossed on the centre of the bowl. The master exhibited great skill, especially in his figure of the queen. This bowl, which was used only as a decoration, is one of the finest silver-gilt masterpieces held at the National Museum.

78. Queen of Sheba's cup

79. Goblet

**80.** The tankard–a mug with a lid–was probably the most typical product of seventeenth-century goldsmiths' work. Generally, the entire drinking vessel was made from gold or silver; consequently, this relatively rare tankard of cut rock-crystal is especially valuable. Its form is typical for tankards; the frame of the crystal work is covered with Transylvanian enamel, coloured with especially delicate hues.

Enamelled leaves and flowers encircle the base and the rim of this ornate tankard. A castle with six towers, daisies, floral designs with hearts, a pair of pigeons perched on a branch, and a bunch of flowers in a rosette alternate with each other on the twelve-sided, polished crystal glass body of the tankard. The bottom of the frame and the dome of the lid are embellished with cloisonné enamelled, reticulated flowers.

Inside the lid, on an embossed plaque the coat-of-arms of the Rákóczis is engraved with the legend: FRANCISCUS DEI GRA(TIA) PRINC(EPS) RAKOCZI COM(ES) DE SAAR(OS) DUX MUNK(ACIENSIS) ET MAKOV(I-CENSIS) DOM(INUS) PER(PETUUS) DE SAROSP(A)TOK REG(ECZ) EC(SED) SOM(LYO). Tradition has it that Ferenc Rákóczi II presented the tankard to a member of the Luzsénszky family at around 1700. Although it has no stamped initial, the typical Transylvanian enamel proves that it was certainly produced in Hungary.

80. Tankard

**79.** Goblets and beakers with floral ornamentation are often mentioned in inventories of aristocrats' possession during the sixteenth and seventeenth centuries. Many of these were embossed, but even more displayed magnificent enamel decoration. They were covered with so-called Transylvanian enamel, which was coloured with meticulous care after the first firing and then fired once again. This seventeenth-century goblet is made even more valuable by the fact that, since this kind of enamel was very delicate and the network of tendrils and flower bunches was easily damaged in use, only a few similar examples have survived.

The silver-gilt surface is covered with reticulated webbing. The enamel plaques, which cover the entire surface of the goblet, are fastened onto the plain base by means of tiny screws. The unknown Transylvanian goldsmith who made the object placed an enamelled flower with a bead in its centre on the top of the small lid. Plain goblets of this type (goblets not enamelled, that is) have survived in large numbers.

# Modern Age Department

81. Throne carpet

**81.** In the 1470s King Matthias ordered from the Florentine Francesco Malocchi's workshop several ornamented tapestries to be hung behind his throne. One of the tapestries, all of which were designed by the famous painter and designer Antonio Pollaiuolo (1433–1498), somehow ended up in the possession of Bishop Tamás Bakócz (1442–1521), who replaced the royal emblem with his own coat-of-arms made of similar woven fabric. Later this tapestry was passed on to the bishop's relatives, the Erdődy family, and was kept in their castle in Galgóc until the end of the nineteenth century, when the family donated it to the National Museum.

The base of the rectangular drapery is woven in yellow and green silk thread. The design is outlined with green cut velvet and brocaded in gold; some areas of the surface are composed of uncut loops of gold thread. The wide border is adorned with wings, cornucopias and ears of wheat. Branches of wild roses growing out of a cornucopia fill in the central zone. In the upper half, surrounded by a wreath of oak leaves, the crowned coat-of-arms of King Matthias is shown, with the raven of the Hunyadi family at the centre; the coats-of-arms of Hungary, Dalmatia and Bohemia are included in its four quadrants. Underneath the knots of ribbon attached to the wreath, there is an ornamental vessel standing on a Renaissance marble base decorated with winged angels' heads and flanked by two eagles about to fly off.

This article is an outstanding example of Florentine tapestry art. Several tapestries of similar design and technique are found in other collections, but this is the only completely preserved example of large-size golden tapestry with a coat-of-arms, despite the fact that similar carpets were frequently mentioned in contemporary inventories, and were often depicted in contemporary paintings.

**82.** The first mention of Wladislas II's (1490–1516) papal ceremonial sword was in an inventory of the famous Ambras Castle, drawn up after Archduke Ferdinand of Tyrol's death on May 30, 1596. After passing through many hands, the sword was handed back to Hungary in accordance with Venice ruling of November 27, 1932. The sword, one of the most notable examples of Italian Renaissance goldsmith's art, was made by Domenico de Sutrio in 1509. The lavishly chased hand-guard is made of gilded silver. The hilt ends in a large, silver-gilt pommel. The papal della Rovere coat-of-arms was painted in gold over the enamel ornaments, which are now rather worn. The reticulated scabbard is made of gilded beaten silver. Masks, dolphins and grotesque heads alternate against a pattern of artistically distributed acanthus leaves and foliage. On the locket of the scabbard there is a slightly convex enamel plaque, on which reappears the Rovere coat-of-arms outlined with niello decoration on the bottom half and with champlevé enamel on the upper half. The parallel application of the two different enamelling techniques on the same plaque bears witness to the virtuosity of Domenico de Sutrio.

The gold brocade belt, which belongs to the sword, is also a masterpiece. The design of the belt consists of three motifs: the Rovere coat-of-arms, the papal tiara with the keys of St. Peter, and foliage which unites the two heraldic elements. The key placed further down is woven of silver petals, the crest is of blue silk. The belt is the work of Bernardo Ser Silvano, whose name–together with that of Pietro Mancino, who made the sheath–has been preserved for posterity in the account-books of the papal treasury for the year 1509.

82. Ornamental sword of King Wladislas II

83. Chasuble

**83.** This chasuble was purchased by the National Museum from the church of Sztropkó (Stropkov) with assistance from Bishop Ágost Fischer-Colbrie (1863–1925). Gold filet lace on a blue background was appliquéd on the crimson velvet, violin-shaped front of the chasuble. A cross is embroidered on the back. Its long limb is lengthened at the base; this piece at one time probably decorated the front of the chasuble. The embroidery was done on a golden base. The figures were worked in coloured silk thread with so-called needle-stitches, a technique which creates the effect of painting. On the top, under a trefoil arch, Christ is enthroned in Judgment. At the centre,

also under a trefoil arch, is Golgotha, with Mary Magdalene giving support to Mary, the Apostle John and a praying woman. The upright piece of the Cross ends at the bottom with the scene of the Annunciation. On the left side of the transverse beam of the Cross kneels the Virgin; behind her are the blessed souls. On the right side is St John the Baptist with the damned.

The chasuble, which may be identical to the one made in a Kassa workshop for the church of Sztropkó and which is mentioned in an inventory drawn up in 1474, was manufactured in the second half of the fifteenth century in Hungary. It reveals strong Flemish influence.

72

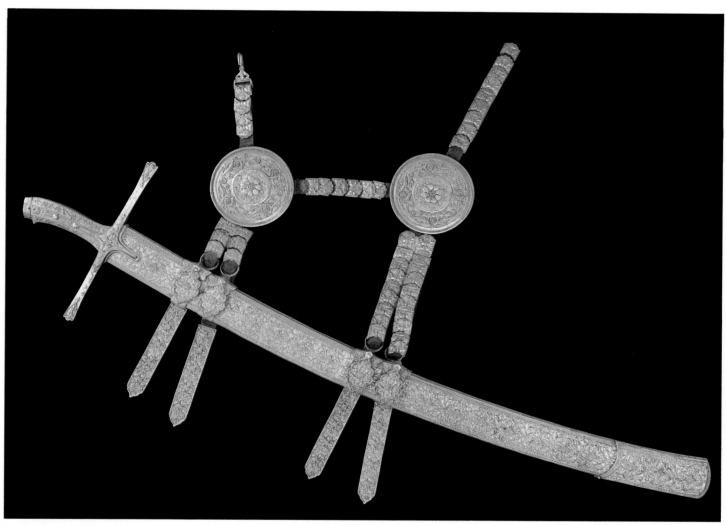

84. Ferdinand of Tyrol's sabre

**84.** The most magnificent and the most completely preserved example of a mediaeval Hungarian sabre, which by any standard makes a unique treasure, was made in 1514. It is believed to have been presented to Ferdinand of Tyrol by members of the Hungarian aristocracy. The hilt, the elongated cross-guard and the belt's mountings are made of gilded silver. The palmette leaves on the hilt and the scabbard are reminiscent of the style of decoration used in the period before the Turkish occupation. On the pommel cap, which was replaced with a new one in the sixteenth century, there is the inscription I[esus] H[ominum] S[alvator], with the monogram IF beneath it, which–despite the oriental motifs used–excludes the possibility of Turkish origin. The sabre was brought back to Hungary from Vienna in accordance with the November 27, 1932 ruling of the Venice Court of Justice.

85. Suit of armour of King Louis II of Hungary

**85.** The principal feature of the armour presented here is the 'Burgundian' armet composed of six separate parts. Due to a remarkable feat of craftsmanship, the armet and the neck-guard seem to form a single piece. The decorative squares contain embossed floral leaf motifs, which were first embossed, then chemically etched and, finally, gilded. The floral leaf motifs imitate the split decoration typical of the *Landsknecht* style. A peculiar feature of the armour is that it was put together from rectangular pieces, with each piece split in four places; this allowed the shirt, made either of cotton or of coloured silk and embroidered with gold thread, to show. The solleret also resembles the *Landsknecht* style with its bluntly cut toe cap. Along the edges of the armour there runs imitation braiding, together with a strip, etched and gilded, recalling embroidery. On the breastplate appears a *Jungfrauenadler* with a female head, which resembles the figure on one of the three heraldic shields which make up the coat-of-arms of the city of Nuremberg. Consequently, it may be assumed that the suit of armour was made there, and that it is of German workmanship. Another interesting feature of the armour is the monogram ES, etched on the breastplate using the above-mentioned technique. The same monogram appears on both the front and the back pommel of the Küris saddle that also belongs to the armour. According to one view, the monograph refers to King Andrew II's daughter, St. Elizabeth; others believe that the monogram denotes the the craftsman who made the armour; yet another view associates it with St Emeric. A previous assumption was that on July 23, 1515 the armour had been given by Emperor Maximillian I (1493-1519) to Louis II, aged nine at the time and slightly underdeveloped for his age. Bruno Thomas, who is one of the best-acclaimed experts on armour today, claims that the armour was made for the wedding of Ferdinand I's daughter, the four-year-old Princess Elizabeth, with the ten-year-old King Sigismund.

The first catalogue ever to describe the weapon collection of Ferdinand of Tyrol referred to the armour as the finest piece to be found there. It was handed back to Hungary in accordance with the Venice ruling.

86. Lady's gown and chemise

**86.** The robe and the shirt of King Louis II (1516–1526), together with his wife's, Queen Mary of Habsburg's, dress and chemise, were purchased from the Church of Mariazell by the National Museum in 1928. The couple most probably wore the costumes at their wedding in 1522. In accordance with the customs of the times, the clothes were then donated to the holy place of Mariazell, in order to be made into ecclesiastical vestments. Although they were ideally suited for the purpose, the clothes were in the end never altered; this was probably due to the respect generally felt for the original owners and their place in history.

The queen's shirt is made of white linen, or cambric, and is adorned with a geometric pattern embroidered using silver thread in a stitch called Hungarian point. The square panels of the shirt were fashioned by the dense gathering of the material. The neckline is oval, the puffed sleeves are held together at the wrist by a band. The garment follows what was the Renaissance fashion between 1520 and 1530. The pattern of the light green, Italian silk damask, which consists of of pomegranates, pineapples, rosettes and floral ornaments, was very popular after the late fifteenth century. The bodice is open on the front; the trapezoid décolletage is trimmed with a band woven from gold, yellow and red silk thread. The funnel-shaped cuffs of the long and tightly fitting sleeves, which were probably worn folded up, were made of the same material. The skirt was cut in a circular pattern; the pleats softly descend from the waist to the ground, ending in a circle on the front and in a graceful train on the back.

A pair of costumes such as these can be found in no other collection. Queen Mary's dress is the second oldest example of a completely preserved female garment in Europe.

87. Folding sundial

The instrument comprises two sundials with different functions. The sundial with the vertical plate–the so-called seasonal sundial–indicates the length of the day, and also the current zodiac position of the Sun. The sundial with the horizontal plate tells the local time only when the gnomon is pointed towards the North Star. A thread pulled taught by a weight is used as the gnomon, led through one of five holes, marked with the numbers 54, 51, 48, 45 and 39, according to the geographical latitudes nearest to the observer's position. The geographical latitudes of the major towns are given in a table underneath the seasonal sundial.

The centre for the production of collapsible sundials made of ivory was in southern Germany, most notably in Nuremberg, where the craftsmen making sundials were allowed to form a guild in 1535. Their products were sold all over Europe. This particular sundial was made by Master I. H. in 1588, as indicated by the monogram inscribed next to the snake-shaped stamp of his guild on the back cover of the object. An additional hole pierced approximately at the position of 49 degrees suggests that the sundial was used in Northern Hungary.

**88.** The pride of the National Museum's watch collection is a man's watch, rather on the large side and worn hanging from the waist pocket, which was acquired together with the Jankovich Collection. The octagonal watchcase was made by soldering copper sheets together and gilding them. The Báthori

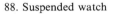

88. Suspended watch

**87.** Until the middle of the eighteenth century–when reasonably priced mechanical clocks appeared–time was measured with the help of sundials of various sizes and types; some were designed to be fixed to the walls of public buildings, some to be placed on a table, and some to be kept in people's pockets. The most important of the small-sized sundials is this four-hundred-year-old multipurpose pocket sundial made of ivory which, according to the German rhyme etched on it, was designed to help the travellers to orient themselves, as well as to measure time.

On the outside of the closed lid there is a sixteen-point compass rose, with the four cardinal points indicated in both German and Latin. The North point of the compass inside the sundial was found by looking through a tiny hole, and a gilded dial shaped in the form of a human hand helped to register the chosen direction. Originally, the sundial also had a small flag to indicate the direction of the wind. On the back of the sundial the various phases of the moon and the days of the lunar month are written. With the help of a rotating perforated sheet, the night-traveller was even able to calculate the number of moon-lit nights during any given period.

family's coat-of-arms with the Order of the Golden Fleece and Dragon's Teeth is shown on the lid, which is decorated with filigreed and chiselled foliation. The back cover, made using a similar technique, is adorned with foliation and stylized flowers growing from a Renaissance flower-pot. The dial plate is made of iron, the digits are Roman and the watch has only one hand. Inside the watchcase once used to be an alarm mechanism which was replaced in the late seventeenth century.

The watch was owned by Zsigmond Báthori (1581–1602), prince of Transylvania. It is not hallmarked, but it was probably made by a Transylvanian master. Zsigmond Báthori was awarded the Order of the Golden Fleece in 1597; therefore, the watch must have been made after this. With only one hand fitted, it was unlikely to have been used after 1700.

89. Pillow-case

**89.** The pillow-case shown here is made of thin white cambric, and is embroidered in coloured silk and silver thread with masterly stitches, which are the same both on the front and the reverse, a technique which is referred to as Hungarian point. Carnations, tulips and acanthuses blossom; tiny birds with hooked beaks are sitting on s-shaped tendrils adorning the four borders of the rectangular pillow-case. The face of the pattern shows that the pillow was used lengthwise, and wreaths of flowers surround the person lying on it, who may have received guests in such ornate bed during recovery from an illness or perhaps after giving birth to a child.

This Transylvanian pillow-case from the middle of the seventeenth century is a wonderful example of the art of so-called domestic embroidery which flourished during this period.

**90.** In the seventeenth and eighteenth centuries, long after the first appearance of the cupboards that eventually made them obsolete, chests continued to play an important role in Hungarian households. A typical kind of chest, the one that remained in use for the longest time, was the hope chest, the nineteenth-century popular version of which was usually decorated with tulip motifs. The chest shown here is an interesting and in many respects a unique example of a seventeenth-century hope chest.

Made of pinewood and decorated with floral and figural motifs, this chest was produced in a Hungarian workshop around the middle of the seventeenth century. The carpenter, a skilful man with a feel for style and balanced composition, most probably worked somewhere in Upper Hungary. Despite the Renaissance architectural ornamentation of Dutch and German origin (shell ornamentation), the chest reveals the unmistakable signs of a mature Hungarian style. The carved and painted ornamentation is complemented by a carved and painted full-figure composition of a couple dressed in Hungarian costumes, which in fact gives the hope chest its unique importance. Only half-length portraits are known besides the figures on this chest; whole-length representation of brides and grooms are known only in two-dimensional representations.

From the viewpoint of cultural history, it is of interest that the chest was once owned by the archaeologist Baron Jenő Nyáry (1836–1914). Unfortunately, the first owner of the hope chest has not yet been identified.

90. Trousseau locker with the figures of the bride and the bridegroom

**91.** According to the evidence of the coat-of-arms, this ornate spoon was made for Count Elek Bethlen II and his wife. It was either in 1678 or in 1679 that Elek Bethlen married his second wife, Klára Nagy, who brought quite a large dowry into the marriage. (The spoon remained largely unknown until it was purchased by the Museum; prior to its acquisition it was never on public display, nor was it ever mentioned in the inventories of the Bethlen family.)

The golden spoon weighs 66 grams. Its handle and the back of its oval-shaped dip is covered with champlevé enamel. The surface is lavishly decorated with golden leaves and pomegra-

**92.** The magnificent book-shaped box was exhibited as the backgammon board of Mihály Apafi, prince of Transylvania (1632–1690), at an exhibition held in the aid of the victims of the 1876 flood, and then at another one organized in connection with the Millennium festivities at the end of the nineteenth century. It was exhibited by Dezső Prónay (1848–1940), who acquired it in the middle of the century from Domokos Bethlen de Iktár. The National Museum later purchased the board from Prónay's daughter.

The large box is made from wood covered with silver both inside and out. The outside and the side panels inside are entirely covered with floral Transylvanian enamelling. In the centre of both its front and back panels, huge (165x125 mm), oval-shaped, polished agate plaques are set in gilded ribbon frames. Around these plaques numerous and differently shaped agate and heliotrope stones are framed in black enamel wreaths of petals. There are a total of 106 agate plaques (67x53 mm) on the front panels, the back panels, and on the sides–both inside and out. The entire surface of the inside, where the game was played, is covered with filigree. The points are made of alternating gold and silver plates. The runners were probably

91. Ornate spoon

92. Backgammon board

nate flowers set against a black background. On both sides of the spearhead-shaped prop which runs halfway up on the bottom of the bowl there are the coats-of-arms of the Bethlen and the Nagy families. The legends around the two coats-of-arms read as follows: ALEXIUS II. DE BETHLEN–CLARA NAGY 1685. The stem ornamented with scrolls and foliage continues in a flattened cylindrical heliotrope. There are three rings around the handle, made of gold and enamelled. The last ring caps the handle, and features a small statue of a green enamelled frog.

This enamelling technique was hardly used during the last years of the seventeenth century in Transylvania, but it was flourishing in German-speaking regions. A very similar piece was auctioned by Sotheby's in 1985; this was a hexagonal spice-holder bearing the coats-of-arms of Mihály Teleki and Judit Vér.

of bone or semi-precious stones. This game of Arabian origin, which called "tric-trac" in French and "Puffspiel" in German, was brought into Europe through either Spanish or Italian mediation in the course of the thirteenth century. It became very popular across the continent and many varieties were played. According to various written sources, the nobility of Transylvania in the seventeenth century liked to amuse themselves with this game of logic, although luck also plays an important role. Only tradition connects this object to Mihály Apafi, but the article shows such superior craftsmanship that it probably did belong to a prince. The ornamentation of the board exhibits elements of oriental taste, but the exact place of origin is unknown.

93. Chest of a guild

**93.** One of the first trades awarded guild privileges in the free royal borough of Modor was the blacksmiths'. The Renaissance chest of the guild was made in 1654. The wooden chest, which is carved and painted, has a tin-plated wrought-iron locking device, braces, handles and a drawer, and comes complete with a Gothic legend running across its sides. According to the inscription, the chest was owned by the honourable blacksmiths of the free royal borough of Modor: "Eines Gantzen Ehrsamen Handtwerch / der Huff Schmidt in der Königlichen Frey Statt / Modor in Ungern." On the outside of the top board, in a field outlined with a lathe-frame, there is a fragmented legend, interrupted by one large and two smaller horseshoes: the symbols of the trade. It is written on the inside of the lid in a field formed by three reticulated, lobular, engraved and tin-plated iron mountings that the chest had been made in 1654 by Michael Könnig for the honourable guild of blacksmiths: "Michael Könnig / hatt diese zech / ladt auffgeri / cht den ehrsamen / handtwerch / der huffSch / midt / 1654." On the left-hand side of the chest, beneath the handle, a red heart cut into two with a saw is shown. On the back the names of the guild officials are listed, and on the right-hand side a bouquet of five tulips is shown. The chest was most probably acquired by the National Museum either immediately after the abolition of the guilds in 1872, or following the sudden upsurge of interest in guild memorabilia which began in 1877.

**94.** This historical Hungarian costume was made for Catherine of Brandenburg, the second wife of Gábor Bethlen, prince of Transylvania (1580–1629). The material is Italian, the higher, cut, shining pattern stands out splendidly against the shorter thickly woven loops of the base. The textile used for the two parts of the garment, while looking indistinguishable from a distance, is in fact different. The bodice is blue with patterns of flowers with pomegranates at their centres. The plum-coloured skirt is decorated with deltoid fields framed in double weaves, and filled with large bending flowers with tulips and pomegranates. The bodice is cut in a wide rectangular shape and laced with snake-shaped metal clasps. The front, the cur-ved back and the armholes are trimmed with carnations, tulips and daisies under arcades embroidered in gold and silver thread with satin stitches and Hungarian point. The bottom of the loose and richly pleated skirt is similarly lavishly embroidered.

It seems likely that Gábor Bethlen had ordered this Transyl-vanian-style dress for his foreign fiancée as early as 1623 or 1624, since a large trousseau awaited her on her arrival. The wedding took place in 1626; the prince died three years later, in 1629. The widow could not easily have had such an exquisite dress made: the material, the cut, and the decoration were all characteristic of the ladies' attire popular in Hungary in the first half of the seventeenth century.

94. Lady's dress

**95.** This *mente*, which is said to have been worn by Gábor Bethlen, prince of Transylvania, was preserved by the Zichy family and sold to the Museum in 1950. The material is light red and is probably Italian patterned velvet; the design consists of diagonal zig-zags and poppy-heads. The short front, which widens towards the waistline, and the back and the fun-nel-shaped sleeves are ornamented with gold and silver cords appliquéd in floral shapes and loops and with embroidery in satin stitches.

The luxurious *mente* is a typical example of special Hungarian men's wear during the seventeenth century.

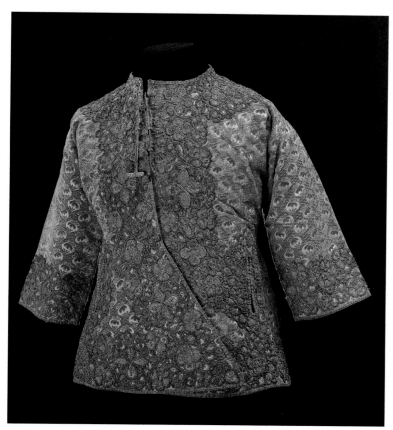

95. Gentleman's *mente*

**96.** At a sale held in Debrecen, Miklós Jankovich's agent bought a musical instrument from a Countess Bethlen who claimed that the instrument, which was concealed in an ornamental box, had once belonged to Catherine of Brandenburg, Gábor Bethlen's second wife. The prince ordered a large number of treasures and articles from abroad, and he usually ordered them from a place known to produce the articles in question in good quality. In the account books of both Gábor Bethlen and his wife, Catherine of Brandenburg, several virginals are mentioned, and although from the brief description it is not possible to identify this particular virginal with any of the ones listed there, the possibility that it was once owned by the prince cannot be discarded.

The virginal of the reigning princess of Transylvania stands out among similar instruments made in the seventeenth century. On the top of the box the velvet-covered cushion hides a small drawer, while the part under the keys conceals a larger drawer divided into compartments, which were probably used to keep jewelry. The box of the instrument is stained black, and covered with silver and gold foliation coiling around different-sized enamelled and etched pictures and medallions, which are partly inlaid and partly appliquéd. Each one of the champlevé enamel pictures is a masterpiece. There are compositions of flowers, fruit, instruments, birds, and angels on the smaller ones; figures playing various musical instruments and allegories of the four seasons, seven arts, and four senses are painted on the larger plaques. The latter are lids of other wonderful pictures in the centre of the cover. In the inside of the little doors the Visitation, the Adoration of the Magi and the Adoration of the Shepherds are painted; behind the two doors on the sides scenes from the Bible are etched using spotting and corrosive technique, and behind the central door there is a mirror. The style and the quality of the ornamentation suggest that the virginal originates from southern Germany, or rather from Augsburg. The initials of the goldsmith are recorded in one of the pictures: "1617 LKI IKF", which probably means, "Lucas

96. Virginal

Kilian Invenit Johannes Klebiller Fecit". This assumption is affirmed by the fact that Lucas Kilian etched a portrait of Gábor Bethlen on copper in 1620. The virginal is more of a toy than a musical instrument: the keyboard extends only to three octaves. Originally, the instrument was played by plucking the short strings.

Nothing is known about the person who made the instrument. Five organ-builders are known to have been working in Augsburg during this period, one of whom was Samuel Bidermann (1540–1622), who made several similar virginals with drawers, sometimes combining them with an automatic playing mechanism. Another virginal, much simpler in design but similar in appearance and in proportion, is preserved in the collection of the Victoria and Albert Museum, but unfortunately that one is not identified either. Looking at the silver mounts, the etching and the enamelling of the virginal in London, the two instruments seem similar.

**97.** An early and fine example of Hungarian baroque furniture is this two-door cupboard made around 1700; it combines the styles of two different periods. The carved cornice reveals marks of seventeenth-century taste, while the rich marquetry—consisting of ribbons, birds and floral ornaments—is characteristic of the eighteenth century. The cupboard with canted corners is supported on five bun-feet beneath a lobular base made of walnut. The surface is decorated with walnut root marquetry, yew-wood, and maplewood inlays outlined by burning; the decorative design is composed of naturalistic birds and various other animals among floral ornaments. The vertical articulation of the structure and the fractured line of the carved framing of the ornamented fields of the doors are emphasized. The cupboard is crowned by a reticulated cornice placed on a slightly protruding corbel. The cornice is made up of acanthus leaves; there is a square-shaped section in its centre with a lathe-turned ornament on the top. The hinges are engraved and tinned. The cupboard was acquired by the National Museum from the descendants of the Rosos family from Szentkirályszabadja.

97. Two-door cupboard

98. Theorbo lute

**99.** The ceremonial dress styled in French fashion was worn by Mrs Gábor Muslay, neé Anna Vay, probably on the occasion of a court ceremony. The dress is a typical example of the "grand habit de cour", or the "robe à la francaise", popular between 1760 and 1770. It seems quite plausible that Anna Vay had the dress made for the occasion of her husband's appointment as Deputy Lord Justice of Pest county in 1768. The National Museum bought the dress from Mrs Rudolf Majthényi, neé Anna Muslay, in 1935.

The material of the dress is French silk, a kind which was very fashionable around 1760–1765. Against a green background an undulating lace-motif and bouquets of flower are woven in the textile with a technique imitating embroidery. It is decorated with a stitched border of green and pink chenille, which used to be covered with lace. The front of the bodice is cut out in a square shape; it is like a small vest, overlaps the skirt a little, and unbuttons in the centre with buttons covered with the material of the bodice. The double skirt is flat both on the front and the back, wide on the two sides and longer at the back; its train is curved. The cloak-like back of the dress is gathered in wide pleats–so-called Watteau-pleats–from the shoulders down. Double rouffle completes the end of the tight sleeves reaching along to the elbows.

99. Lady's dress

**98.** Theorbo-type lutes were especially popular from the sixteenth to the eighteenth centuries. This theorbo and other precious musical instruments were acquired by the National Museum in 1902, as part of the bequest of István Delhaes (1845–1901), a Viennese art collector.

The elongated pear-shaped instrument was made of palisander wood. Masterly bone inlays in tortoise-shell and engraved mother-of-pearl plaques embellish the back of the neck and the pegbox; the little pictures are encircled by leaves, flowers, grotesques, and by sitting and standing figures.

The instrument was made by the renowned master Joachim Tielke of Hamburg. The characteristic feature of his instruments is that he embellished with carved and inlaid ornaments every little place on the entire surface except where the ornaments would have altered the sound. He made the inlays with a method widely used in the seventeenth century, whereby two or more lighter and darker coloured, thin bone and tortoise-shell plates were placed on top of each other. The design was drawn on the top one, and all the pieces were cut out together. By cutting the patterns this way, no material was wasted, and by putting the darker and lighter sections in pairs, every single piece was used. The bone inlays were also decorated with engravings. The compositions were taken from the works of famous copper etchers, such as Otto van Veen (1556–1629). One hundred and thirty-seven works by Tielke are known, seven of which are theorbos. The bone inlays on one of them—made in 1707—were cut at the same time as the one held at Budapest, so the two instruments were produced at the same time, or at least definitely by using the same pattern.

**100.** This nobly proportioned piece of furniture, which was made in the eighteenth century, unites the characteristic types of the period: the commode, the writing cabinet is and the glass-fronted book cabinet. The book-cabinet is in the place usually occupied by the tabernacula found in writing cabinets. This veneered and marquetry-decorated item of Rococo furniture is treasured as one of the finest products of eighteenth-century cabinetmaking in Upper Hungary. The subdued walnut root marquetry is in harmony with the gilded sections. The bookshelves stand on a commode-like base consisting of three drawers with winding contours; the writing board in the centre folds up, and there is a small drawer on each side of it. The tall, glass-fronted upper part has two doors and shelves inside, and its frame is gilded. The playfully buoyant Rococo cornice incorporates shells. The splendour of the Rococo ornamentation is enhanced by the fine gilded brass mounts and the hinges of the glass-panelled section, to compete in exquisiteness with the reticulated brass mounts on the book bindings.

100. Rococo bookshelf

**101.** This strange musical instrument is primarily associated with two names: those of Prince Miklós Esterházy (1714–1790) and Joseph Haydn (1732-1809). The prince, himself an excellent baritone player, was partial to this soft-toned instrument and constantly urged his conductor to write pieces for it. In compliance with the demand, Haydn, in the space of ten years, wrote more than one hundred and fifty works in which a baritone (that is to say, the prince) took the leading part. Haydn's first works for the baritone were written in 1765, suggesting that this precious instrument was already in the prince's possession by that time. One hundred and fifty years later the eminent cello player Béla Csuka (1893–1957) revived interest in the long-forgotten instrument, playing it at a concert with the permission of Dr. Pál Esterházy. During the Second World War the baritone, together with other art treasures, was stored in the Esterházy Palace in Buda, and it was only by good fortune that it survived undamaged. In 1949 it was taken over by the National Museum on the order of a government commissioner.

The baritone belongs to the group of gambas. In addition to numerous bowed strings on the finger-

101. Baritone

board, it also has resonant strings, which have to be plucked by the player's left thumb, by which the player is able to produce unique effects. This baritone is made of pine and maple and lacquered in light yellow. The sides and the back are decorated with undulating lines of inlay; on its extra finger-board there is a foliated scroll inlay of bone and wood. The peg-box ends in a carved, painted moustachiod head wearing a shako. The original case is covered with leather studding with gilded nails. The musical instrument was produced by the renowned Viennese violin maker Johann Stadlmann, as proven by the signature "Johann Joseph Stadlmann Kaiserl. Königl. Hof Lauten- und Geigenmacher in Wien 1750".

The Kunsthistorisches Museum in Vienna has a baritone made by Daniel Achatius Stadlmann, the father of the master who made the one in the Hungarian National Museum: this instrument–as tradition has it–used to belong to Haydn.

**102.** This typical Rococo chalice was produced by one of the most excellent enamel painters of the eighteenth century, János Szilassy. The legend on the patera belonging to the chalice has "FECIT JOANNES SZILASSI LEUTSCHOVIAE ANNO 1763". Szilassy was the master of the silversmiths' guild in Lőcse from 1747 until his death in 1782; so far 108 of his artworks are known, the most magnificent of these being the one-meter-tall monstrance–for which he was commissioned by Kassa Cathedral. The National Museum purchased the monstrance from an antique dealer, Fülöp László (Löwy) in 1895. The chalice was first on display at the Millennium exhibition, but since then it has been exhibited many times. There are three painted and enamelled medallions among the embossed shell-shaped ornaments on both the base and the cup; on the base the portraits of three Hungarian saints, St Stephen, St Elizabeth and St Margaret, and on the cup itself Ecce Homo, St Francis of Assisi and St Nicholas, are painted. Between the medallions, enamelled angels stand under baldachins. The entire surface is embellished with tiny enamel flowers and precious stones.

Painted enamel ornaments were often used by Baroque goldsmiths at Augsburg and Vienna. The talented master of Lőcse was probably influenced by their example when he designed and painted his enamel plaques, but he also added a Hungarian flavour to the decoration by including the characteristic minute flowers.

**103.** The chastiser–quite rare in Hungary–was a guild emblem. The example shown here was carved from hardwood; it has the shape of a spoon with a long three-lobular handle. Looking at the painted emblem and tools and products of the trade, it becomes apparent that this chastiser used to belong to a bootmakers' guild. A copper tool for flattening the leather and a curved knife for cutting out the pattern are placed by the boot, which is cut high under the knee. The date, 1778, is either the time when the guild was founded, or the year the chastiser was manufactured. The place where it was made is not indicated; the fact that it is Hungarian is proved by the coat-of-arms of the country, with the crown painted on the back. It might have served several purposes: it could have been an emblem representing power, or a means of administering punishment, which was between one and twelve strokes. The variety developed in the the Czech and the Moravian regions and in Vogtland in the Erzgebirge also played the role of trade-certificates: by presenting it, the person proved that he was authorized to bring a message or mandate from the master of the guild.

**104.** Trade certificates are probably the most decorative and–owing to the figural representations on them–the most colourful documents in the history of crafts. After 1731, in the Holy Roman Empire their use was ordained by a decree, and as the culmination of a journeyman's study-trip abroad, these written documents soon became widely used in Hungary also. After the seventeenth century it was a general policy of the guilds to ask journeymen to show written proof of their probity and of the work they had performed during their previous employment.

102. Chalice

103. Chastiser

The handwritten and elaborate manuscripts–which were embellished with ornamental designs, drawings of tools and working scenes according to the style of the period–had become common in Hungary by the last third of the eighteenth century. Starting from the beginning of the next century, the use of printed trade certificates became more and more widespread; the finest were decorated with cityscapes. Following the 1816 decree of the Council of Lieutenancy, the certificates were made out in a book format; this remained in use until the abolition of the guild system in 1872.

As shown by the elaborately written certificate, and confirmed by the stamp of the guild, the harnessmakers of Sárospatak accepted into their guild one János Szabó, who in 1776 had just completed his study years. The certificate is framed with folkloristic flowers and ornamented with a picture of a harnessmaker at work. The man in the picture is wearing the clothes typical of the time, and he is sitting with his leg thrown over the special stool constructed for harness-makers, with the harness he is working on held in place by a vice in front of him. He holds a pair of compasses in his hand, and uses them to measure the width of the strip of leather. In front of him, on the bench, a punch and a curved knife are shown. Above the man hangs an example of the the most obvious product of the trade, a barble-bit and harness.

104. The trade certificate of the Harnessmaker's Guild at Sárospatak

105. Bowl

**105.** The first and most important faience manufactory in the Habsburg empire was founded by Queen Maria Theresa (1740–1780) and Francis of Lorraine (1745–1765) at Holics; this later stimulated the development of such establishments in Hungary.

The manufactory of Holics produced primarily for the court, the households of the nobility, and the Church; its style was influenced by northern Italian, French and German porcelain factories. The harmony of coloured and blue flower bouquets, lambrequin ornaments of the Strasbourg and Rouen factories, the landscapes which covered the entire surface in the manner of Castell, and genres and Chinese ornaments gave a peculiar flavour to Holics porcelain. In addition, the various animal, flower and fruit-shaped trays, boxes with lids, and the antique and religious statuettes were patterned with infinite charm.

The large Chinoiserie-style bowl which was made in the 1760s–the most prosperous period of the manufactory–was one of the most exquisite pieces produced in the works. The ornamentation bears the traces of baroque animation: in front of a throne made up of shells under a baroque parapet wild animals are seen resting. Sea boats in a harbour appear vaguely in the distance among foliage bearing clusters of grapes and flowers. In the foreground a powerful Chinese gentleman is smoking his pipe and servants are hurrying towards him. This bowl, which is important even in comparison with other European masterpieces, was acquired from the collection of Count Géza Andrássy (1856–1938).

**106.** Typical historical evidence of Hungary's feudal period includes the letters patent of nobility awarded by Hungarian kings and Transylvanian princes, as well as other letters featuring coats-of-arms. Initially, parchment paper sheets were used; then, from the eighteenth century onwards, the documents were issued in book form, mostly in an ornamental style fitting the style of the period. The title of nobility of the Andrássy family–a familiar name in Hungarian history–was made out in the latter format. The rank of count was conferred on Károly Andrássy and his children by Maria Theresa in 1779; the diploma was bound in red leather, with the royal seal confirming the act securely protected in a copper box. The Latin text lists the virtues of the person awarded it and describes the coat-of-arms of the Andrássy family. Each of the parchment paper sheets is framed using finely-drawn Rococo ornamentation mixing with military trophies composed of various weapons and scenes of encampment, thus referring to the glorious military tradition of the family. The most striking feature of the diploma is the painted coat-of-arms on the first page. In line with the custom of the age, the miniaturist painted a baroque architectonic frame around the coat-of-arms. In the foreground, again, arms and soldiers of Antiquity are depicted. Beneath the crest, there are naked natives holding the cartouche-shaped shield with the nine-pointed coronet denoting

the rank of count together with the Andrássy family's coat of arms: against a blue background, two lions facing each other stand on a green mound, holding a closed crown. Two of the helmet crests repeat the lion featuring on the coat-of-arms; the one at the centre shows a knight who, according to a family myth, during the knightly contest held on the occasion of King Stephen's coronation, cut off the head and arm of his opponent with one blow. The legend beneath the shield also refers to the family's military virtues and bravery FIDELITATE AT FORTITUDINE (By means of loyalty and courage).

The Andrássy de Krasznahorka family was of Szekler ancestry; it acquired its family estates, including the one which lent the name Krasznahorka, in Gömör county in the sixteenth century. The Andrássys were raised to the rank of barons in 1676, then one branch of the family was given countship in 1766, the other in 1779. In the past two centuries the Andrássy family has provided several prominent personalities in the country's political and scientific life: Count György Andrássy (1797–1872) was one of the founding members of the Hungarian Academy of Sciences, Count Gyula Andrássy the Elder was the first Hungarian prime minister after the Compromise of 1867 (he then became foreign minister of the Monarchy); and Count Gyula Andrássy the Younger was the last foreign minister of the Monarchy.

106. The letters patent of the Count Andrássy de Csíkszentkirály et Krasznahorka family

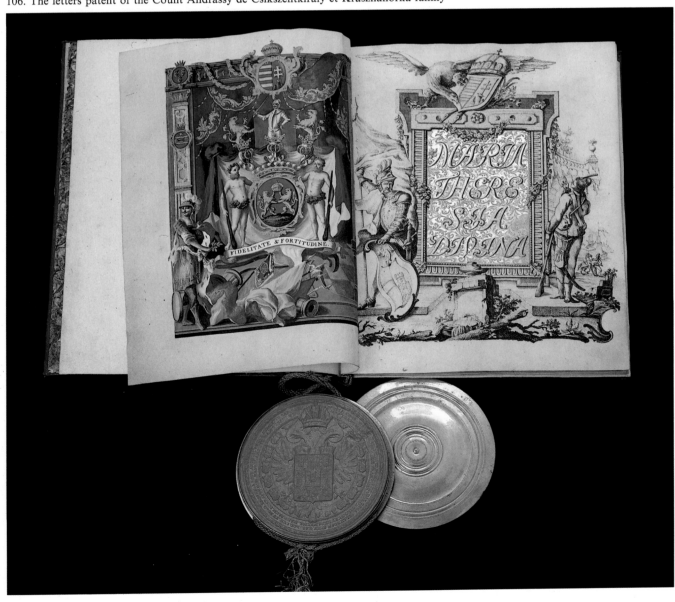

107. Empire drawing-room suite

**107.** The fifteen-piece suite of Empire-style sitting-room furniture was made in the 1820s for the manor-house at Tengelic, the property of Dániel Csapó (1778–1844), Tolna county's deputy to the reformist sessions of the Diet and the first vice-president of the Hungarian Economics Association; he was also an eminent agriculturalist. It was bequeathed to his daughter, Ida, who was the wife of Pál Kiss de Nemeskér, the governor of Fiume, who entertained Széchényi and Kossuth in his palace on several occasions. The next lord of the manor was Vilmos Csapó (1798–1879), a nephew who was a colonel in the Hungarian army during the War of Independence of 1848, and who distinguished himself at the Battle of Ozora. The suite of furniture remained in the possession of the family until 1963 when it was acquired by the National Museum.

The suite represents a Hungarian variation on the French Empire style; it developed in the 1820s on the basis of the Classicist style of furniture. Its formation was helped by the current flourishing of the Classicist style in architecture; the cold, ceremonial and pompous French Empire was transformed into a simpler and more homely version more in accordance with the demands of the progressive and independently-minded members of the middle and small nobility, and which was also more appropriate to the atmosphere of the mansions of the higher nobility. The sofa and armchairs of the polished black wooden suite are upholstered, their backs are arched, and their legs end in shells. Each leg of the sofa stands on a gilded caryatid. The backs of the upholstered chairs end in a three-lobed arch with a cross-rail; their prismatic legs narrow towards the ground. The table is of a plain rectangular shape, a narrow rim beneath the tabletop is ornamented with gilded open-work in rectangular deepened fields, the prismatic legs narrow towards the ground. The suite is complemented by poufs, hassocks, and flower-stands.

108. Set of jewellery, pendant and pair of earrings

**108.** When the Emperor Napoleon Bonaparte (1804–1815) was sent to exile, he was not accompanied by his wife, the Habsburg Archduchess Maria Louisa (1791–1847). At the Congress of Vienna the Duchy of Parma was chosen as her future place of residence. She was living there when she married again, this time to Karl, Graf de Bombelles, Lord Chamberlain of the Court of Parma. No children resulted from this marriage. From his first marriage, Bombelles had a son, Louis, who married Countess Franciska Hunyady in 1850. The jewelry, accompanied by a letter, was said to have been given by Maria Louisa to her stepdaughter-in-law on that occasion.

The large polished citrine stones are set in yellow, green and red eighteen-carat gold mounts which form the arms of the cross-shaped pendant, as well as the earrings which are made up of two parts. The settings of the stones of the earrings are decorated with minute rosebuds. A Parisian initial is stamped in each piece (Rosenberg 3 Nr. 5868); this was in use between 1809 and 1819. The chain which used to belong to the pendant was lost during the Second World War, together with the certificate of donation. The claim that the jewelry was given to Countess Hunyady as a wedding present by Maria Louisa is probably unfounded, since Maria Louisa died in 1847 and the wedding took place in 1850. Nevertheless, the jewelry can still be associated with Napoleon's second wife.

109. Writing desk with clock

**109.** This writing cabinet is an example of the Hungarian variety of Empire style. The prototype of this kind of furniture was developed during the eighteenth century. The more compact types with larger drop-leaves and two doors at the bottom appeared in the 1810s and the 1820s. The writing cabinet with a clock, previously owned by the archaeologist József Hampel (1849–1913), the director of the Coin and Antiquities Collection of the National Museum, forms an interesting variant of this compact type. A harmonious design both in its proportions and in its decoration, the cabinet has a curving outline and resembles some urn-shaped writing desks. The drawers and compartments hidden behind the drop-leaf can be regarded as the substitutes for the drawers of the compartments. At the bottom there is a rectangular base on four rounded feet, on which the four volute legs actually supporting the body of the cabinet rest. The bottom part of the cabinet forms a semicircle, with the two doors corresponding to two quarter-circles. On top of it there is a rectangular piece, rounded at the corners, with the drop-leaf. Moving further up, we find the vaulted top with the round-shaped clock resting on an oblong base. "Joseph Lechner in Pest" is engraved in the glass of the round-shaped clock. The ornamentation of the cabinet, which is made of walnut with mahogany and maple-wood marquetry, is very diversified: it incorporates marquetry laid in a radial pattern, black painting, carved and gilded ornaments and copper mountings.

91

**110.** The sabre shown here has a carefully elaborated blade, with both sides lavishly etched. The dedication surrounded by ornate motifs reads: "As a token of their deepest respect and gratitude, the Hungarian Lifeguards offer this [sabre] to their beloved and much-respected Lieutenant Count Ferencz Haller de Hallerkő". On one side the dedication ends with the Hungarian royal coat-of-arms, and on the other with the Haller family's coat-of-arms adorned with a count's nine-pointed coronet. On both sides, broken up into four lines, the names of the thirty-two officers presenting the sabre are listed. Beneath the hand-guard, in two semi-circular chased-base oak wreaths, the coats-of-arms of Hungary and Transylvania are shown. The etch-work of the seven castles built on seven mounds, the sun, the crescent moon and the eagle looking to the right is just as elaborate as the Hungarian coat-of-arms. In the given form, the emphasized elements of the sabre undoubtedly reflect the emperor's policy of "divide et impera". At this time Transylvania was treated as a principality separate from Hungary; therefore, the insignia of the Guard, and even the Vienna Palace of the Lifeguard, were obliged to reflect the dividedness of the Empire–regardless of the feelings on the subject entertained by the young men wishing to gain acceptance by the refined circles of the Viennese Court. On the blade-extension and on the mounts of the sheath decorated with scenes taken from the life of the unit, there is the stamp of the Viennese goldsmith I. H. Haussman, with the year 1849 marked next to it. The decoration featuring large leaves, a favourite motif during the early nineteenth century, as well as every detail of the Haller family's coat-of-arms on the octagonal smoke-stone seal which substitutes for the buttons, pays tribute to the goldsmith's artistic skill and his gift for balanced composition.

110. Ferenc Haller's sabre

**111.** On the blade of the sabre the words "Georg Rákótzi II 1643" are written next to the coat-of-arms of Rákóczi, who was prince of Transylvania. The hilt is plated with silver-gilt decorated with engraved foliage. The coat-of-arms of the Rákóczi family adorns the scabbard-straps: the principality's coat-of-arms with the Szekler eagle flying towards the sun combined with the seven castles of the Saxons. The scabbard bears a total of 164 corals. In 1849 the women of Transylvania bought the sabre to present it to József Bem in recognition of his heroic attempts to defend Transylvania. After occupying Bem's camps, the Russians discovered the sabre in a red leather casing, complete with the words "A souvenir for the heroic commander Bem, from the women of Kolozsvár, 1849". The sabre was taken to Russia as booty, and was kept in the imperial weapon collection at Tsarskoe Selo for a while; it then was moved to the tsar's museum in St Peterburg. The Hungarian state borrowed the sabre for the Millenium Exhibition. On August 7, 1896 the Russian ambassador to Vienna addressed a letter to Austria-Hungary's common foreign ministry, revealing that the Russian empire wished to present the sabre to the Hungarian National Museum: "By this presentation, His Imperial Majesty wishes to express his appreciation for the cordiality which characterizes relations between the Russian Empire and Austria-Hungary".

111. The sabre of György Rákóczi II and József Bem

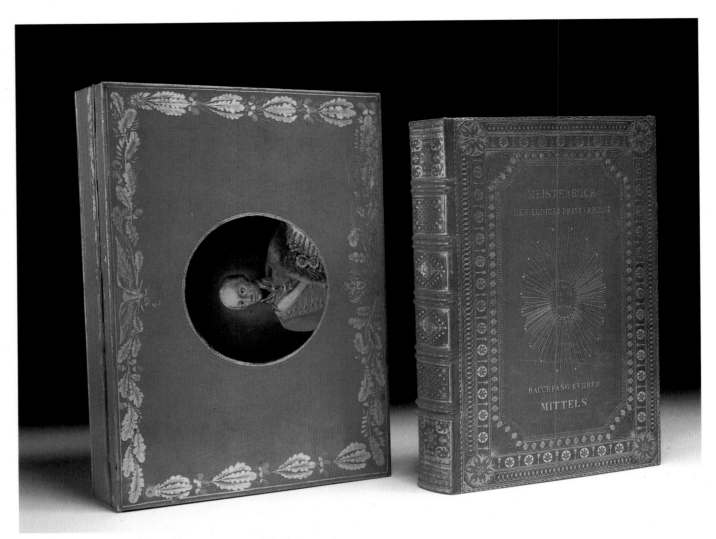

112. The Master Book of the Chimneysweeps' Guild of Pest-Buda

**112.** The guilds which—on the basis of their privileges—were allowed to organize their internal life, laid a great emphasis on the dignified holding of initiation ceremonies for new members. Accordingly, most of the guilds had a master-book specifically for the purpose of registering the particulars of their accepted members. The master book of the chimneysweeps of Pest-Buda is unique both for its artistic execution, and for the fact that no other master book of the same trade is known. Only a few chimneysweep guilds are known to have existed in Hungary. Chimneysweeps formed guilds only in a few larger towns, for example in eighteenth-century Pozsony and in the mining towns of Northern Hungary. In Pest-Buda (as the twin cities were called before their unification), they were given the royal letters patent in 1818. In the first half of the nineteenth century, there were usually nine to ten masters working at the same time in the two cities of Pest and Buda. Their master book, which dates back to 1828, and its accompanying case are masterpieces of contemporary bookbinding and leatherwork made in Pest-Buda. The gilded red leather binding with ray ornaments in Empire style was produced by József Szidarits of Pest. The workmanship of the frontispiece is also noteworthy. On the tin case, which was also made in 1828, a gold wreath of oak leaves on a red background adorns the portrait of emperor-king Francis I (1792–1835). Another jacket to protect the tin case was made by Ferenc Oláh in 1835.

**113.** To decorate this masonic master's apron, which itself was made from white goat-skin with black cotton lining, the same method was used as in the production of coloured copper etchings. This item reflects the ideas and the mysterious symbolism of the Free Masonic Order—a movement in the forefront of the Enlightenment. On the apron we find motifs taken from Ancient Egyptian culture and the Jewish religion, the components of deism, mediaeval mysticism, rationalism and the Enlightenment combined with the traditions of the guilds of mediaeval church builders, a group recognized by the freemasons as their forerunners. The Sun, depicted as a radiating human face, and the Moon rising from the clouds are shown on the apron; at the centre, beneath stars, we see Solomon's temple. Standing next to a locust-tree are Corinthian columns on both sides of the picture, with the letters J and B–the initials of the master builders Jachin and Boaz respectively. The desolate landscape in the foreground is filled with the seemingly complicated symbols of the masonic order: the half-opened compasses, the bevel-square, the architectural plan, the hammers, the stones both carved and uncarved, the pyramid, the snake coiling around a globe, the bee-hive with bees, the sword, the trowel and the pick-axe: the symbols of human knowledge, effort, creativity and labour.

In the freemason's order, the apron distinguished the officials of the movement. In the second half of the eighteenth century beautiful Masonic Order aprons were made by English, French and German craftsmen. This particular example of such an apron arrived in Hungary with Austrian help. The apron, which for decades was worn during the ceremonies, finally became a precious relic even for free masons. The apron was acquired by the National Museum as part of the Auer collection in 1981.

113. Freemason's master cloth

114. Statue of a Freemason

**114.** This porcelain statue shows a masonic master. The procedure of being accepted by the organization of freemasons led from acceptance by the lodge–through being inaugurated first as an apprentice then as a journeyman–to being raised to the level of mastership. Leaning on a stump surrounded by grass, the male figure stands on a square base with rounded corners. The figure is that of a typical eighteenth-century freemasonic master wearing a grey wig under a black hat, a white ruffled shirt, and a green waistcoat and terracotta jacket, which is slit up to the waist at the back and buttoned the whole length of the front; a large master-apron covers his black breeches. He lifts his hand protectively towards a mop on the top of a pillar. The mop is a secret reference to the "Order of the Mop" found in German-speaking regions which united the wives and daughters of freemasons. The original of this statuette was fashioned in Meissen by Johann Joachim Kändler (1706–1775) around 1745. Another version of this sculpture–dating from 1925–is held by the Berlin Museum of Freemasonry.

**115.** The first doll's house was made according to the ideas of Albert V, prince of Bavaria in the 1550s; however, it was made not for the merriment of his children, but to represent the grandeur of his court. Later on, doll's houses played an important role in the education of rich, upper-class girls. At the beginning of the nineteenth century–together with other toys–doll's furniture, doll's rooms, kitchens and shops were manufactured, and these miniatures soon became popular items on the European market.

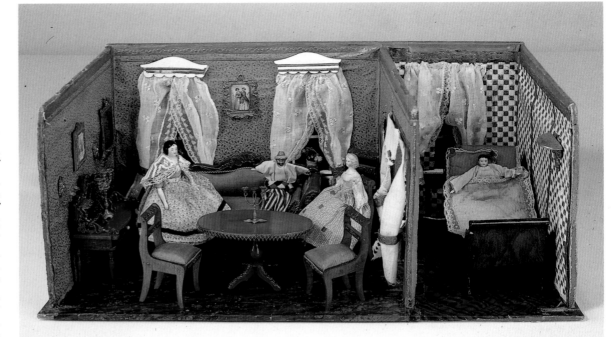

115. Doll's house

This Biedermeier doll's flat–with elegant furniture and porcelain-headed dolls–used to belong to the children of the Baron Prónay family. The walls are made of wood, the floors are covered with marbled paper. The living-room has two windows (the pattern of the wallpaper is gold on blue), and a gold paper-trimming with embossed ornamentation runs along the top of the walls of both rooms. The smaller room's wallpaper is checkered blue and white; in front of its single window hangs a flower-patterned tulle curtain adorned with lace. An opening is cut between the two rooms. The living-room furniture–consisting of a settee, an oval table, six chairs, an ottoman and a dressing table with mirror–is upholstered with blue silk and decorated with copper mountings. The walls are decorated with

116. Portrait of Baron Gábor Kemény

a religious picture, a fashion design and mirrors in embossed metal frames. Newspapers, candle-holders and a shelf on the wall create the illusion of a real home. In the corner of the bedroom stands a white metal stove, in the bed–made of metal painted brown–a doll baby wrapped in a silk blanket rests on silk pillows. The ladies are sitting in the living-room together with a male doll dressed in Turkish clothes. The dolls have white-glazed and biscuit porcelain heads, their limbs and bodies are made of stuffed linen. Their modelled painted coiffure, painted little faces and their dresses indicate that the doll's flat was made in the 1860s. The following is written in ink on the back of the wall: "From 1855 or 1856. I received this from my dear unforgettable Mother on the day of Christmas in 1858 or 1859 upholstered anew by my beloved governess Jenny Louise–Baroness Róza Prónay". This doll's flat was displayed at an exhibition organized during the First World War to aid of the children of those who had been called up, and the newspapers mentioned it as a special, antique piece. After the Second World War this doll's flat–as an object of historical value–was first deposited at the National Museum, then, in 1960, it was donated to the collection by Mrs. Tibor Patay.

**116.** The original of this porcelain plate was decorated with flowers encircled by a band of animals. Then the decoration at the centre was replaced with a portrait of Baron Gábor Kemény (1830–1888), landowner, minister, member of the Hungarian Academy of Sciences, and many other scholarly or charitable institutions. The photograph was taken by Ferenc Veress, the first photographer to open a studio in Transylvania; Veress photographed Transylvania's most beautiful regions, most interesting historical monuments, and most notable personalities. He set up a muffle in his Kolozsvár studio in 1868, where he started to produce his porcelains, decorated with characteristic golden-brown photographs. On the occasion of a national craft exhibition held at Székesfehérvár in 1879–which was opened by its sponsor, Baron Kemény–he exhibited more that 300 photoceramics executed using a technique developed by Veress himself. At the same time he published in German the first book to describe this procedure. The plate was acquired in 1949 by the Museum as part of the collection of the Museum of the Parliament.

**117.** The first and still the most renowned porcelain factory in France is the one at Sèvres. Louis XV (1715–1774) contributed to its success by declaring it a royal factory in 1753. Based on famous artists' designs, elegant cutlery, statues and ornate vessels were manufactured there; many new colour shades were developed at the works, and the Sèvres gilding technique achieved a very high standard. The participants of the second conference of the International Measurement Society organized in 1872 in Paris–at which Hungary was represented by Kálmán Szily (1838–1924) and István Kruspér (1818–1905)–were presented with a vase made at Sèvres. The two gentlemen were also delegates on the four-member commission which, in 1867, worked out a detailed scheme for the Hungarian Academy of Sciences concerning the adoption in Hungary of the French metric system of measures –a system which at that time was being implemented by many European countries. The dark-blue, marbled and gilded vase of classical shape consists of three parts; the neck and the foot were screwed onto the vase using brass underplates. The gilded brass handle consists of the delicate face of a girl, whose long hair is let down, and of a bunch of palmette leaves. Surrounded by branches of laurel tied together with a gilded ribbon, the following words are inscribed on the base of the vessel: COMMISSION INTERNATIONALE DE MÈTRE / PARIS – 1872/ E DE KRUSPER / ( Professeur à l'Ecole Polytechnique / de PESTH / DELEGUE de la HONGRIE.

The vase–similar pieces are held in France and in Belgium–was donated by the Kruspér family to the National Museum.

117. Vase

118. Pipe

**118.** Meerschaum pipes rival even ivory ones in beauty. The best quality meerschaum is found in Anatolia. What makes it an extremely suitable material for carving pipes is the fact that, if soaked, meerschaum becomes very easy to carve, and if heated afterwards, it turns stone-hard. The first person ever to carve a pipe out of meerschaum is said to have been a Hungarian named Károly Kovács. In 1723, on returning home from the Ottoman empire, where he had been sent as an envoy, István Andrássy brought back a slab of meerschaum and gave it to Kovács, who carved it into a pipe. Moreover, he discovered that, if dipped in wax, a Meerschaum pipe obtains an "aged" colour in use.

Buda, Pest and Vienna soon became the centres of meerschaum pipe carving. The pipes carved in these cities, either by professional pipe makers or by artists who did this as a diversion, bear the marks of contemporary styles: baroque, rococo, national romanticism and historicism. Besides floral ornamentation, elaborate monograms and coats-of-arms, these pipes were often decorated with hunting scenes, portraits, historical events, or simply with genre scenes.

The half-length figure of a huntress embellishes this cigar-holder. One end of the holder juts out from the curls of hair behind her little hat. The delicate lady wears a tightly-fitting dress, a sporting gun is thrown over her right shoulder, and she holds a dagger in her left hand. A powder-horn hangs from her shoulder.

This object was acquired by the Museum from the collection of István Bárczi (1866–1943), a mayor of Budapest.

97

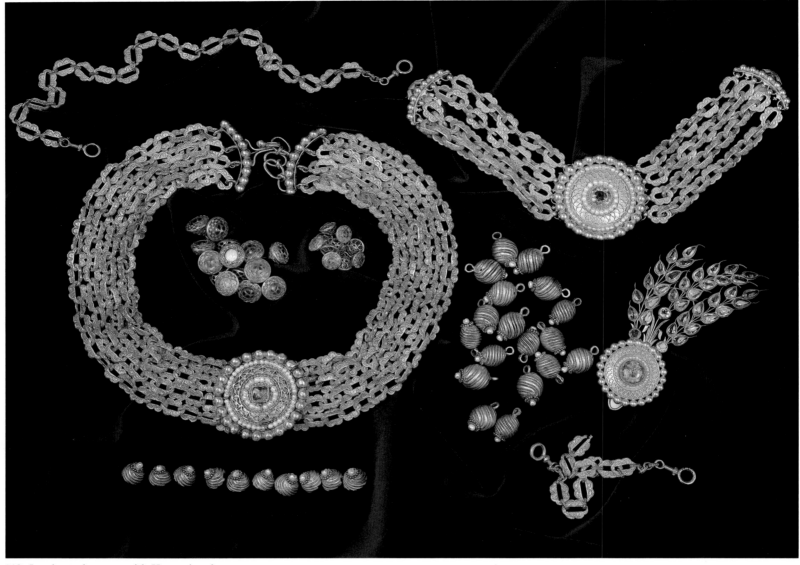

119. Jewelry to be worn with Hungarian dress

**119.** After the necessary alterations, this clasp (which dates from the Great Migrations period) and the seventeenth-century chain–both owned by the Prónay family–were incorporated into an item to be worn as part of Hungarian gala dress. The daring idea was executed with taste. The set of jewels was commissioned by Gábor Prónay (III) from the Chr. F. Rothe workshop in Vienna for the occasion of the coronation ceremony in 1867; the set was later purchased by the National Museum.

The round clasp from the Great Migrations period was refashioned to form the buckle of the belt. A large citrine surrounded by concentric circles of pearls, filigree and gold open-work decorates the clasp sited at the centre of the belt. The belt itself is formed of Renaissance chains formed by sections known to Hungarians as the "nut-kernel" pattern. Each end is a semi-circle decorated with a row of very small gold beads. The belt of the *mente* was made in the 1860s as a copy of this ornate belt. The circles of golden open-work in the clasp are substituted for by neo-Gothic pierced decoration. The citrine at the centre of the aigrette's rosette has a claw setting, otherwise it is quite similar to the clasp of the *mente* belt. Three plumes, their fronds shaped like ears of corn with seeds formed of thirty-six teardrop-shaped citrines, branch out of the rosette.

On the stem and on the back of the clasp the master's initials F. R. are stamped. The sword holders are formed from the eyes of the original Renaissance "nut-kernel" chain sawn into two and joined with an oval ring between each link. There is a longer and a shorter chain with carabiners on the ends. The set of twenty-four buttons is made of polished, cone-shaped citrines in gold mountings decorated with minute flowers and a netted pattern. The same master's initials–F. R.–and the eighteen-carat hallmark are stamped on the back of the buttons. The other set of buttons consists of twenty-eight gilded silver pieces decorated with pearls. They are sewn onto the dolman, the *mente* and the sleeves. The buttons of the dolman and the sleeves were made in Pest in 1818 and are stamped with the initial N.I. The oval buttons are decorated with twisted fluting, the grooves of which are filled in with twisted wire. The single baroque bead on the top of each button is fastened by a minute plate consisting of eight petals and surrounded by a row of beading.

The tradition of wearing this collection of jewels with a man's Hungarian gala dress originated in the nineteenth century. A great many of these sets were made for the occasion of the coronation ceremony in 1867 and for the Millennium, but only a few of the gold ones have survived.

**120.** The splendour of historical costumes lived on in Hungarian gala dress both for men and women; this was especially spectacular on the occasions of festivities held at Court.

This ornate attire was commissioned by the wife of Lord Chief Justice Count György Majláth in 1867 to be worn at the coronation ceremony of Franz Joseph I (1848–1916); this is what she wore at the Millennium parade of 1896, and probably also in November 1906, when the ashes of György Rákóczi II were brought home (because in 1907 the royal photographer Strelisky took a photograph of her wearing this dress). Her daughter-in-law inherited the attire from her, and in 1916 at the coronation ceremony of Charles IV (1916–1918) the daughter wore it, too. The costume was sold to the National Museum by her husband, Count György Majláth the Younger.

The costume consists of pieces dating from different times and bearing the traces of alterations. The very loose, richly pleated repp-silk skirt–which was originally worn with a crinoline–, the white tulle apron, and the tulle veil were probably made in 1867, because these three pieces are embroidered with the same golden flowers. The crimson velvet bodice is also embroidered in gold; its huge puffed, tinselled sleeves and the white silk shirred front are made in accordance with 1896 fashion. Probably the original corset which in the meantime had become too tight to wear was adjusted at the Göttmann and Mérő Salon at this time, too. In 1916 the young Countess Majláth ordered from the Monaszterly and Kuzmik firm the red velvet *mente*, which is decorated with eighteenth-century golden lace and golden braid.

120. Ornate attire to be worn during the Coronation ceremony

121. a) Hungarian-style lady's dress
b) Hungarian-style gentleman's suit
c) Gentleman's belt
d) Neck-tie

**121.** In 1933 a movement was launched to promote the Hungarian style in the fashion trade. The movement, which had a distinct anti-Hitlerite undertone, was led by Ferenc Ferenczy, a Ministry of the Interior civil servant, and by Klára Tüdős, a dress designer at the Opera House. The aim was to introduce Hungarian traditional folkwear, and ornamentation, to the changing world of men's and women's fashion. In 1933, within the framework of the Union of Public Associations which brought together right-wing groups, Ferenczy announced a competition to design Hungarian-style fashion-wear. Klára Tüdős also entered the competition and won second prize. In 1934 Ferenczy founded the National Committee of the Movement for Hungarian-style Fashion-wear, and organized further successful competitions–giving a boost to a newly-emerged branch of designer art: fashion design. To promote Hungarian-style fashion abroad, Ferenczy organized a Hungarian Ball in London in 1936, followed by another one in Warsaw in 1937, inviting on both occasions members of high society. Klára Tüdős was the most talented activist and designer of the movement, and her dresses, which combined the traditional elements of Hungarian wear with the latest trends in Parisian fashion, were always popular with the public. In 1936 she opened a fashion salon named the Pántlika (Ribbon), which became a regular meeting place for fashionable ladies, both from Pest and from abroad. Tüdős also founded the Hungarian ready-made fashion industry by opening Hungarian-style fashion departments, the first one in the Hungarian Fashion Hall, and then another one in the Corvin Department Store. Due to the efforts of the Pántlika salon and the movement, the export of Hungarian embroidery and Hungarian-style dresses grew considerably, and Budapest became one of the fashion centres of Europe.

The black woolen suit decorated with green agate buttons and braiding was made for Ferenc Ferenczy by Pál Mohácsy, the well-known men's tailor who also participated in the work of the movement. It was sold to the National Museum by Ferenczy in 1973.

The evening gown was made in the Pántlika salon around 1938. The blue satin sleeveless dress with shoulder-straps and a pink woollen jacket–embellished with floral embroidery in gold and blue silk thread–is a good example of Klára Tüdős's principle: "A dress should show Hungarian characteristics either in the material used, or in the cut, or in the decoration, but never in all three at the same time."

# Department of Coins and Medals

122. Tetradrachma. Imitation of the Philippos II Tetradrachma.
Mászlony-puszta type

**122.** The area of the Carpathian Basin, territory that all used to belong to Hungary, is very rich in Celtic coin finds. The Celtic tribes arrived in this region from the West during the fourth century B.C., by which time they had encountered the influence of Greek culture. Celts were hired as mercenaries in the Macedonian army, and so they became familiar with Greek money. After the third century B.C., the Celts minted their coins patterned after Greek coins, mainly Macedonian tetradrachmae. They were the first people to mint money in the Carpathian Basin. Celtic coins imitated the tetradrachmae of Philippos II (359–336), usually with Zeus's portrait showing a laurel wreath on the obverse and with a rider on the reverse. They also counterfeited Alexander the Great, Lysimachos, Audoleon, Larissa and Thasos coins, which were usually silver tetradrachmae weighing 14–15 grams. Another group of Celtic coins was patterned after the Roman Republic's denarius, but

the weight–about 17 grams–equalled that of the Greek coins. The third group of Celtic coins reproduced both the weight and the design of the Roman Republic's denarius. These were struck by the Celtic Araviskus tribe, as evidenced by the stamps RAVIS, IRAVIS, etc. Such stamps help to establish which particular Celtic tribe occupying the Carpathian Basin minted these coins. Since in most cases it is not possible to tell which tribe the coins belonged to, the different types are named after the sites of discovery.

The tetradrachma reproduced here is known as the Mászlony-pusztai type. The right profile of Zeus is on the obverse, and a galloping horse and rider are on the reverse. As a result of the many copies made of the original tetradrachma, the classical features of the Zeus portrait have almost entirely vanished. This coin was probably minted in the second century B.C.

**123.** Except for the fact that it was found in the river Danube somewhere in the territory of Hungary, nothing more is known about the site of discovery of the only engraving die owned by the National Museum. The truncated cone-shaped die is made of bronze, with its edges broken off. The legend says: CONCORDIA MIL-ITUM, in the exergue the letters are: AXXI.

The emperor is shown standing on the left side of the obverse, with his head turned to the right. Facing him stands Jupiter, wearing a cloak fastened at his left shoulder; the emperor is holding a sceptre and presenting Jupiter with a statue of Victory standing on a globe. This variety of representation was used on the antoninianuses minted for Diocletian (284–305) and his co-emperors: Galerius Maximian, Constantinus I and Severus II. This variety of representation is found on coins minted between 284 and 307. The minter's stamped

123. Late third-century engraving die of the neverse of an Antoninianus

101

initials–AXXI–prove that the engraving die was in use before the monetary reforms of Diocletian (294). One of the regulations introduced in the course of this reform was that the minters had to be indicated by the initials or the first syllable of their names on the reverse of the coins. The type, the legend, and the stamp ascertain that the die was in use between 284 and 294. The same stamp is found on contemporary coins minted in Antiochia, Kyzikos, and Siscia. The possibility of Siscian origin is excluded, since during that period antoninianuses with this type of reverse were not struck there. On the basis of its style, and also by the analysis and the comparison of the letters, it may be established that this engraving die was made in Antioch. The dies used for striking the reverse of the coins were always the movable ones. The flan was placed on the bottom die–with the engraving of the obverse–, then the other die–with the engraving of the reverse of the coin–was placed over it.

124. Maximianus Herculius. Medallion

**124.** This medal is a unique piece in the collection. It weighs four times as much as did the concurrently used aureuses, thus it rightly could also be called a quaternion. This coin, in almost mint condition, was discovered at the beginning of the twentieth century in Szár, a village in Fejér county.

The portrait of Emperor Maximianus Herculius (286–305) is on the obverse with the legend IMP C MA MAXIMIANVS P F AVG. As shown by his name–HERCVLIVS–, the emperor worshipped Hercules therefore, he is represented with lion's skin, an attribute of the Greek hero who, as one of his twelve labours, killed the Nemean lion. The reverse shows the standing figures of the two emperors facing each other and offering a sacrifice with a patera over a tripos. The stamped initial in the exergue is the impression of the mint at Tricinum (Sacra Moneta Tricenensis). When this medallion was struck in 294, it was among the first in Tricinum after the monetary reform. The finely contoured hair and beard, together with the individualized features of the emperor, have remained almost unmarred. The precise engraving of the die shows that it was made by a superb craftsman. The workmanship of the reverse is much less refined; nevertheless, the portrait quality of the emperors' heads is undeniable. It is atypical that the design on the reverse is rather two-dimensional and not as plastic as usual. The slightly eroded state of the coin's surface indicates that it must have been in intensive circulation.

125. Half Aureus of Maximianus Herculius. Subaeratus imitation

**125.** Gold coins of the value of a half aureus were quite rare at the beginning of the fourth century; many among them are unique copies. This "half-aureus" is in fact a gold-coated bronze coin; the original coin, after which this one was cast, is unknown, or has not been published yet.

Adorned with a laurel wreath and wearing a helmet, the half-length portrait of Maximianus Herculius, co-emperor of Diocletian, is struck on the obverse of the coin, accompanied by the legend MAXIMI-ANVSAVG. In the left field of the reverse, the Sun-god Sol is shown standing, his cloak is fastened at his left shoulder; he holds a whip in his left hand and raises his right. On the reverse, are the letters ORIEN-S AVGG; on the exergue the letters SIS are seen. Many differences can be detected when this coin is compared with the only similar example, held at the collection of the Kunsthistorisches Museum in Vienna. The styles of the representations and the hyphenation of the words are different, and the emperor wears a helmet on the medallion of the National Museum, which is not the case in the Viennese portrait. The different hyphenation of the legend and Sol's holding the whip on the reverse also make them dissimilar. There must have been at the time a half-aureus piece, after which this fake copy was made in a weight below that of a usual half-aureus.

This coin, which was probably struck between 302 and 305, is a subareatus. The method of counterfeiting these coins was that only the outside of the coins was plated with gold or silver coins; the inside, the "soul" (*anima*) was made of bronze. If the plating remained intact, measuring the coin's density was the only way to identify it as a fake. Mostly silver coins were forged this way. It may rightly be assumed that these so-called subareatuses were struck in an official mint. Naturally, the profit was increased, since less gold and silver were needed to produce the same face value.

126. Anastasius I. Medallion

**126.** Medallions are rare kinds of coins, made of gold, silver or bronze, which were usually struck to commemorate an event or to be given as a present, and were not intended to be used as money. Their weight was a multiple of the coins used as currency.

The portrait of Anastasius I (491–518) is represented on the obverse of this medal, with a diadem of beads adorning his head. He wears a cuirass and a cloak. The legend reads D N ANASTA-SIVS P AVG [Dominus Noster ANASTASIVS Pius AVGustus]. On the reverse, surrounded by a laurel wreath, are the letters VOT (XXXX) MV < T/XXXX; the mint's initials are CONNOS. There are several mistakes in the inscription: for example, the letter "L" in MV < T is awry and the repetition of the number forty (XXXX) is wrong. Judging by these mis-

takes it may be concluded that this medallion was not an issue. Year-numbers in wreaths of laurel, which referred to an anniversary, were often used after the last third of the fourth century, and later by Byzantine mints. These medallions were usually made to commemorate the 5th, 10th, 15th, 20th, and 30th anniversaries of an emperor's reign. The letters MVLT and the number afterwards refer to the next anniversary. For example, coins with the letters VOT V MVLT X were made to commemorate the fifth anniversary of an emperor's reign, thus suggesting that the tenth jubilee was to come. This is why it is inaccurate, and makes no sense, to repeat the number XXXX twice on the Anastasius Medallion. The emperor did not even reign for forty years, only for twenty-eight. This unique piece in the collection weighs 12 scruples.

**127.** Engraving dies are among the most treasured pieces in the collection, because only a very few of them have survived. To curb the spreading of forgery, these minting tools were very scrupulously guarded, and when they were not in use any more (either because they were too worn or because new types were issued), these dies were destroyed. Money minting during the reign of the Árpád Dynasty was kept under close control by the authorities, and only the king's mint was allowed to issue coins, a consideration making the three engraving dies in the Museum even more precious. The most outstanding among them is the die used for casting the obverse of the King Solomon (1062–1074) denarius. The fact that the eleventh was the first century when money was minted in Hungary, and the artistic quality of the figural representation enhance the value of the die. Before Solomon, there was only a simple cross

127. Die of Salamon's denarius number CNH.I.19

103

on the coins, encircled by the name of the king and the imprint of the mint.

The schematic figure of a king from knee up with a fillet on his head is engraved in the die. The legend on the side has + SALOM - ONI REX. In the Middle Ages the lower section of the die used for striking the reverse had a truncated cone shape; the negative of the coin was on top. The die ended in a spike on the bottom, by which the tool was secured into a wooden block reinforced with metal bands. The upper die was cylindriform, with the engraving on one end. After putting the flan between the two, the minter placed the top die over the bottom one either by hand or using a grip, and the coin was struck by hammering the upper die. The engraving die shown in the photograph is only 3.5 cm long, and 2.2 cm in diameter. On both of its sides indentations made by a vice are visible. The engraving is a little worn and corroded, so the more delicate details are hardly seen; nevertheless, the artistic design and the superb engraving are apparent.

128. Wladislas II, king of Hungary and Bohemia. Gold coin

**128.** During the fifteenth century the countries abounding in silver issued silver coins. The value of these was as high as for gold coins. The first such silver coin, the guldiner–or the thaler, as it came to be called later–was issued in 1486 by Sigismund, duke of Tyrol (its weight was about 28 grams). In 1499 Wladislas II, king of Hungary and Bohemia, was the first to have guldiners minted in Hungary; more came in 1500, 1501 and 1504–1506. Hungary was rich in silver and especially in gold, which explains the fact that these guldiners were also struck from gold at the very beginning.

On the obverse of Wladislas II's guldiner the coat-of-arms of the king is seen, and on the reverse the equestrian figure of Wladislas I (1077–1095) is portrayed. Although MOnETA WLADISLAI REGIS VnGARIE is struck on the obverse of the coin, these medals were not used as means of payment, as proven by the fact that these coins did not have a constant weight, which is a basic condition for any currency. The one minted in 1499 was the first Hungarian guldiner, and only a few examples are known of these in the entire world. The gold version, which was acquired by the National Museum as part of the Niklovits Collection, is the only one of its kind.

129. Fifty-ducat piece of Mihály Apafi, prince of Transylvania

**129.** It is very characteristic of seventeenth-century coinage that gold coins of extremely high value were minted, up to one-hundred ducat weight. These medals were issued only in a very few copies; rather than being used as means of payment, they were given as presents by sovereigns. Sigismund III, king of Poland (1587–1632), Ferdinand III, emperor of Austria and king of Hungary (1619–1637) and Mihály Apafi, prince of Transylvania all had such coins minted.

In Transylvania, where taxes were levied by two emperors, gold was abundant. The gold recovered from its mines and washed out of its brooks were minted to pay the army, the taxes, and tribute, but there still remained enough for trade, and even for valuable artworks to be given away as presents. We know of a hundred-ducat piece, minted for Apafi, consisting of a ten-ducat coin at the centre of a gold plate and surrounded by one-ducat coins. The medal shown here, however, is even more notable. It was stamped with a large engraving die made in 1677 by the minter of Fogaras in two sizes: in one-hundred and in fifty-ducat weight. The flan used for the hundred-ducat piece was thicker.

Mihály Apafi's portrait wearing splendid armour, a princely head-dress and sceptre is stamped on the obverse, and the prince's coat-of-arms is on the reverse. The one on display in the Hungarian National Museum is a fifty-ducat variant. The person to whom Apafi intended (or was forced) to present the item is unknown. In the nineteenth century this gold medal was in Prince Coburg's collection; then, after many adventurous years during which time the medal was taken to America and Japan, it was returned to Hungary and in 1977, on the three-hundredth anniversary of its issue, it took its place in the strong-box of the Hungarian National Museum.

130. Lajos Kossuth credit note issued during his emigration in London

**130.** Following Hungary's defeat in the War of Independence of 1848–49, Lajos Kossuth (1802-1894), then regent of Hungary, resigned and fled the country. He and his followers continued, however, to work for the cause of the revolution even after the Hungarian military command's decision to avoid further bloodshed and surrender their weapons at Világos. Kossuth and his followers tried to boost popular support for Hungarian independence abroad among people already sympathetic towards the Hungarian cause. To fund a war of liberation, though, a great deal of money was required, which Kossuth hoped to be able to raise by issuing bonds underwritten by the revolutionary government repayable after the victory of the revolution. The first bonds were issued in New York and in Philadelphia in two currencies: the dollar and forint. Kossuth attempted to do the same in London in 1860. In December

1860 and January 1861, twenty tons of paper watermarked with the word RESURGO were delivered to the Day company to print bonds in one-, two- and five-forint denominations. However, the Austrian government discovered the transaction and on February 3, 1861 called upon Lord John Russell to have the printing stopped. After this was done, a British court of justice ruled in favour of the Austrian government, and seventeen tons of bonds and three tons of watermarked paper, were burnt in the furnaces of the Bank of England. A few copies, together with an unknown quantity of watermarked paper were somehow rescued, however. The latter was used to make envelopes, of which one copy is owned today by the Museum of Miskolc. The very few surviving bonds constitute a tragic memento of the Hungarian War of Independence.

**131.** The oldest Hungarian-made medals discovered so far were made during the reign of King Matthias. Under the influence of the Italian Renaissance, King Matthias, too, ordered medals showing his own image; these were mostly large pieces made of cast metal. The reform of the monetary system–a switch-over from the small denarius and grossus to the much larger thaler–resulted in an increased area to be filled, thus providing an opportunity for the medalists to design coins showing portraits and scenes. In the sixteenth century a large proportion of the medals were made in mints, using the same technique as for coins and most of the time in a weight either equal to or a fraction of, and sometime even a multiple of, the weight of the coins. This is why the sixteenth-century memorial medals are often called memorial thalers.

105

131. Medallion with the portraits of Louis II and Queen Mary

In Hungary, the mint at Körmöcbánya always played an important part in the country's coin and medal minting. Around 1532 it was there that Christoph Fuessl designed the memorial Mohács Thaler, with the pictures of the king, who had perished in the battle, and his wife. On the obverse of the medal, framed in a twined border, the profiles of King Louis II and Queen Maria face each other, with floral ornamentation in the background. In the exergue there are the letters LU-DO:UNGAR:BOHE:QUE / REGIS·ET·MARIAE·RE / GINAE· DULCIS CON/ GIS·AC·PROCES·/IN FLAN: On the reverse of the medal, in a twin border the Hungarian and Turkish cavalries are shown fighting each other, with Turkish guns in the background. In the exer-gue the letters are: LUDO:HUNG:BOEM:ZC·REX / ANN:AGENS·-XX·IN·TURCAS / APUD·MOHAZ·CUM·PAR / VA·SUORUM·MANU·PU / GNAS·HONESTE OBYT·M·XXVI. Although the year 1526 is given on the medal, reference is made to Maria's journey to Flanders, which could only have been after 1531, when–at the request of her brother, Charles V (1519–1556), also king of Spain–, she accepted the regency of Flanders.

The medal shown here is a very early masterpiece of Hungarian coinage–of a craft previously almost non-existent in the country.

132. Holy Trinity medal

**132.** The coin made by Hans Reinhart the Elder is of outstanding value. On the obverse of it are the letters PROPTER$_x$SCELUS$_x$ POPULI$_x$MEI$_x$PERCUSSI$_x$EUM·EASIÆ LIII. In the company of angels, the enthroned Almighty God is shown crowned and holding a sceptre and an orb; in front of him, the crucified Christ is shown, with a pigeon sitting on the Cross. On the reverse, between two plain borders the letters are: REGNANTE·MAURI-TIO:D:G:DUCE·SAXONIÆ $\underset{JZC}{\Omega}$:GROSSUM HUNG·LIPSIÆ HR CUDEBAT: ANºM·D·XLIIII MENSE·JANU:. There is a small Saxon shield on the top; in the field, written in twenty-two lines on a board held by two angels, are the letters HAEC EST /FIDES CATHOLICA,/ UT·UNUM DEUM IN TRINI,/TATE ET TRINITATEM IN UNITATE...etc.–the words of the Athanasian Creed.

The fact that Almighty God was depicted wearing the vestment of the Holy Roman emperor can undoubtedly be linked to the European prestige of Charles V at the peak of his power. The emperor managed to have the Council of Trent summoned in the face of opposition by Pope Paul III. The aim of this Council was supposed to be the restoration of the Church's unity; in fact, it achieved just the opposite and the existing rifts grew even deeper. Charles V succeeded in dividing the German prince-electors, gaining the support of the Saxon Prince Moritz who tried to arbitrate between Charles V and the Protestant German princes. He did this with the help of emphasis on the Holy Trinity, a dogma also accepted by the Reformists. Therefore, the coin expressed the fundamental political problem of Europe, outlining at the same time the solution using the coinage.

133. Biblical medal

**133.** The Bible played a very important part in sixteenth-century intellectual life, and this was especially so during the Reformation period. There were frequent bans on reading the Bible, imposed by the Church itself. The ancient texts denouncing the rich, the powerful and the tyrannical were suitable to form the ideological foundation of a heretical movement. Luther took a firm stance against reading anything written by clergymen and commentators. He was of the opinion that the Bible itself ought to be read, because the commentators often perverted the originally-intended message of the Bible. The origin, and the popularity, of sixteenth-century scriptural coins is partly rooted in this circumstance. The pictorial representation of the coins can be traced back to the *Biblia Pauperum,* a book published with pictures, where each picture combined two scenes from the Old Testament with one scene from the New Testament, and was surrounded by the Prophets. A similar arrangement was often used by the designers of scriptural coins, whereby scenes from the Old Testament were presented on the obverse, and a New-Testament scene of similar moral message was depicted on the reverse. The minting of scriptural coins actually began in a mint at Joachimstal in Bohemia, also

exerting an influence on the Hungarian mint at Körmöcbánya. Almost every important scene from the Old Testament was depicted on coins minted at Joachimstal, the legends for which were mostly taken from the Bible.

Hieronimus Magdeburger's coin presents the Annunciation and the Crucifixion–the first and the last episode of Christ's temporal journey–on the same side. On the obverse, to the right, we see Mary on a kneeling chair, with a dove above her head and the angel approaching her. At the centre the crucified Christ is shown, with Mary and John standing at the bottom of the cross. The legend refers to both episodes: AIT✳ANGELUS✳ AVE✳GRACIA✳PLENA ♣ IN✳HOC✳SIGNO✳VINCES✳1537. The expression in the second half of the legend is attributed to Constantine the Great (307–337), who said it before going to battle against Maxentius. On the reverse side, between two plain borders, is the name ↩ ✾ FRIEDRICH ✿ PRUNSTERER, ✿ with a shield at the centre. Originally, the reverse of the coin, which then was the obverse, showed the Fall of Adam and Eve. This was later removed and was replaced with the present image. The coin was most probably a present to Prunsterer.

134. Chain and emblem of the English Order of the Bath

**134.** The Order of the Bath was established in 1399 by the king of England, Henry IV (1399–1413). It has been suggested that the foundation of the Order had its origin in the King's interrupting his bath to receive two ladies who sought the King's clemency towards their relatives. A more likely explanation has also been put forward whereby the order was established to commemorate the ritual bath preceding the coronation ceremony. During the reign of Henry IV, the Order had 46 knights. The coronation of the queen and the birth or the wedding of the heir were the usual occasions to admit new knights. After 1661 the admission of new knights was suspended. In 1725 the Order was renewed, after which both military and civil merits were recognized with this award. This reform also brought changes in the appearance of the Order. The Military Order of the Bath was cross-shaped; the Civil Order was an oval-shaped medallion. On certain occasions the knights wore the lavishly-adorned formal dress of the Order, part of which was the richly embellished chain.

135. Cross of the Russian Order
of St. Anne, Third Class

**135.** The Order of St Anne was established by Prince Carl Friedrich Holstein-Gottorp in 1735, in memory of his wife, the Grand Princess of Russia Anna Petrovna, and was meant to be awarded to members of the nobility who distinguished themselves in honesty, in piety and in services rendered to the sovereign. At that time the Order had only one class, and at any given time no more than fifteen knights were admitted to it. With the succession to the Russian throne of their son, Tsar Peter III (1762), the Order was included among the Russian orders. As a result of the changes made by Tsar Peter I (1796–1801), the number of classes was increased to three, and foreigners also became eligible to receive the Order. In exceptional cases, the insignia was decorated with precious stones to express the tsar's special favour.

On the obverse of the Order shown here there is a red enamelled cross standing on a base, with a larger teardrop-shaped diamond and eleven smaller diamonds between each of the two arms of the cross. The standing figure of Anne is in the central circular field of the medal, surrounded by twelve diamonds. On the reverse, there is a monogram. The Russian hallmark for gold and the year 1856 are stamped on the ring by which the medallion was hung. The Order, which was among the articles stolen in 1947 from the Esterházy family, was handed back by the Austrian embassy in Budapest in 1985.

# Historical Gallery

**136.** On the East-Central-European family estates of the aristocracy, the galleries featuring the impressive portraits of ancestors formed an important part of appearances. On the basis of their wealth and jealously guarded feudal rights, members of the Hungarian aristocracy could have pretended to be sovereign rulers of larger areas; in any case, their portraits give an impression to that effect. Ferenc Nádasdy (1623–1671) was one of the greatest art collectors and patrons in seventeenth-century Hungary. All his property was confiscated and he himself was beheaded in Vienna for involvement in high treason organized by Count Wesselényi. Benjamin Block was on his way to Italy when he met Nádasdy in Vienna. Nádasdy took him into his service for a while, and on releasing him, provided him with letters of recommendation and money. Having completed his study trip, the artist took service with the emperor in Vienna, painting and engraving several portraits in the eclectic style typical of the Court artists. In addition to its artistic merits, the Nádasdy portrait also makes an important document of the garments worn by members of the aristocracy in those days. The crimson broad-cloth pelisse decorated with golden soutache and black trousers, the red leather foot-cloth and yellow slippers are characteristic pieces of seventeenth-century man's attire. The clock standing on the table, together with the large buttons of the pelisse, refers to the affluence of the sitter. The dog, as an attribute expressing fidelity, is a recurring motif in the portraits of this period.

136. Portrait of Ferenc Nádasdy, by Benjamin Block

137. Kuruc–Labanc Battle Scene

**137.** After some preliminaries in Renaissance art (Leonardo da Vinci, Michelangelo), it was in Baroque art that the painting of battle scenes reached the highest point in its development. In order to be able to solve the problem, the artist had to possess proficiency in dynamic composition and in the painting of strongly foreshortened moving figures, as well as in achieving various lighting effects. It was a new sensation for the spectators to see the familiarly-outfitted armies of the European powers fighting an exotic-looking enemy. This was how the soldiers of Ferenc Rákóczi, and their battle tactics of cavalry attack from ambush, became one of the favourite subjects of the Augsburg artist Georg Philipp Rugendas the Elder. As a result of the artist's ingenious compositions and his popularity with the public, the pictures of Rugendas were often copied or incorporated in other painters' compositions. The small drawing reproduced here, in which the difference between the uniforms and the weaponry of the bitterly fighting adversaries can be studied in detail, testifies to the influence of Rugendas.

**138.** Count Dénes Bánffy (1723–1780), Master of the Horse and lord lieutenant of Kolozs county, was a close confident of Francis of Lorraine, the husband of Maria Theresa. His portrait was painted by Martin van Meytens, an artist born in Stockholm who studied in Holland and England. Meytens worked in Sweden, Paris, Dresden and Italy, before finally settling in Vienna. He became Maria Theresa's Court painter and, after 1759, followed Jakob van Schuppen as director of the Art Academy. His miniature and oil paintings were very popular at the time. The painting shown here is an eighteenth-century version of the pictures displayed in the Hungarian ancestral galleries. The artist evidently takes much delight in painting the golden soutache of the blue pelisse trimmed with fur. The posture assumed by the sitter reveals self-confidence; with his right hand, he points to the castle of Bonchida, the centre of the family estates.

138. Portrait of Count Dénes Bánffy,
by Martin van Meytens

139. Dwellings in the Tihany Caves, by Joseph Fischer

**139.** Joseph Fischer was an outstanding landscapist of the late-eighteenth-century Viennese art scene. He stayed in Paris and London between 1802 and 1804: in the French capital he met Prince Miklós Esterházy, whom he also accompanied on a trip to England. After 1804, Fischer first became the inspector, then the director, of the Esterházy Gallery in Vienna. Concurrently with performing his official duties, Fischer continued developing his own art. He first came to Hungary in 1800, when he visited Pest; probably the drawing presented here also originates from this period. Fischer's compositional technique already shows the influence of Romanticism: the threatening intrusion of the rock into the field of vision, the steeply declining foreground and the mysteriously mirroring pond hidden behind the rock all suggest it. The birds flying through the air emphasize the impressive perspective and the dimensional differences existing between the various forces of Nature, in the same way as do the two discoursing figures in the foreground.

**140.** Vinzenz Georg Kininger was born in Regensburg. He continued his art studies at the Viennese Academy. The skills he learned there were put to good use in the genres of miniature painting and lithography. He was on friendly terms with Ferenc Kazinczy, one of the leaders of the Hungarian cultural scene at the turn of the nineteenth century. In the first decade of the nineteenth century, the Hadik family commissioned the artist to paint several portraits. In this particular portrait, Gusztáv Hadik is shown wearing simple garments, with his barbered locks falling over his forehead. The flowerpot he holds in his hands shows the continued application of a centuries-old attribute of child portraits. The rich drapery painted on both sides is a usual feature of Baroque portraits, while the objects of the interior show the characteristics of Classicist style. The restrained use of colours, the unaffected pose of the sitter and the realistic and reserved composition are, again, the marks of the Classicist style.

141. Portrait of János Batsányi, by Friedrich Heinrich Füger

140. Portrait of Gustav Hadik as a Child, by Vinzenz Georg Kininger

**141.** János Batsányi (1763–1845) was one of the most important poets of the Hungarian Enlightenment. He was jailed for taking part in the Jacobin movement, then exiled for translating Napoleon's proclamation addressed to the Hungarian people. Throughout their adventurous lives, the poet and his wife, the popular Viennese poetess Gabriella Baumberg, always entrusted only the best Austrian artists with the painting of their portraits. In addition to Friedrich Heinrich Füger's work, the couple also had their portraits painted by Vinzenz Georg Kininger, as well as by Johann Niedermann. In Füger's picture, the attributes referring to the poetic discipline, such as the books displayed in the background, remain inconspicuous in order to allow the face, which is the most important element of the characterization, to receive as much attention as possible. This is also stressed by the grey of the hair, the white of the neckerchief and the brownish yellow of the drapery. The lighting which comes from the left increases the plasticity of the representation. With this painting, the great exponent of Viennese Classicism produced one of the finest portraits ever painted of a Hungarian literary figure.

142. View of Buda and Pest from the Gellért Hill, by Antal Fülöp Richter

**142.** The joint rule of Maria Theresa and Joseph II (1780–1790) meant a new chapter in the development of Pest and Buda. The Queen ordered the relocation of the University of Nagyszombat to Buda Castle, while her son sent government officials from Pozsony. András Petrich, an army officer in the engineering corps with an artistic bent and, also, the first commandant of the Ludovika military academy, captured the Hungarian capital at its early stage of boom. From the vantage point at the top of Gellért Hill, we get an excellent view of the two banks of the Danube and the bridge connecting them. On the flat side, the expansion of Pest has not yet reached the Margaret Island. On the other side, between the towering bulk of Buda Castle and the row of houses of Tabán at the bottom of the hill, there was still nothing but meadow. In the foreground, we see János Pasquich, the director of the observatory on Gellért Hill, inviting the promenaders to take a view through his telescope.

143. Peasant Women from Veszprém County,
by Franz Jaschke

**144.** Ferenc Bene (1775–1858), professor of medical sciences and a honorary member of the Hungarian Academy of Sciences, established the practice of smallpox vaccination in Hungary. He also played an important part in the introduction of physical education to the school curriculum. It was probably through his interest in sport that he met Vilmos Egger, the painter of his portrait. Egger had left his job in Pestalozzi's institute in Yverdon at the invitation of János Váradi Szabó to instruct the children of Baron Vayk in music, drawing and physical education. He arrived at the house of the Vayk family in Felsőzsolca in 1813, and soon moved to Pest with the family. He was given a job at the Evangelical school as a drawing and physical education instructor; it was he who introduced the practice of doing physical exercises in public in the capital. He was also much in demand as a portrait painter, working primarily for scholars and aristocrats. Through his familiarity with the art of G.F.A. Schöner and A. Graff, he transmitted the achievements of French painting to Hungary. The picture of Ferenc Bene is one of the finest scientist portraits painted at the time. The head and the trunk of Professor Bene are shown depicted in front of his bookshelves, as he turns towards the viewer. The greatest names in medical science can be found written on the spines of the books, giving those unable to recognize him a clue about the profession of the sitter.

144. Portrait of Ferenc Bene, by Vilmos Egger

**143.** The Silesian-born Franz Jaschke began his studies at the Viennese Academy in 1794. In 1807-1808, and then again in 1810, he accompanied Archduke Louis and Archduke Rainer, respectively, on journeys in Hungary and the adjacent provinces to the east and the south. During these trips, he drew sketches of the towns they visited and the population groups they encountered. The resulting engravings were published in Vienna in 1821, accompanied by János Csaplovics's commentary. The engraving showing the womenfolk of Veszprém county has a counterpart displaying the menfolk. The woman on the left, possibly the sheriff's wife, wears a curiously-folded, white cotton head-dress. She is accompanied by her daughter wearing a lavishly ornamented dress. A plainly dressed servant walking one step behind completes the group, which is probably on its way to the church. In the background, we see the Castle of Csesznek, which Jaschke drew after sketches made on the spot.

145. Portrait of Kázmér Batthyány, by Miklós Barabás

**146.** Ferenc Pulszky (1814–1897) was a politician, archaeologist, art historian, a member of the Hungarian Academy of Sciences and the director of the National Museum. His portrait was painted by a childhood friend, Wolfgang Böhm, who had studied in Rome and London before settling in Vienna. Pulszky's memoirs reveal that the two met in London, where Pulszky lived as a political exile. The art of the old English portrait painters and Van Dyck had the greatest influence on Böhm's painting. This particular picture, with its freshness and sketchiness, might strike the viewer as modern. The cloudy sky in the background at the same time refers to the age in which the picture was painted and the personal fate of the sitter.

146. Portrait of Ferenc Pulszky, by Wolfgang Böhm

**145.** The prominent figures on the political and cultural scene of the Reform Age were portrayed by Miklós Barabás. He adjusted the compositional technique and the ambience of the Viennese Biedermeier style to the taste of his Hungarian sitters, also incorporating in his method the earlier traditions of Hungarian portrait painting. There are, however, works in his oeuvre which prove him an outstanding master of the pure Viennese style. One such work is the miniature portrait of Count Kázmér Batthyány (1807–1854), an opposition politician dedicated to reforms who was also the chairman of the Union for Protective Tariffs. The style of this painting showing Batthyány striking an elegant pose in front of an elaborate landscape is somewhat reminiscent of the style of Ferdinand Waldmüller. The overall light tone of the miniature painting, too, evokes the world of Biedermeier. The grey trousers, the light-orange vest and the white shirtfront are set in the dark coat, which also serves to separate the figure from the background; the dark tie leads the eye towards the intelligent face, framed in beard and hair.

147. Electioneering in front of the National Museum by Ferenc Weiss

**147.** The Parliamentary elections for the Diet of 1847–1848 were marked by a great struggle between the reformers and the conservatives. Decisive victory was achieved in this political contest with the election of Lajos Kossuth as deputy for Pest county. In the early nineteenth century, Hungarian artists were already capable of capturing the important events of their age in works of high standard. This lithograph showing the mass demonstration of law students canvassing for Lajos Kossuth originated from the distinguished workshop of Frigyes Walzel Agost. People on horseback and on foot are shown carrying flags inscribed with Kossuth's name, as they march past the recently completed building of the National Museum. We see among the participants Lajos Batthyány on horseback, while in the colourful group of spectators people from all walks of life are represented.

148. View of Visegrád, by Károly Klette

**148.** Visegrád was a favourite subject of nineteenth-century Hungarian artists not only for its beautiful natural surroundings, but also for its memory of King Matthias, who spent much time there. In the Hungarian Reform Age, people liked to relive this finest age of Hungarian national history, gaining inspiration from literary and art representations describing the period. The scenery has paramount importance in this drawing by Károly Klette, an artist from Dresden who first moved to Vienna, then to Hungary. The mediaeval ruins at the centre harmoniously fit into the gently rolling hills of the river bank, all lit by diffused light. The dark tones at the centre turn into the greyish-blue patches of the distant mountains through greyish-green transitions. At the front, two peasants returning from the fields are shown in tranquil natural surroundings.

149. Battle of Nagysalló, by Mór Than

**149.** The final phase of one of the victorious battles of the 1849 Spring Campaign is captured by the young Mór Than in this aquarelle using, for the first time in the artist's career, a horizontally elongated canvass. This particular arrangement enabled the painter to depict the dynamic movements of the fighting masses and the light effects produced by the burning village and the explosion. In the foreground, the tension of the moment is achieved with the help of the sketchily arranged figures of groups of soldiers ready to see action on the one hand, and those returning from it with wounds on the other. The forward thrust of the attacking companies in the smoke-covered distance continues at the centre in the movement of the charging Hunyadi Hussars, who are about to destroy the fleeing Austrian infantry. The fact that the dead horse and the scattered objects to the fore became recurring compositional elements for Viennese lithographers depicting battle scenes proves Mór Than's influence.

**150.** The scientist Ágoston Kubinyi (1799–1873) was a member of the Hungarian Academy of Sciences and the director of the Hungarian National Museum. His portrait was painted by the Prussian-born Friedrich Lieder, who had been a pupil of David in Paris. Lieder went to work in Vienna first, then moved on to Pozsony before coming to Pest in 1820. He painted miniatures and oil paintings, and also made lithographs. In this particular painting, he managed to capture the sitter's character. Evidently, he took delight in painting the details of Hungarian costume. The excellent still-life on the left, beside its decorative function, also indicates the sitter's interest in botany. The building of the National Museum in the background refers to Kubinyi's position as head of that institution.

150. Portrait of Ágoston Kubinyi, by Frigyes Lieder

151. Portrait of Bertalan Szemere, by Sándor Kozina

**151.** Bertalan Szemere (1812–1869), a Hungarian politician who became prime minister in 1849, was also a writer and a member of the Hungarian Academy of Sciences. His portrait was done by Sándor Kozina, who had been a student of Peter Krafft in Vienna. Later, Kozina settled in Pest, working as a portrait painter, although he spent a great deal of his time travelling. Bertalan Szemere's diary sheds light on the origin of the portrait. The two already knew each other from Hungary when they met in Paris; Szemere was there as a political emigré, while Kozina was on a study trip. This particular painting is probably Kozina's best picture. The coat, the hair and the beard serve to emphasize the face of the sitter, while the title of the newspaper in Szemere's hand (*Respublica*) shows him to be a progressively-minded politician.

152. Pécs Cathedral, by Ludwig Rohbock

**152.** The German landscapist Ludwig Rohbock arrived in Hungary to illustrate Pál Hunfalvy's book entitled *Ungarn und Siebenbürgen in Bildern*. The author's intention was to give a geographical and cultural historical account of Hungary and its people. The illustrations included views of towns and castles, mediaeval ruins and important historical monuments. Every picture is elaborately drawn in monochrome colours, since these usually served as the originals of black-and-grey steel-plate engravings. However, there are drawings such as the one showing the western front of the cathedral in Pécs, in which the composition is built on the overall harmony of the green landscape, the deep-blue sky and the white buildings. The aquarelle is also remarkable from the point of view of architectural history: the reconstruction of the cathedral in the early nineteenth century by Mihály Pollack (1773–1855) was completely effaced during a subsequent reconstruction in 1882–1892. Rohbock's picture remains the only evidence of the previous reconstruction, showing how this eminent Hungarian exponent of the Classicist style incorporated Romantic elements in his design.

153. Royal Hunt, by Wilhelm Richter

**153.** Wilhelm Richter specialized in hunting and battle scenes. The hunt in this particular picture took place in Gödöllő in December 1872. The painting has several versions: this one was transferred to the National Museum from the Royal Palace. To the right of the queen, the following persons can be identified: Lord Buchanan, Count Gyula Andrássy, Count István Keglevich and Count Aurél Dessewffy. People standing or sitting: Leopold, prince of Bavaria, Count Miklós József Esterházy, Baron Béla Wenckheim, Dénes Pázmándy, Ferenc Tihanyi, Miklós Jankovich, Nándor Éber, Baron József Rudics. The queen's equerry, Holms, is seen behind the king. The group of four next to them: Count Tasziló Festetich, Count Pál Festetich, Lajos Tisza and Count István Károlyi. Behind and to the left: Prince Alexander of Liechtenstein and his suite. People next to the tree: Elemér Batthyány, János Harkányi, Lajos Simonyi, Ernő Blaskovics, Géza Rohonczy, Count István Szapáry, Prince Czetwertinsky, Count István Sztáray, Count Géza Szapáry, and the little girl Mici Van-Son.

154. Portrait of Pál Rosty, by Bertalan Székely

**155.** The most important contribution of the Nagybánya Art Colony to art history was that, by attaching importance to the study of Nature and thus rejecting the official academic style, its members helped the twentieth-century renewal of Hungarian painting. István Réti, who had studied under Hollósy in Munich, was one of its organizers and, later, the chronicler of the Nagybánya Art Colony. As teachers at the Academy of Art, he and Károly Lyka introduced educational reforms at that institute; later Réti went on to become the director of the Art Academy. This unpretentious self-portrait by the young Réti is one of the outstanding works of turn-of-the-century Hungarian portrait painting.

155. Self-portrait, by István Réti

**154.** Bertalan Székely studied in Vienna under Waldmüller. Later, he became one of the most distinguished Hungarian artists in the genre of Romantic historical paintings. He also gained recognition as a teacher. Primarily, he painted monumental pictures, although he also made some good portraits: this particular painting is an example. It shows Pál Rosty (1830–1874), who took part in the War of Liberation, then emigrated. He was widely travelled; he published his impression, including a diary written during a journey to South America. The Hungarian Academy of Sciences recognized his achievements by awarding him the title of associate member. He also took pictures on his journeys; these photographs today are regarded as valuable documents. The portrait shows a man with an arresting face in natural position. The books, the globe and the exotic plants in the background refer to the sitter's scientific interests.

# Additional Items of Importance in the Museum

*1. Spearhead*   *2. Spearhead*   *3. Bomb-shaped bowl*

*4. Sacrificial vessel with human figure*   *5. Painted bowl*   *6. Libation table*   *7. Bowl with hollow pedestral*

*8. Lid with zoomorphic handle*   *9. Statue of a goddess*   *10. Libation vessel*   *11. Clay model of a wagon with solid wheels*

*12. Suspension vessel*   *13. Bird-shaped vessel*   *14. Bowl*

*15. Disk-shaped pectoral*

*16. Bracelet ornamented
with a bull's head*

*17. Bird-shaped vessel with human face*

*18. Vessel shaped like
a human being with a dagger*

*19. Swords*

*20. Diadem*

*21. Spiral-shaped armrings*

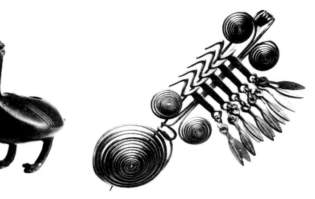

*22. Bird-shaped vessels*

*23. Fibula with stylized bird figures*

*24. Bronze bucket*

*25. Sceptre with a horse's head*

*26. Cauldrons and cup*

*27. Urn*

28. Statue of a deity

29. Hydria from Sparta

30. Mirror

31. Quiver mounting

32. Stag-shaped shield ornament

33. Vessel with handles ending in the head
of a bull or a ram

34. Jar with a handle in the shape
of a female figure

35. Jug with handle surmounted
by a plastically rendered head

36. Torques with rich plastic decoration

37. Antropomorphic knife-handle

38. Scabbard engraved with dragon figures

39. Bracelet

40. Belt chain with zoomorphic clasp

41. Bronze lamp

42. *Plated ornamental dagger*

43. *Military diploma*

44. *Statuette of Victory*

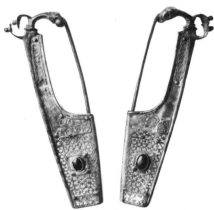

45. *Glazed vessel*

46. *Gravestone of a native*

47. *Pair of fibulas with openwork decoration*

48. *Waxed table*

49. *Chariot ornament*

50. *Chariot ornament*

51. *Wheel-disk with the head of a swan*

52. *Decorated helmet*

53. *Statue of Liber Pater*

54. *Emblem of a native official*

55. *Head of Hygieia*

56. *Relief of Athene*

57. *Leda and the swan*

58. *Relief depicting the myth of Ganymede*

59. *Relief of Iphigenia*

60. *Heracles and Alcestis*

61. *Orpheus among animals*

62. *Baking mould with the figure of Victory*

63. *Sarcophagus*

64. *Milestone*

65. *Bust of Trebonianus Gallus*

66. *Necklace*

67. *Mithras tablet*

68. *Table with a rescript*

69. *Bronze casket mountings*

129

70. Tripus

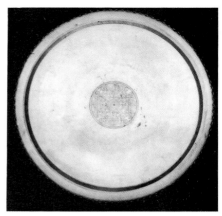

71. Moesian plates

72. Engraved glass

73. Christ monogram

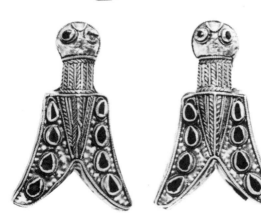

74. Inscription on a sepulchral monument

75. Cauldron

76. Cicada pair of fibulas

77. Electron cup

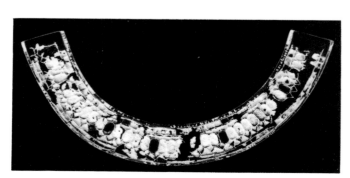

78. Shield mounting

79. Buckle

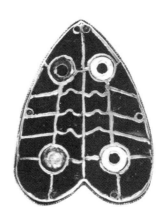

80. Hearth-shaped pommel

130

*81. Necklace*

*82. Glass cup*

*83. Belt buckle*

*84. Fibula*

*85. Eagle-shaped fibula*

*86. Belt buckle*

*87. Pair of fibulas*

*88. Pendant*

*89. Torque*

*90. Pair of fibulas with lions*

*91. Pair of disk-shaped fibulas*

*92. Pair of fibulas*

*93. Scabbard mounting*

131

94. S-shaped fibulas

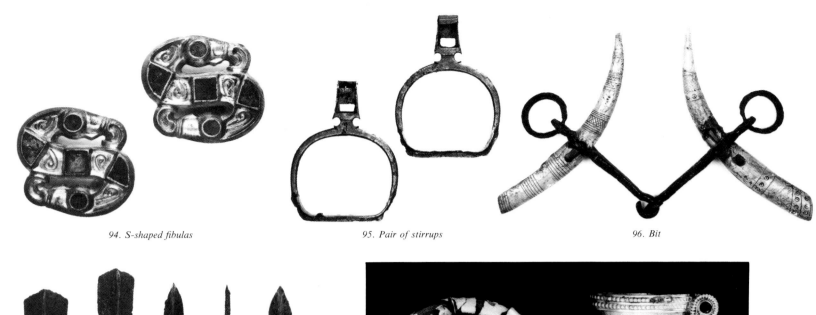

95. Pair of stirrups

96. Bit

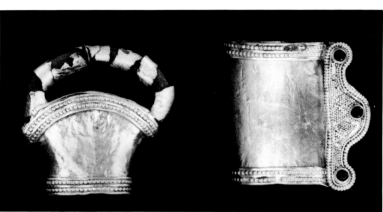

97. Arrow-heads

98. Handle of a sword and scabbard mounting

99. Necklace

100. Pressing moulds

101. Basket-shaped earrings

102. Head-dress

103. Belt ornament

104. Earring

105. Finger ring

107. Large strap-end

106. Belt mounting

108. Large strap-end

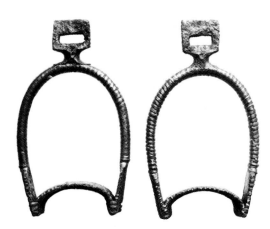

109. Strap-end shaped like a boar's head

110. Disk

111. Pair of stirrups

112. Phalera

113. Phalera

114. Jar with a spout

115. Corpus

116. Summoning sigil of the Veszprém
    Collegiate Church

117. Aspersorium

118. Head of a crosier

133

119. Ring

120. Aquamanile decorated
with a female head

121. Aquamanile decorated
with a riding scene

122. Base of a cross

123. Reliquary in the form
of a patriarchal cross

124. Processional crucifix

125. Censer

126. Candlestick in the form of a siren

127. Funerary crown of Béla III

128. Funerary crown of Anne of Antioch

129. Funerary sceptre and sword
of Béla III

130. Bracelet and pair of spurs of Béla III

131. Enkolpion from the grave of Béla III

132. Processional cross from the grave
of Béla III

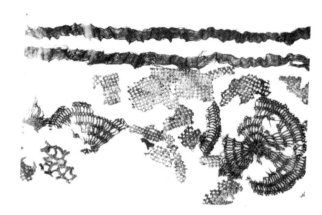

133. Rings of Béla III
and Anne of Antioch

134. Gold lacework from the grave
of Anne of Antioch

135. Cup

136. The Golden Bull of Béla IV

137. Clasp (Fürspan)

138. Clasp

139. Earthenware cauldron

140. Earthenware pot

141. Bowl from the Körmend Find

143. Reliquary from Trencsény

142. Engraving die

144. The Sigismund Crown

145. Baptismal font

146. Gravestone
of Zsuzsanna Kompolthy

147. Stove tile

148. Trough pan

149. Iron tools

150. Bell

151. Monstrance

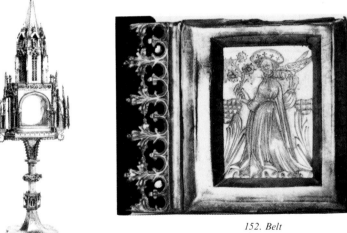

152. Belt

153. The Matthias Glass Goblet

154. Waffle-iron

155. Easter candlestick

156. Earthenware
drinking cup

157. Chalice

158. Ciborium

159. Reliquary
of Balázs Besztercei

160. Section of a Gothic iron door

161. Capital

162. Bookstand

163. Book binding from the former
library of the St. Egidius
Church of Bártfa

164. Stove tile

165. Iron door

166. Choirstalls (two seats)

167. Trousseau locker

168. Earthenware jug

169. Earthenware
drinking cup

170. Stove tile

171. Crest-tile of a stove

137

172. Corner tile

173. Crest-tile of a stove

174. Cup

175. Gild badge from Brassó

176. Queen Mary's ring

177. Flagon

178. Beaker with standard

179. The Barcsay Plate

180. Spice-container with mine scenes

181. Can

182. Candlestick

183. Pair of slippers

184. Scales weight

185. Turkish memorial stone-slab

186. Mehmed Ali's ring

187. Goblet belonging to a guild

138

188. Helmet (Hundsgugel)

189. Seal of the Rudabánya mining town

190. Seal of the Újbánya mining town

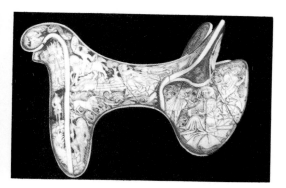

191. Saddle

192. Shield

193. Pair of spurs

194. Shield

195. Tournament armour

196. Suit of armour

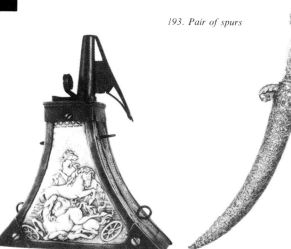

197. Powder-horn

198. Dagger

199. Can of the Shoemakers'
Guild at Gölnicbánya

200. Can of an unknown
Blacksmiths' Guild

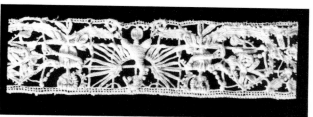

201. Lace

202. Homespun material

139

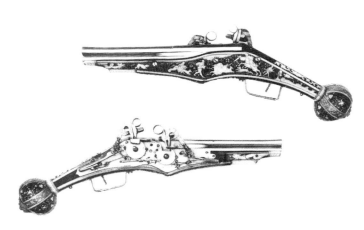

203. Pistol (puffer)

204. György Thurzó's helmet

205. Sand-clock

206. István Thököli's harpsichord

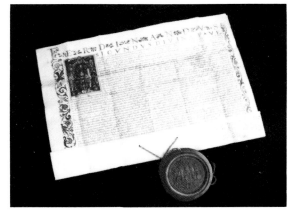

207. The Szapárys' letters-patent
from Ferdinand II

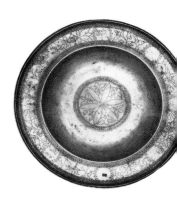

208. Platter with engraved
decoration

209. Wall-clock

210. Seal of Ferdinand II

211. Ship's cannon

212. Embroidered table-cloth

213. Saddle cloth

214. A fragment of a cannon
of György Rákóczi I

217. Stirrup

218. Deer antler powder-horn
with the Telekis' coat-of-arms

215. György Rákóczi's
chain-mail shirt

216. Quiver

219. Pistols of King Matthias Corvinus

220. Cloth for Communion-table

221. Chasuble

222. Beaker with István Apor's
coat-of-arms

223. Tankard with a merchant scene

224. Seal of the Rimaszombat Guild
of Merchants

225. Princely seal
of Ferenc Rákóczi II

226. Pocket-watch
of Ferenc Pápai Páriz

228. Can of the Érsekújvár
Butchers' Guild

229. Privileges of the Debrecen Guild
of Merchants

227. Long-case clock

230. The armchair
of Ferenc Rákóczi II

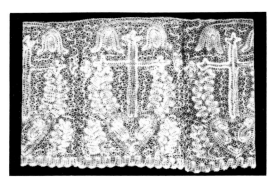

231. Strip of lace

232. Covered beaker

233. Bottle
with a screw-in cork

234. Haban plate

235. Lock and key

236. Table ornament
from the Esterházy Castle at Tata

237. Table sundial

238. Mulled wine decanter
with the Torockai coat-of-arms

239. Certificate of the Diószeg Guild of Tailors

240. Mozart's clavichord

241. Gala suit for a young
Hungarian man

242. Lady's gala dress with apron

243. Hungarian gentleman's gala
suit and shoes

244. *Aigrette*　　　245. *Lady's belt*　　　246. *Aigrette*　　　247. *Chalice*　　　248. *Haban pitcher*

249. *Falconer's tote*

250. *Grain measure*

251. *Trumpet*

252. *Trade-sign*

253. *A meeting of freemasons*
*for the admission of masters*

254. *Palatine Joseph's armchair*

255. *Saxon jug*

256. *Oil and vinegar bottles*

257. *Necklace*

258. *Mente belt*

259. *Coffee pot*

260. *Covered pan for hot milk*

261. Piano that belonged to Beethoven
and then to Liszt

262. Chest of a Pest Guild of Masons

263. Medal and coin cabinet
of Count Ferenc Széchényi

264. The first seal of the Hungarian
National Museum

265. Bowl

266. Sugar bowl

267. Glass

268. Meerschaum pipe

269. Gentleman's Hungarian gala
suit and boots

270. Imre Madách's desk

271. Desk

272. Seal of the National League

273. Seal of the first Hungarian
government's Prime Minister

274. Count Lajos Batthyány's
prime-ministerial chair

*275. Teapot*

*276. Glass*

*277. Plate*

*278. Bottle*

*279. Glass commemorating Pál Almásy's imprisonment at Olmütz*

*280. Platter*

*281. Episcopal pectoral cross*

*282. Armchair from the Upper House of Parliament*

*283. The chairman's seat from the last dietal session in Transylvania*

*284. Guitar of Kornelia Lotz*

*285. Freemason's watch pendant*

*286. Portraits of Mór Fischer and his wife*

*287. Pipe*

*288. Seal of Franz Joseph I*

*289. Queen Elizabeth's bodice*

*290. Armchair from Queen Elizabeth of Hungary's sitting-room furniture*

*291. Chandelier from the former Royal Palace*

*292. Chalice*

*293. Beaker with lid commemorating Lajos Kossuth*

*294. Broach*

*295. Necklace*

*296. Flag of the "Progressio" masonic lodge*

*297. Freemason's watch*

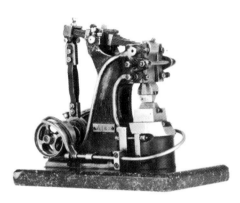

*298. Model of a spring hammer*

*299. Beaker of the "Világ" masonic lodge*

*300. Beaker commemorating Imre Steindl*

*301. Field marshal's baton*

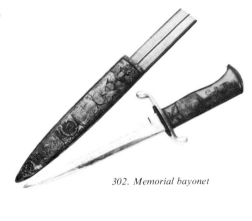

*302. Memorial bayonet*

*303. Necklace*

*304. Fashion design*

146

305. Leontino. Tetradrachma

306. Syracuse. Decadrachma

307. Tetradrachma. Sikelo-pun

308. Thasos. Tetradrachma

309. Croisos. Stater

310. Artaxerxes I. Dareikos

311. Tetradrachma. Zichy-Újfalusi type

312. Tetradrachma. Regöly type

313. Tetradrachma. Audoleon type

314. Tetradrachma. Noricum type

315. Tetradrachma with Apollon's portrait. Fertőrákos type

316. Tetradrachma. Alexandros type

317. Barbarian tetradrachma. The so-called Transylvanian sciphatus (bowl-shaped type)

318. Barbarian tetradrachma. Thasos type

319. Boi tetradrachma with the inscription BVSV

147

*320. Boi drachma. Tótfalusi type*

*321. Eraviskus denarius*

*322. Tiberius. As*

*323. Vitellius and Son. Denarius*

*324. Faustina II. Sestertius*

*325. Septimus Severus. Quinar*

*326. Clodius Albinus. As*

*327. Plautilla. Denarius*

*328. Paulina. Denarius*

*329. Pacatianus. Antoninianus*

*330. Laelianus. Antoninianus*

*331. Magnia Urbica and Carinus quinar*

*332. Diocletianus. Denarius argenteus*

*333. Reduced follis. Alexander Tyrannis*

*334. Constantinus II. Medallion*

*335. Valens. Centenionalis*

*336. Byzantine coin weight. Eighteen solidus*

*337. Contemporary imitation of an Antoninus Pius denarius*

*338. Contemporary imitation of a fourth-century follis*

*339. Avar imitation of a Byzantine silver coin. Constans II*

340. King Stephen denarius

341. Imitation of a King Andrew I denarius

342. Three-ducat gold coin issued by Ladislas V

343. Gold groat coin issued by Matthias I

344. Guldiner coin issued by Ladislas II

345. Essay plate of a Ferdinand I denarius

346. Three-ducat coin issued by Rudolf

347. Three-thaler coin issued by Matthias II

348. Five-thaler coin issued by Ferdinand III

349. Three-ducat coin issued by Leopold I. XV-kreutzer gold coin

350. Two-ducat coin issued by Leopold I. VI-kreutzer gold coin

351. Maria Theresa fifteen-kreutzer gold coin

352. 10,000 crown weight

353. Design of the ten-crown coin of the Hungarian Republic of Councils

354. Two-pengő gold coin to commemorate Péter Pázmány

149

355. Ten-ducat coin showing
Count Miklós Esterházy

356. Ten-ducat coin issued
by John Szapolyai

357. Double thaler issued by John Sigismund

358. Five-ducat coin issued
by Zsigmond Báthory

359. Szeben ten-ducat coin

360. Ten-ducat coin issued by Mózes Székely

361. Six-ducat coin issued
by Gábor Báthory

362. Two-ducat coin issued
by György Rákóczi I

363. Essay-plates of a György Rákóczi thaler and denarius

364. Crescent-shaped ten-ducat coin issued by Leopold I

365. Ducat issued by Ferenc Rákóczi II

366. Denarius of Bernhard,
duke of Carinthia

367. *Real issued by Maximilian I*

368. *Three-ducat gold coin issued by Ladislas II*

369. *Hundred-ducat coin issued by Ferdinand III*

370. *Hundred-ducat coin issued
by Sigismund III, king of Poland*

371. *Fifteen-ducat coin issued
by Sigismund III, king of Poland*

372. *Denarius issued by Juga,
prince of Moldavia*

373. *Ducat issued by Heraclius,
prince of Moldavia*

374. *The Wass-Molitor Company's fifty-dollar coin*

 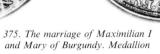

375. *The marriage of Maximilian I
and Mary of Burgundy. Medallion*

376. *Portrait of Maximilian I. Medallion*

377. *Portrait of Tamás Bakócz. Medallion*

151

378. Portrait of Martin Luther. Medallion

379. Louis II. Relief

380. Queen Mary of Hungary. Relief

381. Biblical medal from Joachimstal.
Last Supper—Last Judgement

382. Biblical medal from Joachimstal.
The Temptation—The Expulsion

383. Portrait of Gianbattista Castaldo. Medallion

384. Biblical medal from Körmöcbánya.
The Temptation—The Expulsion—The Adoration of the Shepherds

386. Portraits of Ferdinand I, Maximilian II
and Mary. Medallion

385. Portrait of Maximilian II.
Medallion

387. Portraits of Rudolph II and Prince Ernst. Medallion

388. Portrait of Rudolph II. Medallion

389. Portrait of David Hohenberger.
Medallion

390. Portrait of Georg Basta. Medallion

391. Matthias II riding a horse. Medallion

392. Portrait of Catherine of Brandenburg.
Medallion

393. The Peace of Westfalia. Medallion

394. Death of Ferdinand III. Medallion

395. Coronation ceremony of Joseph I,
king of Hungary. Medallion

153

396. Homage paid by Transylvania at the coronation ceremony
of Maria Theresa. Medallion

397. Maria Theresa's medal issued on the occasion of founding
the Royal Hungarian Order of St. Stephen

400. Coronation ceremony of Queen Elizabeth
of Hungary. Medallion

398. Cross of the Royal Hungarian
Order of St. Stephen

399. Chain of the Order
of Leopold

401. Medallion issued in commemoration
of the death of Hans von Bülow

402. Kelemen Mikes. Medallion

403. Sándor Kőrösi Csoma. Medallion

404. Portrait of Konrad Röntgen. Medallion

*405. View of Buda, from the Shedel Chronicle*

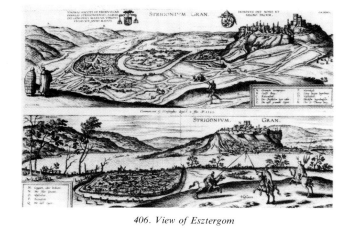

*406. View of Esztergom*

*407. Portrait of István Báthory, by J. Amman*

*408. The Recapture of Győr, 1598, by Franz Hogenberg*

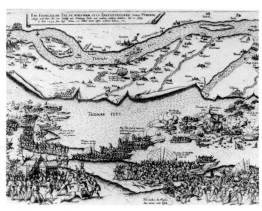

*409. Footsoldiers' attack in Tolna, 1599, by J. Sibmacher*

*410. View of Buda from the North, by W. Dilich*

*411. Portrait of Miklós Zrínyi, the hero of Szigetvár, by G. B. Fontana and D. Custos*

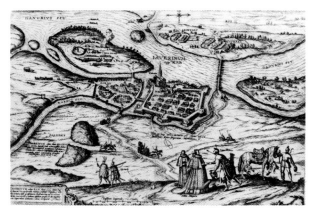

*412. View of Győr*

*413. View of Kassa*

155

414. *View of Eger*

415. *Portrait of Gábor Bethlen, by E. Sadeler*

416. *Portrait of Péter Pázmány, by Gy. Szelepcsényi*

417. *Portrait of Gáspár Lippay, by E. Wideman*

418. *Turkish–Hungarian combat, by I. Major*

419. *Gáspár Illésházy on his catafalque*

420. *View of Pozsony*

421. *View of Tokaj, by L. G. Saicha and K. Merian*

422. *View of Hatvan, by W. Hollar*

423. *Portrait of Miklós Zrínyi, by J. Thomas and G. Bouttats*

424. *Portrait of Imre Thököly, by D. Plaas and P. Stevens*

425. *Portrait of Kristóf Batthyány*

156

426. *The Siege of Esztergom, by J. Nypoort and J. M. Lerch*

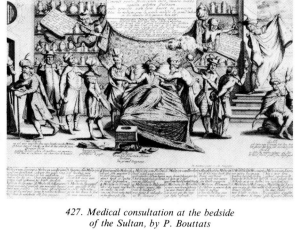

427. *Medical consultation at the bedside of the Sultan, by P. Bouttats*

428. *The Siege of Buda*

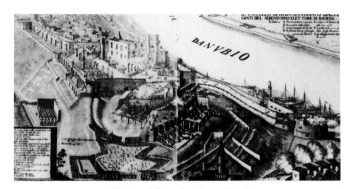

429. *Detail from the Siege of Buda, by L. N. Hallart and M. Wening*

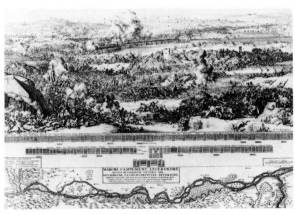

430. *The Battle of Nagyharsány, by R. Hooghe*

431. *Allegory of the successful wars for freedom, by J. Onghers*

432. *Portrait of Ferenc Rákóczi II, by Á. Mányoki*

433. *Kuruc horseman, by G.P. Rugendas*

434. *View of Esztergom, by J.C. Leopold*

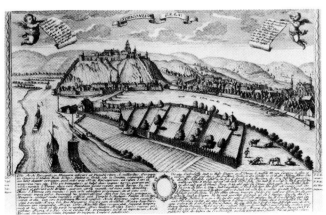

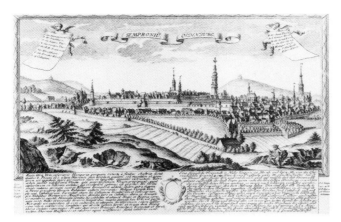

*435. View of Sopron, by B. Werner and J.C. Leopold*

*436. View of Székesfehérvár, by B. Werner and C. Leopold*

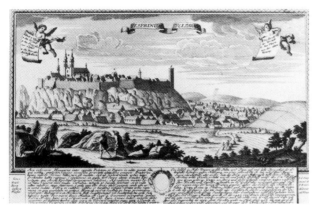

*437. View of Veszprém, by B. Werner and C. Leopold*

*438. Maria Theresa's coronation procession
in Pozsony, by J. D. Herz*

*439. The wife of a hussar officer,
by M. Engelbrecht*

*440. Portrait of Kristóf Migazzi,
by F.A. Palko*

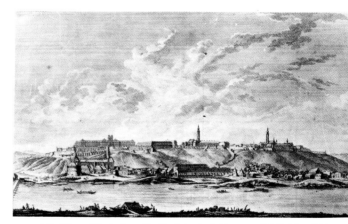

*441. View of Buda from the East, by J. J. Meyer and J.E. Mansfeld*

*442. Allegory of the Patent issued
by Joseph II, by J.F. Beer*

*443. View of Pozsony, by J. and P. Schaffer*

*444. Portrait of András Hadik,
by G. Weikert and J.P. Pichler*

445. The inauguration of Lord Lieutenant Antal Esterházy,
by C. Schütz and J. Berkeny

446. The execution of Martinovics and
his associates on Vérmező, 1795

447. The Marczibányi mansion
in Tornya by I. Marczibányi and S. Czetter

448. Portrait of Sándor Bárótzi,
by S. Czetter

449. Portrait of Count
Ferenc Széchényi,
by S. Czetter

450. The Tarpatak Falls in the Tatra
Mountains by E. Schrött and J. Ziegler

451. Portrait of Ferenc Kazinczy,
by V.G. Kininger and F. John

452. Portrait of Mihály Csokonai Vitéz,
by J. Erőss and F. John

453. Portrait of Count Ferenc
Barkóczy, by P. Krafft

454. View of Kecskemét, by J. Szokolai Hartó and F. Karancs

455. Portrait of Benedek Virág,
by J. Donát

456. A peasant and a maidservant,
by J. Bikkessy-Heinbucher

159

457. *Portrait of János Bihari, by J. Donát*

458. *Portrait of Colonel József Simonyi*

459. *View of Mohács, by J. Alt and A. Kunike*

460. *Horse-racing in Pest, 1827,*
*by J.G. Prestel, S. Clarot and J. Schmid*

461. *Blasting at the Iron Gate, by J. Lántz and A. Mink*

462. *Kálvin tér during the flood in 1838 by F. Collar*

463. *Portrait of András Fáy,*
*by A. Ehenreich*

464. *Portrait of Palatine Joseph,*
*by A. Einsle*

465. *The Vigadó building in Pest,*
*by R.v. Alt and F.X. Sandmann*

466. *Portrait of Franz Liszt,*
*by M. Barabás*

467. *Portrait of István Széchenyi,*
*by M. Barabás*

468. Portrait of Sándor Petőfi,
by M. Barabás

469. The flight of Metternich

470. The distribution
of the first publications of free press in Pest,
by V. Katzler

471. Portrait of Richárd Guyon,
by J. Perger

472. Portrait of Lajos Kossuth,
by A. Prinzhofer

473. Portrait of József Bem,
by M. Barabás

474. Portrait of Artúr Görgey,
by M. Barabás

475. A group of horseherds

476. Hussars breaking out of Komárom, by V. Katzler

477. Battle of Szolnok, by M. Szerelmey

478. Battle of Isaszeg, by M. Than

479. The recapture of Buda, by A. Pettenkofen

480. Portrait of László Józsefné
Mimi de Caux, by M. Barabás

481. Self-portrait of F. Lieder

482. Portrait of Lázár Mészáros,
by K. Brocky

483. Portrait of Gereben Vas,
by A. Canzi

484. Szentháromság tér in Buda,
by R.v. Alt and F. X. Sandmann

485. Portrait of Imre Székely,
by B. Kiss

486. Prison cell in Olmütz, by L. Berzsenyi

487. The shore of the Danube, by R.v. Alt and F.X. Sandmann

488. Shepherd by T. Valérie

489. Detail of Balatonfüred, by K.L. Libay and R.v. Alt

490. Portrait of Ferenc Erkel,
by A. Györgyi-Giergl

491. *View of Miskolc, by J. Poppel*

492. *Portrait of Mihály Horváth,*
*by B. Székely*

493. *Portrait of Miklós Izsó,*
*by B. Székely*

494. *Portrait of Géza Mészöly,*
*by B. Pállik*

495. *Portrait of Gyula Andrássy,*
*by B. Székely*

496. *Portrait of Lajos Kossuth,*
*by V. Parlaghy*

497. *Portrait of Queen Elisabeth*
*of Hungary, by Gy. Benczur*

498. *Rail production in the Diósgyőr Factory,*
*by Á. Feszty*

499. *The first May-day parade in Budapest,*
*by K. Cserna*

500. *Portrait of Kálmán Tisza,*
*by L. Horovitz*

501. *Portrait of Mór Jókai,*
*by A. Ferraris*

502. *Portrait of Madame Révai,*
*by K. Ferenczy*

503. *Portrait of Ödön Lechner,*
*by B. Pór*

504. *View of the Servite Church from the Kristóf tér in Pest, by I. Zádor*

505. *Dr. László Sipőcz*

506. *Hunt in Sárpentele, by F. Czakó*

507. *An election speech given by Count István Tisza, by O. Kallós*

# Catalogue. Colour Plates

## The Hungarian Coronation Insignia

### 1. Crown
Inv. No.: None
1074–1077 and second half of the 12th century, two parts assembled before the 13th century, Byzantine Gold, cloisonné enamel, precious stones and pearls, beaten, chiselled, with filigree and pearl-wire
Height: 17.8 cm, Diameter: 20.3 cm and 21.6 cm
Ref.: Kovács–Lovag; Bárány–Oberschall; Deér

### 2. Coronation mantle
Inv. No.: None
1031
Byzantine silk with gold and silk embroidery, pearls on the neck-piece
Length: 134 cm, width: 268 cm
Ref.: Kovács–Lovag; Bárány–Oberschall

### 3. Sceptre
Inv. No.: None
10th century and last quarter of the 12th century, Hungarian rock crystal, cut, set in gold and gilded silver, filigree
Length: 37.5 cm
Ref.: Kovács–Lovag; Bárány–Oberschall

### 4. Orb
First quarter of the 14th century
Silver, gilded, beaten, chiselled with enamel blazon
Height: 16.2 cm, diameter: 8.7 cm
Ref.: Kovács–Lovag; Bárány–Oberschall

### 5. Sword
Inv. No.: None
Early 16th century, Venetian
Iron, wrought, etched, velvet case cover with copper-plating
Length: 97.3
Ref.: Kovács–Lovag; Bárány–Oberschall

## Department of Archaeology

### 6. Bowl with pedestal
Inv. No.: 51.7.205
4th millennium B.C.
Clay, engraved, embossed
Height: 21.5 cm
Site: Lebő-Alsóhalom,
Csongrád county
Ref.: Korek, J.: "A Lebő-halmi ásatás 1950-ben" (Excavations in Lebő-halom in 1950). *AÉ* 85/1958. 140, Plate 40, 6; *MNM*, 1977. pp. 32-33

### 7. Disk-shaped pectoral
Inv. No.: 58.38.1–2
First half of 3rd millennium B.C.
Gold, punched
Diameter: 12.5 and 10.5 cm, weight: 81.6 and 59 g
Site: Zalaszentgrót-Csáford, Zala county
Ref.: Korek, J.: Die Goldscheiben von Csáford. *FA* 12/1960. pp. 27–33, Plates 6–7; Bóna, I.: "Javarézkori aranyleleteinkről.—Über Goldfunde aus der Hochkupferzeit." *Veszprém Megyei Múzeumok Közleményei* 18/1986. pp. 65–66, Illustrations 19–20

### 8. Antropomorphic urns
Inv. No.: 59.14.7–9
Second half of 3rd millennium B.C.
Clay
Height: 48.4 cm; 40. 6 cm; 23.9 cm
Site: Center, Borsod-Abaúj-Zemplén county
Ref.: Kalicz, N.: *Die Péceler (Badener) Kultur und Anatolien.* Budapest, 1963. Plates 1–3; Kalicz Illustrations 65–69; Kovács, 1977. Illustrations 45–46; *MNM*, 1977. pp. 36-37

### 9. Bell-beaker
Inv. No.: 143/1878.1
Early 2nd millennium B.C.
Clay
Height: 10 cm
Site: Tököl, Pest county
Ref.: Tompa, F.: *Budapest az ókorban* (The Ancient Budapest) I. Budapest, 1942. Plate 7, 2; Kovács, 1977. Illustration 6; *MNM*, 1977, pp. 38–39

### 10. Bracelet
Inv. No.: 72.5.1
Middle of the 2nd millennium, B.C.
Gold
Length: 13.9 cm, weight: 287.2 g Site: Dunavecse, Bács-Kiskun county
Ref.: Kovács, 1977, Illustration 28; *MNM,* 1977. pp. 40–41

### 11. Battle axes
Inv. No.: 60.41.1–3
16th century B.C.
Bronze, engraved
Length: 21.6, 20.5, 15.7 cm
Site: Szeghalom-Károlyderék dűlő, Békés county
Ref.: Mozsolits, A: *Die Bronze und Goldfunds des Karpatenbeckens.* Budapest, 1973. Plate 12

### 12. Jewelry
Inv. No.: 55/1878.1, 19–24,29–30
8th century B.C.
Gold, repoussé, with strands
Diameter: 7.3, 7.6, 7.7, 7.8, 8.6, 8.5, 5.5, 5.6, 5.7, 5.7, 5.8 cm; height: 54.6 cm
Site: Besenyszög-Fokorúpuszta, Jász-Nagykun-Szolnok county
Ref.: Harmatta, J.: "Le probleme cimmérien." *AÉ* 1946–48. Plates 16–20

### 13. Golden stag
Inv. No.: 2/1929.1
4th century B.C.
Gold, glass-paste, repoussé
Length: 37 cm
Site: Mezőkeresztes-Zöldhalompuszta, Borsod-Abaúj-Zemplén county
Ref.: Fettich, N.: *A zöldhalompusztai szkíta lelet–La trouvaille scythe de Zöldhalompuszta.* Budapest, 1928; *MNM,* 1977. pp. 48–49

### 14. Rattles with animal decorations
Inv. No.: 67.7.1–2
4th century B.C.
Bronze, cast
Length: 23.1 and 22.2 cm
Site: Nagytarcsa, Pest county
Ref.: Bakay, K.: *Scythian Rattles in the Carpathian Basin and their Eastern Connections.* Budapest, 1971. p. 1, Plates 4-5; *MNM,* 1977. pp. 50–51

### 15. Ornamental plates
Inv. No.: None
5th-4th century B.C.
Silver, engraved, repoussé
Length: 83 and 87.8 cm
Site: Titel
Ref.: Márton, Plate 16, p. 4

### 16. Statuette of a boar
Inv. No.: 88/1893
2nd century B.C., Celtic
Bronze
Length: 10.9 cm
Site: Báta, Tolna county
Ref.: Hunyady, Plate 38, p. 4

### 17. Gold spheres decorated with masks
Inv. No.: 71/1891, 67/1890
1st century B.C., Celtic
Gold, hammered
Diameter: 2.5–3.5 cm
Site: Szárazd and Regöly, Tolna county
Ref.: Hunyady, Plate 3, pp. 1–5; Plate 39, p. 8; *MNM,* 1977, pp. 54–55

### 18. Pitcher and patera
Inv. No.: 10/1951.104–105
1st century A.D.
Bronze, gold, silver, niello decoration
Height of pitcher: 24.3 cm, Diameter of patera: 23.4 cm
Site: Egyed, Győr-Moson-Sopron county
Ref.: Hekler, A.: "Die hellenistischen Bronzegefässe von Egyed." *Jahrbuch des deutschen Archäologischen Instituts* 24/1909. pp. 28–40; Wessetzky, V.: *Die ägyptischen Kulte zur Römerzeit in Ungarn.* Leiden, 1961. p. 42

### 19. Dolichenus triangle
Inv. No.: 10/1951.106–107
Second half on 2nd century –3rd century A.D.
Bronze plated with gold and silver
Height: 36 cm, width: 27.5 cm
Site: Kömlőd-Bottyánsánc, Tolna county
Ref.: Rómer, F. –Desardins, E.: "A Magyar Nemzeti Múzeum feliratos emlékei" (Inscriptions on Some Objects Held in the Hungarian National Museum). In: *Acta Nova Nationalis Hungarici.* Budapest, 1873. pp. 11-13, Plates V-VI; Láng, F.: *Das Dolichenum von Brigetio.* Laureae Aquincenses 2. DissPann Ser.II:11. Budapest, 1941. p. 177; *MNM,* 1977. pp. 68–69

### 20. Model of a gateway
Inv. No.: 66.1906.352
Around the beginning of the 3rd century, A.D.
Pannonia
Clay, fired
Height: 31 cm, width: 50 cm, depth: 20 cm
Site: Dunapentele (Intercisa), Fejér county
Ref.: Nagy, L.: *Az aquincumi polgárváros tűzoltóságának székháza (schola collegii centonariorum)* (The Headquarters of the Fire-Brigade in the City of Aquincum) Laureae Aquincenses 2. DissPan Ser.II:11. Budapest, 1941. p. 191; *MNM,* 1977. pp. 66–67

### 21. Veriuca's tombstone
Inv. No.: 56.1911.3
Around the beginning of the 2nd century A.D.
Limestone
Height: 149 cm, width: 87.5 cm, depth: 16 cm
Site: Dunapentele (Intercisa), Fejér county
Ref.: Erdélyi, G.: "Kőemlékek. Intercisa / (Dunapentele-Sztálinváros) története a római korban I" (Stone Finds. The History of Intercisa [Dunapentele-Sztálinváros] in the Roman Era. Part I). *ArchHung* 33/1954. p. 155; Erdélyi, G.–Fülep, L.: *op. cit.* p. 240, No. 49; *MNM,* 1977. pp. 60–61

### 22. Ivory statuette
Inv. No.: 22.1888
Around the beginning of the 3rd century A.D.
Height: 29 cm, without addition: 20 cm
Site: Szombathely (Savaria), Vas county
Ref.: Kádár, Z.: "A szombathelyi bacchikus elefántcsont szobor" (Statue of Bacchus from Szombathely). *FA* 14/1962. pp. 41–50

### 23. Cultic insignia
Inv. No.: 58.12.33
End of 3rd century–beginning of 4th century A.D.
Silver, coated with gold and decorated with niello
Height: 33.1 cm
Site: Szőny (Brigetio), Komárom-Esztergom county
Ref.: Barkóczi, L.: "New Data on the History of Late Roman Brigetio." *Acta Antiqua* 13/1965

### 24. Gold textile
Inv. No.: 59.1894.6

4th-5th century
Site: Kosztolác
Ref.: Paulovics, I.: "Római kori gyűjtemény" (The Roman Age Collection). In: *Hungarian National Museum–Hungarian Museum of History. Guide to the Archaeological Collection.* Budapest, 1938. p. 73

**25. Bust of an emperor**
Inv. No.: 108.1912.66
Middle or second half of the 4th century A.D.
Height: 12.2 cm
Ref.: Fülep, F.: "Sopianae. The History of Pécs during the Roman Era, and the Problem of the Continuity of the Late Roman Population." *ArchHung* 50/1984. p. 74, o. 70; Beck, H.–Bol, P.C. (eds.): *Spätantike und frühes Christentum. Ausstellung im Liebighaus Museum alter Plastik.* Frankfurt/Main, 1984. p. 453, No. 61; *MNM*, 1977. pp. 74–75

**26. Fragment of a table top**
Inv. No.: 54.20.1
4th century A.D.
Marble
Length: 34 cm
Site: Csopak-Kőkoporsó dűlő, Veszprém county
Ref.: B. Thomas, E.: "Későrómai márvány asztallap Csopakról" (Late Roman Marble Table Top from Csopak). *FA* 6/1954. pp. 74–85, 205–206

**27. Belt ornaments**
Inv. No.: 103.1864.
II.5–9, 11
4th century A.D.
Silver plated with gold and niello decoration
Width: 6.9 cm
Site: Budapest-Budaújlak
Ref.: Radnóti, A.: "Buda régészeti emlékei" (Archaeological Finds in Buda). In: *Budapest Műemlékei I* (Budapest Monuments I). Budapest, 1955. p. 30

**28. Fondo d'oro**
Inv. No.: 3.1934
End of 4th century A.D.
Glass, sheet gold
Diameter: 8.7 cm
Site: Dunaszekcső, Baranya county
Ref.: Fülep, F.: "Ókeresztény üvegedények a Magyar Nemzeti Múzeumban" (Old Christian Glass Wares in the Hungarian National Museum). *Antik Tanulmányok,* 14/1964. pp. 239–248; Fülep, F.: "Early Christian Gold Glasses in the Hungarian National Museum." *Acta Antiqua* 16/1968. pp. 401–412

**29. Cage cup**
Inv. No.: 23.1849.2
Early 4th century A.D.
Glass
Height: 11.6 cm, diameter: 15.9 cm
Site: Szekszárd, Tolna county
Ref.: Barkóczi, L.: "Pannonische Glasfunde in Ungarn." *Studia Archaeologica,* 9/1988. pp. 219, no. 556

**30. Helmet**
Inv. No.: 110.1899 End of 4th century A.D.
Iron covered with gilded silver
Height: 23.5 cm
Site: Budapest: Eskü (today Március 15) tér
Ref.: B. Thomas, E.: Der Helm von Budapest, Ungarn. *Spätrömische Gardehelme.* (Edited by Klumbach, H.) München, 1973. pp. 39–50

**31. Diadem**
Inv. No.: 55.36.1
5th century
Sheet gold, stones in mountings
Length: 26.7 cm, width: 3.6–4.2 cm
Site: Csorna, Győr-Moson-Sopron county
Ref.: Hampel, pp. 12–14; Alföldi, A.: "Leletek a hun korszakból és etnikai szétválasztásuk - Funde aus der Hunnenzeit und ihre ethnische Sonderung." *ArchHung* 9/1932. p. 59, table 19; Kovrig, I.: "Das Diadem von Csorna." *FA* 36/1985. pp. 107–148; *MNM*, 1977. 80–81

**32. Pair of bracelets**
Inv No.: 19/1860.1
First half of the 5th century A.D.
Sheet gold, repoussé, inlaid garnet
Diameter: 8.5 cm
Site: Dunapataj-Bakodpuszta, Bács-Kiskun county
Ref.: Hampel, table 2; Fettich, M.: "Régészeti tanulmányok a késői hun fémművesség történetéhez–Archäologische Studien zur Geschichte der spathunnischen Metallkunst." *ArchHung* 31/1951. Plates XV-XVI; Kovrig, Illustration 31b; Kiss, pp. 95-131, Illustrations 5:3, 8; *MNM,* 1977. pp. 84-85

**33. Buckle**
Inv. No.: 10/1927
5th century
Sheet silver, gilded and niello decoration
Length: 10 cm, width: 7.8 cm

Site: Szabadbattyán, Fejér county
Ref.: Fettich, 1953. Plate LVII, 1

**34. Fibula**
Inv. No.: 122/1895.1
Second half of the 4th century
Sheet gold, repoussé, onyx, crystal, amber, karneol
Length: 17 cm, widest diameter: 11 cm
Site: Szilágysomlyó
Ref.: Fettich, 1932. Plate VII; Kovrig, Illustration 46.a; Bóna: "Dáciától", p. 134, Colour Illustration 3; *MNM*, 1977. pp. 76–77

**35. Cups**
Inv. No.: 122/1895.16–17
First half of the 5th century A.D.
Sheet gold, repoussé, tinted, with almadine inlay
Diameter: 12 and 10 cm, height: 4.5 and 3.5 cm
Site: Szilágysomlyó
Ref.: Fettich, 1932. Plates XXVIII-XXIX

**36. Vessels**
Inv. No.: 8/1927;
43/1884.5; 75/1893.111
6th century A.D.
Clay, fired, with stamped and smoothed in patterns
Height: 9 and 8 and 12.4 cm, diameter at the rim: 6.1 and 5 and 6.4 cm, diameter at the bottom: 5.1 and 4.5 and 6 cm
Site: Gyula, Mezőberény, Szarvas, Békés county
Ref.: Csallány, D.: "Archäologische Denkmäler der Gepiden im Mitteldonaubecken (454–568)." *ArchHung* 38/1961. Plates XCXIV, 4 and CCXX, 5 and CXCIII, 13

**37. Jug and beaker**
Inv. No.: 69/1858.10
7th century A.D.
Sheet silver, hammered
Height: 21 and 10.7 cm, diameter at the mouth: 10.7 and 9.5 cm, diameter at the bottom: 6.3 and 4 cm
Site: Kunágota, Békés county
Ref.: Hampel, pp. 339–343, Plates 260–262; Bóna, 1982–83, pp. 88–98

**38. Pair of earrings**
Inv. No.: 14/1895.1–2
6th–7th century A.D.
Gold, stamped, granulated
Length: 5 cm
Site: Debrecen, Hajdú-Bihar county

**39. Pseudo buckle**
Inv. No.: 65/1912.4
7th century A.D.
Gold, partially cast, pressed, repoussé
Length: 5.3 cm,

width: 3.1 cm
Site: Tépe, Hajdú-Bihar county
Ref.: Supka, G.: "A tépei népvándorláskori leletről" (On the Finds at Tépe from the Age of the Great Migrations). *AÉ* 33/1913. pp. 395–408; László, Plates LVII-LVIII

**40. Buckle, strap end, belt and saddle accessories**
Inv. No.: Orn.Jank.49, 50, 51
End of 6th century A.D.
Gold, engraved, semi-precious stone inlays
Length: 5.5 and 4.7 and 1.8 and 5.1 cm, width: 3.5 and 2 and 1.7 and 3.4 cm
Site: Hungary
Ref.: Hampel, p. 687, Plate 257, 4; Bóna, 1982–83, pp. 82–85

**41. Belt loop**
Inv. No.: 131/1881.14
First half of 8th century A.D., late Avar period
Gold, repoussé
Length: 3.6 cm, width: 1.2 cm
Site: Tab, Somogy county
Ref.: Garam, É.: Spätawarenzeitliche "Goldgegenstände im Ungarischen Nationalmuseum." *FA* 35/1984. p. 94, Illustration 5

**42. Pair of clasps**
Inv. No.: 183/1870
Around the beginning of the 8th century
Gold, pressed
Length: 11 cm, height: 2.3 cm
Site: Dunapataj, Bács-Kiskun county
Ref.: Hampel, pp. 389–390, Plate 282; Horváth, T.: "Az üllői és a kiskőrösi avar temető–Die awarischen Gräberfelder von Üllő und Kiskőrös." *ArchHung* 19/1935. pp. 61–62, Plate XLVIII

## Mediaeval Department

**43. Sabretache plate**
Inv. No.: 148/1870.5
10th century, age of the Hungarian Conquest
Silver, gilt
Height: 12.5 cm, width: 11.3 cm
Site: Szolyva
Ref.: *MNM*, 1977. pp. 104–105

**44. Sabretache plate**
Inv. No.: 8/1895.74
10th century, age of the Hungarian Conquest
Silver, gilt
Height: 13.4 cm, width: 12.3 cm
Site: Tarcal,

Borsod-Abaúj-Zemplén county
Ref.: Dienes, pp. 58–61, 80, Illustration 7; Fettich, 1937. pp. 73–74

**45. Sabretache plate**
Inv. No.: 42/1871.13
10th century, age of the Hungarian Conquest
Silver, gilt
Height: 13 cm, width: 11.2 cm
Site: Galgóc
Ref.: Dienes, pp. 58–61, 80, Illustration 2; Fettich, 1937. pp. 76–77)

**46. Sabretache plate**
Inv. No.: 86/1896.236.a
10th century, age of the Hungarian Conquest
Copper, gilt
Height: 13.6 cm, width: 15.6 cm
Site: Tiszabezdéd, Szabolcs-Szatmár-Bereg county
Ref.: Dienes, pp. 58–61, 81, Illustration 11; Fettich, 1937. pp. 76–77; Fettich, N.: "Adatok a honfoglaláskor archeológiájához" (Data on the Archaeology of the Age of the Hungarian Conquest). *AÉ*, 45/1931. pp. 49–72, Illustrations 33–35; Fodor, I.: "Einige Beiträge zur Entfaltung der ungarischen Kunst der Landnahmezeit." *Alba Regia,* 17/1979. pp. 65–73

**47. Apex of a tall fur cap**
Inv. No.: 51/1900.20–21
10th century, age of the Hungarian Conquest
Silver, gilt
Originally about 12.5 cm
Site: Beregszász
Ref.: *MNM*, 1977. pp. 106–107

**48. Plait disc**
Inv. No.: 59.5.3. A 10th century, age of the Hungarian Conquest
Silver, gilt, cast
Diameter: 5.2 cm
Site: Sárospatak, Borsod-Abaúj-Zemplén county
Ref.: Dienes, pp. 53–54, 63–64, 83, Illustrations 36–37

**49. Band-shaped bracelet**
Inv. No.: 3/1938.4
Bronze, gold sheet, red gem
Diameter: 7 cm
Site: Heves, Heves county
Ref.: Dienes, p. 63, 84, Illustration 51; Pataki, V.: "A hevesi honfoglaláskori női sírlelet" (The Female Grave from the Age of the Hungarian Conquest Found at Heves). *FA.* 1–2/1939. pp. 200–203, Plate I. 17

**50. The Monomachos Crown**
Inv. No.: 1860.99.1–4, 1861.37.1–2, 1861.51.1–2, 1870.36.1–2 1041–1050
Gold, beaten, enchased, with cloisonné enamel
Height of the largest section (in the centre): 11.5 cm
Site: Nyitraivánka
Ref.: Bárányné-Oberschall, M.: "Monomachos bizánci császár koronája–The Crown of the Emperor Constantine Monomachos." *ArchHung* 22/1937; *MNM*, 1977. pp. 112–113

**51. Processional Crucifix**
Inv. No.: 58.59.B
Second half of the 12th century, Transdanubia
Bronze, gilt, beaten, engraved, cast
Height: 24 cm
Site: Szerecseny, Győr-Moson-Sopron county
Ref.: Lovag, Illustration 8

**52. Finds from the royal tomb of Székesfehérvár**
Inv. No.: 1885.76, 58.64.1–7.B, 58.65.B
12th–13th century, Hungarian royal workshop
Gold, beaten, engraved, with filigree, granulation, cloisonné enamel and pearls
Height of crown: 1.8 cm, height of strap-end: 1.8 cm, length of bracelet: 17.3 cm
Site: Székesfehérvár, Archbishop's Palace, Fejér county
Ref.: Henszlman, F.: *A székes-fehérvári ásatások eredménye* (The Results of the Excavations at Székes-fehérvár). Pest, 1864; Kovács, 1974. p. 52, Plate 14

**53. Clay bottle**
Inv. No.: 20/1892.4 End of the 12th century
Clay, made on a potter's wheel, fired, yellowish-white colour, brownish-red stripes on the body
Height: 30 cm, diameter at the mouth: 7.8 cm, diameter at the bottom: 11.3 cm
Site: Hatvan, Heves county
Ref.: Höllrigl, J.: "Árpádkori keramikánk I. Fenékbélyeges edények" (Árpád Age Pottery in Hungary. Part I. Vessels Stamped on the Bottom). *AÉ* 44/1930. pp. 146–147, Illustration 101, 1; Höllrigl, J.: "Középkori magyar kerámia" (Mediaeval Hungarian Pottery). *M.Műv.* 7/1931.

pp. 461–462, Figure 1a; *MNM*, 1977. pp. 130–131

**54. Mould for making double-sided seal**
Inv. No.: CimSec.I.V.3
First half of the 13th century
Site: Esztergom
Bronze, gilt, engraved, cast
Diameter: 7.1 cm
Ref.: Vattai, E.: "Az esztergomi latinok kettős pecsétje" (The Double-sided Seal of the Latins in Esztergom). *AÉ* 90/963. pp. 39–45; *MNM*, 1977. pp. 264–265

**55. Finger-bowl**
Inv. No.: App.Jank.186
Around 1240, Limoges
Copper, gilt, beaten, engraved, enamelled
Diameter: 22 cm
Site: Bátmonostor, Bács-Kiskun county
Kovács, É.: *Limoges-i zománcok Magyarországon* (Limoges Enamels in Hungary). Budapest, 1968. p. 26, Illustrations 38–39; *MNM*, 1977. pp. 134–135

**56. Crown**
Inv. No.: 1847.43
Last third of the 13th century
Silver, gilt, beaten, engraved, cast, with amethysts, granites and pearls
Height: 6.2 cm, diameter: 17 cm
Site: Budapest, Margaret Island
Ref.: Vattai, E.: "A margitszigeti korona" (The Margaret Island Crown). *BudRég* 18/1958. pp. 191–207; Feuerné Tóth, R.: "V. István király sírja a margitszigeti apácakolostor templomában" (The Grave of King Stephen V in the Church of the Margaret Island Convent). *BudRég* 21/1964. pp. 11–131; *MNM*, 1977. pp. 136–137

**57. Mantle clasp**
Inv. No.: Orn.Jank.141
1240–1250, Hungarian, royal workshop
Silver, gilt, beaten, engraved, cast, stones and pearls are missing
Diameter: 13.3 cm
Ref.: Kovács, É.: "Über einige Probleme des Krakauer Kronenkreuzes." *Acta HistArt* 17/1971. pp. 231–268; Kovács, É.: "Két 13. századi ékszerfajta Magyarországon" (Two Thirteenth-century Types of Jewelry in Hungary). *ArsHung*/1973. pp. 67–95

**58. Ciborium**
Inv. No.: 1916.31

Around 1360, Szepesség
Copper, gilt, engraved
Height: 39 cm
Site: Szepeskörtvélyes
Ref.: Kolba, J.H.: "Zwei gotische Ziborien im ungarischen Nationalmuseum." *Acta HistArt* 21/1975. pp. 283–332; *MNM*, 1977. pp. 142–143

**59. Chalice from Vízakna**
Inv. No.: 58.173.C
Middle of the 14th century, Italian
Silver, gilt, engraved, with translucent enamel, enchased
Height: 19.8 cm, diameter at the rim: 11.3 cm
Ref.: Mihalik, S.: "Problems Concerning the Altar of Elizabeth, Queen of Hungary". *Acta HistArt* 10/1964. p. 247

**60. The Nyári Chalice**
Inv. No.: 1879.114.11
Around 1460, Transylvania
Silver, gilt, wire enamel, engraved, cast, with filigree decoration
Height: 25.5 cm, diameter: 15 cm
Ref.: Kolba, J. H.: "Der Nyári-Kelch." *Acta ArchHung* 32/1980. pp. 373–402

**61. Trousseau chest**
Inv. No.: 19/1919
15th century, Nagyszeben
Linden wood, painted
Length: 160 cm, height: 107 cm, width: 55 cm
Ref.: K. Csilléry, K.: "Az ácsolt láda" (Wooden chests). *Publications of the Second Department at the Hungarian Academy of Sciences. 3. I/2.* 1953. pp. 231–284)

**62. Bookcase**
Inv. No.: 6/1915
Around 1480, Bártfa
Front made of lime-wood, the other parts of larch; carved, painted; iron fittings coated with tin
Length: 430 cm, height: 238 cm
Place of origin: Bártfa, St. Egidius's Church
Ref.: Kovalovszki, pp. 10–11, 25, Plates I–II; *MNM*, 1977. pp. 158–159)

**63. Missal**
Inv. No.: 63.53.C
1480, Verona, Italy
Incunabulum, handpainted
Length: 37 cm, width: 25.8, thickness: 10.5 cm
Ref.: Soltész, Z.: "Blutfogel Boldizsár miniátor" (Boldizsár Blutfogel, the Miniaturist). *Publications of the National Széchényi Library.* Plate XLI. Budapest, 1957. p. 7

**64. Gothic choir stalls**
1483, Bártfa
Lime-wood, carved, painted
Length: 359 cm, height: 405 cm
Ref.: Myskovsky, V.: *Bártfa középkori műemlékei I.* (Mediaeval Art in Bártfa. Part I.) Budapest, 1879. pp. 89–95

**65. Renaissance choir stalls**
Inv. No.: 67/1933.a.c
1511, Nyírbátor Master Marone
Oak wood, carved, marquetry
Length: 1025 + 200 cm, height: 400 cm
Place of origin: Nyírbátor, Szabolcs-Szatmár-Bereg county, Sanctuary of St. George's Church
Ref.: Oberschall, M.: "A nyírbátori stallumok" (The Choirstalls from Nyírbátor). *Bibliotheca Humanitatis Historica* 2. Budapest, 1937; *MNM*, 1977. pp. 162–163

**66. Earthenware mug**
Inv. No.: 61.65.C
15th century, Site: Lostitze
Clay, made on a turning wheel, fired, under purplish-blue salt glazing tiny blisters on the body, on the base and around the rim, setting made of gold plated bronze sheet
Height: 19 cm, diameter at the rim: 8 cm, diameter at the base: 9.2 cm
Ref.: Divald, K.: *A magyar iparművészet története* (The History of the Applied Arts in Hungary). Budapest, 1929. p. 160; Holl, I.: "Külföldi kerámia Magyarországon. XIII–XVI. század" (Imported Ceramics in Hungary. Thirteenth to sixteenth centuries.) *BudRég* 16/1955. pp. 159–161

**67. Earthenware jug**
Inv. No.: 64.3.C
First half of the 16th century
Clay, made on a turning wheel, fired, yellowish-white colour, incised and stamped decoration on the top and on the handle, brownish-yellow glaze
Height: 29 cm, diameter at the rim: 13.7 cm, diameter at the bottom: 10 cm
Site: Szécsény Castle, Nógrád county
Ref.: Höllrigl, J.: "A középkori magyar kerámika" (Mediaeval Hungarian Ceramics). *M.Műv.* 7/1931. pp. 465–468, Figure 8; *MNM*, 1977. pp. 164–165

**68. Cruets from Nagyvárad**
Inv. No.: Poc.Jank.188–189
End of the 15th century, Transylvania
Silver, gilt, embossed, filigree decoration, enamelled
Height: 25.3 cm
Ref.: Kolba, p. 109, Illustration 44

**69. Pendant**
Inv No.: Pig.Jank.225
Around 1530, Transylvania, perhaps Kolozsvár
Gold, coloured enamel, with almandine and opal
Height: 11.5 cm
Ref.: Kolba, p. 104, Illustration 22

**70. Patrona Hungariae pendant**
Inv. No.: Orn.Jank.127
Gold, colour enamel, with pearl and rubin
Height: 10.6 cm
Ref.: Kolba, p. 104, Illustration 21

**71. The Pálffy Beaker**
Inv No.: 1940.19
1598, Prague, royal workshop
Gold, champlevé and translucent enamel, cast details
Height: 42.8 cm
Ref.: F. Vattai, E.: "Pálffy Miklós győzelmi serlege" (Miklós Pálffy's Triumphal Cup). *Művészet*, 1966. pp. 4–6

**72. Cloak**
Inv. No.: 69.80.C
Turn of the 15th and 16th century, Istambul, imperial workshop
Leather, made up of several panels, the edge and the bottom corners of the two panels on the sides, which are folded back to their full width, are trimmed with leather appliqué
Length: front: 115 cm, back: 125 cm
Ref.: Fehér, pp. 11–13, 29, Plates III–VI, Illustrations 2–10

**73. Writing set**
Inv. No.: 32/1926
Second half of the 17th century, Turkish
Silver
With the certifying imprint of Sultan Mehmed IV and hallmark of Mehmed, goldsmith
Length: 30.5 cm
Ref.: Fehér, p. 23, 35, Illustrations 63–65

**74. Tent**
Inv. No.: 54/1927
Before 1683, Turkish
Canvas, crimson on the outside; twelve posts on the top and on the sides,

colour appliqué between the posts
Length: cc. 600 cm, width: cc. 400 cm
Place of origin: Vienna; captured in the siege of 1683
Ref.: Fehér, pp. 6–10, 29, Plates I–II, Illustration 1

**75a) Canopied bed**
Inv. No.: 6/1947
Pine wood panels in oakwood frame, with walnut and maplewood decoration
Length: 192 cm, height: 195 cm, width: 129 cm
Ref.: Kovalovszki, p. 22, 3, Illustrations 72–73

**75b) Bedspread**
Inv. No.: 121/1932
Second quarter of the 17th century
Silk feather shag embroidered with gold and silver thread
Size: 182 x 200 cm
Ref.: Ember, 1981. pp. 95–96, Illustration 119

**76. Tile stove**
Inv. No.: 65/1927
Last third of the 17th century
Clay, fired, decorated with plastic white tin-glaze leaf and flower ornaments against cobalt-blue background
Tile: length: 36 cm, width: 28 cm; stove: height: 280 cm, width: 144 cm
Place of origin: Liptónádasd, Baán Mansion
Ref.: Divald, K.: *A magyar iparművészet története* (The History of the Applied Arts in Hungary). p. 157, Plate VIII; Voit, P.–Holl, I.: *Old Hungarian Stove Tiles.* Budapest, 1963. pp. 56–57, Plate 42

**77. The Brózer Chalice**
Inv. No.: 1926.90 1640, Kolozsvár, István Brózer (active: 1633–1660)
Gold, enamelled, embossed, engraved, cast parts
Height: 26 cm, diameter at the base: 11 cm
Ref.: H. Kolba, J.: "A Brózer-kehely" (The Brózer Chalice). *Műtör.* 26/1977. pp. 225–240; *MNM*, 1977. pp. 174–175

**78. Queen of Sheba's cup**
Inv. No: 61.2114.C
End of the 17th century, Sebestyén Hann (1644–1713)
Silver, gilt, engraved, embossed, coral, with a few turquoise and pearl ornaments
Height: 25.2 cm
Ref.: Mihalik, S.: "Der Goldschmied S. Hann." *Acta HistArt* 16/1970 pp. 151–200

**79. Goblet**
Inv. No.: 53.46
End of the 17th century, Transylvania
Silver, gilt, painted, (Transylvanian) enamelled ornaments
Height: 26 cm
Ref.: Mihalik, S.: *Emailkunst im alten Ungarn.* Budapest, 1961. Item No. 37; *MNM*, 1977. pp. 170–171

**80. Tankard**
Inv. No.: 1939/27
Around 1700, Transylvania
Rock-crystal, cut, in gilded silver and Transylvanian enamelled setting
Height: 23 cm, diameter at the base: 12.6 cm
Ref.: H. Kolba, J.–Németh, A.: *Ötvösművek. A Magyar Nemzeti Múzeum Kincsei* (Goldsmiths' Art. Treasures of the Hungarian National Museum). Budapest, 1973. p. 19, No. 36; Radvánszky, B.: *Magyar családélet és háztartás a XVI. és XVII. században* (Family Life and Households in the 16th and 17th Centuries in Hungary). 3 vols. Budapest, 1986. vol. I, p. 351, No. 220; *MNM*, 1977. pp. 176–177

## Modern Age Department

**81. Throne carpet**
Inv. No.: 1960.190
Around 1470, Florence
Brocaded in gold, woven of yellow and green silk, uncut loops of gold thread, outlined in green velvet
Length: 252 cm, width: 162 cm
Ref.: Fraknói, V.: "Erdődi Bakócz Tamás műtárgyai" (The Collection of Tamás Erdődi Bakócz). *AÉ* 7/1887. pp. 404–417; Radisics, J.: "Mátyás király trónkárpitja" (King Matthias Corvinus's Throne Carpet). *Magyar Iparművészet* 14/1911. pp. 354–357; Ember, 1980; *MNM*, 1977. pp. 182–183

**82. Ornamental sword of King Wladislas II**
Inv. No.: 55.3235
1509, Italian, Domenico de Sutrio
Silver, enamel, wrought, embossed
Length: 112,4 cm, length of handguard: 43 cm
Ref.: Kalmár, J.: "Dobzse László pápai díszkardja" (Ornamental Papal Sword of László Dobzse). In: *Gerevich Emlékkönyv.* Budapest, 1942. pp. 87–108; Modern, H.: "Geweichte Schwerter und Hüte in den Kunsthist. Samml. des Allerhöchsten Kaiserhauses." In: *Jahrbuch* 22/1901. pp. 136–167; *MNM*, 1977. pp. 218–219

**83. Chasuble**
Inv. No.: 1908.70
Second half of the 15th century, Hungarian
Velvet, crimson, gold filet lace against blue base, embroidered in golden thread, tapestry woven in coloured silk
Back: length: 104 cm, width: 76 cm
Ref.: Báránné Oberschall, M.: *Magyarországi miseruhák* (Hungarian Chasubles). Budapest, 1937; Ember, 1980; *MNM*, 1977. pp. 184–185

**84. Ferdinand of Tyrol's sabre**
Inv. No.: 55.3236
1514, Hungarian
Silver, gilt, engraved, embossed
Length: 107 cm, width of blade: 4 cm
Ref.: *A bécsi gyűjteményekből*, p. 51, Item No. 97; *Arms and Armour*, pp. 57–58, Plate VIII

**85. Suit of armour of King Louis II of Hungary**
Inv. No.: 55.3269
Early 15th century, Nuremberg
Iron, silver-plated, wrought, embossed
Height: 157 cm
Ref.: Kalmár, J.: *Régi magyar fegyverek* (Old Hungarian Arms and Armour). Budapest, 1971. pp. 294–295; Thomas, B.: "Der Knabenharnisch Jörg Seusenhofers für Sigmund II. von Polen." In: *Zeitschrift des Deutschen Vereins für Kunstwissenschaft.* Berlin, 1939. pp. 221–234; *MNM*, 1977. pp. 220–221

**86. Lady's gown and chemise**
Inv. No.: 1928.36, 1928.38 1522
Gown: green silk damask, golden yellow lampas; chemise: white linen, Hungarian point with silk thread
Girth: 56 cm, length: 142 cm
Ref.: F. Dózsa, K.: "Mária királyné esküvői öltözéke az újabb kutatások tükrében" (New Research on the Wedding Attire of Mary, Queen of Hungary). *FH* 13/1987. pp. 7–31; Höllrigl, J.: "A történelmi ruhák a Magyar Nemzeti Múzeumban" (Historical Garments in the Hungarian National Museum). *M.Műv.* 1929. pp. 205–216; *MNM*, 1977. pp. 186–187

**87. Folding sundial**
Inv. No.: 1974.183 1588, Nuremberg, Master I.H.
Ivory, engraved inscriptions in red and black
Length: 10.4 cm, height: 1.2 cm, width: 7.2 cm

**88. Suspended watch**
Inv. No.: Jank.80
Around 1600, Transylvania?
Copper, gilt, repoussé
Length: 9 cm, height: 3.8 cm, width: 6.3 cm
Ref.: *Az időmérés története* p. 8; *MNM*, 1977. pp. 262–263

**89. Pillow-case**
Inv. No.: 1955.456
Middle of the 17th century, Transylvania
White linen-cambric, Hungarian point worked in coloured silk and silver thread
Length: 84 cm, width: 75 cm
Ref.: Ember, 1980; Ember, 1981

**90. Trousseau locker with the figures of the bride and the bridegroom**
Inv. No.: B.1983.11
Middle of the 17th century, Hungarian
Painting and gilt on pinewood
Height: 57 cm, width: 115.5 cm, depth: 55.5 cm

**91. Ornate spoon**
Inv. No.: O.II.74.26 1685
Gold with engraved-base enamel
Length: 16 cm, diameter of the dip: 4.2 x 5.5 cm, weight: 66 g

**92. Backgammon board**
Inv. No.: 1972.114
17th century
Wood, silver-plated both outside and inside, filigree with enamel and precious stones
Length: 39.5 cm, height: 13.5 cm, width: 31.5 cm
Ref.: *MNM*, 1977. pp. 208–209

**93. Chest of a guild**
Inv. No.: 1981.23 1654
Pine, bass-wood
Length: 57.5 cm, height: 34.5 cm, width: 40 cm
Ref.: Szádeczky, L.: *Iparfejlődés és a céhek története Magyarországon* (Industrial Development and the History of Guilds in Hungary). 2 vols. Budapest, 1913

**94. Lady's dress**
Inv. No.: 1954.664.1–2 1624–1629, Transylvania, from Italian material
Velvet, enchased, crimson blue, worked in Hungarian point and satin-stich with gold and silver thread
Girth: 43 cm, length: 140 cm
Ref.: Ember, 1980; Höllrigl, J.: *Régi magyar ruhák* (Old Hungarian Costumes). Budapest, 1938; Varjú–Ember, M.: *Die ungarische Galakleidung im XVI. und XVII. Jahrhundert.* Munich, 1966.; *Waffen- und Kostümkunde*, pp. 23–34; *MNM*, 1977. 194–195

**95. Gentleman's *mente* (short coat)**
Inv. No.: 1950.177 1610–1629, Transylvania
Velvet, enchased, light red, with silver and golden cord appliqué, embroidered in Hungarian point
Width of back: 47 cm, length of front: 70 cm

**96. Virginal**
Inv. No.: App.Jank.243
Ebony with silver and enamel plaques
Length: 43 cm, height: 25 cm, width: 23.5 cm
Ref.: Gábry, Gy.: "Brandenburgi Katalin virginálja" (Catherine of Brandenburg's Virginal). *FA* 11/1959. pp. 179–186; Gábry, pp. 9–10, 33, Illustrations 1–2; *MNM*, 1977. pp. 252–253

**97. Two-door cupboard**
Inv. No.: 1954.472
Around 1700, Hungarian
Walnut wood with walnut root marquetry
Height: 263 cm, width: 205 cm, depth: 80 cm
Ref.: Oberschall, p. 17, Illustration 23; Szabolcsi, H.: *Régi magyar bútorok* (Old Hungarian Furniture). Budapest, 1954. p. 32, Illustration 34; Dévényi, J.: *A Történeti Múzeum XVIII. századi bútorai* (Eighteenth-century Furniture in the Historical Museum). Budapest, 1960. p. 9. Illustration 2; *MNM*, 1977. pp. 230–231

**98. Theorbo lute**
Inv. No.: 1951.44 1707?, Hamburg, Joachim Tielke (1641–1719)
Brasilian rosewood, with mother-of-pearl and tortoise-shell inlays
Length: 104 cm, height: 16 cm, width: 31 cm
Ref.: Gábry, p. 19, 36, Illustrations 19.a and c; Hellwig, G.: *Joachim Tielke.* Frankfurt/Main, 1980. p. 315

**99. Lady's dress**
Inv. No.:1935.110 1768?,
Material French, probably
Hungarian
Green silk, broached, with
coloured patterns
Girth: 62 cm, length of the
back: 163 cm

**100. Rococo bookshelf**
Inv. No.: 1954.473
Middle of the 18th century
Walnut wood with walnut
root marquetry
Height: 265 cm, width:
130 cm, depth: 65 cm
Ref.: Oberschall, p. 17,
Illustration 22; Dévényi J.:
*A Történeti Múzeum
XVIII. századi bútorai*
(Eighteenth-century
Furniture in the Historical
Museum). Budapest, 1960.
p. 12

**101. Baritone**
Inv. No.: 1949.360
1750, Vienna, Johann
Joseph Stadlmann
Pine and maple wood,
lacquered in pale yellow,
marquetry
Length: 130 cm, height:
12.5 cm, width: 36.7 cm
Ref.: Gábry, p. 23, 38,
Illustration 31; *MNM*,
1977. pp. 256–257

**102. Chalice**
Inv. No.: 1961.1159
1763, János Szilassy
(active: 1729–1782)
Silver, gilt, chased, cast,
colour painted enamel
Height: 26 cm, diameter at
the rim: 9.5 cm, diameter
at the bottom: 15.5 cm
Ref.: H. Kolba, J.–
Németh, A.: *Ötvösművek*
(Goldsmiths' Work). p. 27

**103. Chastiser**
Inv. No.: 1961.1296
Hardwood
Length: 62.6 cm,
diameter: 13 cm
Ref.: Nagybákay, P.:
*Magyarországi
céhbehívótáblák*
(Trade-signs in Hungary).
Budapest, 1981. pp. 40–41

**104. The trade certificate of
the Harnessmakers' Guild
at Sárospatak**
Inv. No.: L. 1968.2
1776, Sárospatak
Paper, painted decoration
Size: 34 x 42.5 cm

**105. Bowl**
Inv. No.: 1961.2186
1760s, Holics
Height: 71 cm,
width: 86 cm
Ref.: Kiss, A.: *Barokk
fajanszművészet
Magyarországon* (Baroque
Faience Art in Hungary).
Budapest, 1966. p. 19,
Plate III

**106. The letters patent of
the Count Andrássy de
Csíkszentkirály et
Krasznahorka family**
Inv. No.: Udgy. 1974.14
December 17, 1779, Vienna
Book-format in leather
binding, on parchment
paper, reinforced by
a royal seal secured in
a brass case
Size: 28.2 x 35.2 cm;
diameter of the bull: 15 cm
Ref.: *Magyarország
címeres könyve. Liber
Armorum Hungariae.*
Introduction: Gyula
Andrássy. Budapest, 1913.
p. 13; Nagy, I.:
*Magyarország családai
czímerekkel és leszármazási
táblákkal* (The Families of
Hungary with
Coats-of-arms and
Genealogical Tables). vol. I.
Pest, 1857. pp. 34–40;
*Siebmachers grosses und
allgemeines Wappenbuch.
Der ungarische Adel von
Géza v. Csergheő, Iván v.
Nagy.* Nuremberg, 1893.
p. 12

**107. Empire drawing-room
suite**
Inv. No.: 1963.135.1–15
Pine, larch, and
beechwood, covered with
walnut and basswood
polished to black
Couch: height: 102.5 cm,
width: 183 cm,
depth: 84 cm
Armchair: height: 50 cm,
width: 58.5 cm,
depth: 52 cm
Chair: height: 92.5 cm,
width: 49 cm,
depth: 52 cm
Table: height: 94 cm,
width: 47 cm,
depth: 78.5 cm
Ref.: *Magyaro. tört.* p. 81;
*Három nemzedék,* p. 122

**108. Set of jewelry, pendant
and pair of earrings**
Inv. No.: O.II.85.20.1–3
1809–1819
Gold and citrine, cast,
beaten, enchased
Pendant: length: 7.8 cm,
width: 5.8 cm;
earrings: length: 4.2 cm

**109. Writing desk with
clock**
Inv. No.: 1954.483
1810
Walnut, mahogany and
maplewood marquetry
Height: 160 cm,
width: 80 cm, depth: 37 cm
Ref.: *Három nemzedék,*
p. 126

**110. Ferenc Haller's sabre**
Inv. No.: 56.4293
1840, Vienna,
I.H. Haussmann
Silver, engraved, embossed
Length: 102.2 cm, width of
blade: 2.7–3 cm

Ref.: Temesváry, F.:
"Haller Ferenc
testőrkapitány
ezüstszablyája" (The Silver
Sabre of Ferenc Haller,
Captain in the Hungarian
Life Guard). *FA* 20/1969.
pp. 187–204

**111. The sabre of György
Rákóczi II and József Bem**
Inv. No.: 55.3601
1643, Transylvania
Silver, gilt, engraved, stone
setting technique
Length: 979 cm, width of
blade: 31 cm
Ref.: Szendrei, J.: *Magyar
hadtörténelmi emlékek az
ezredéves országos
kiállításon* (Objects from
the History of Hungarian
Warfare at the National
Exhibition of the
Millenium Celebrations).
Budapest, 1896. pp.
759–762; idem: *Ungarische
Kriegsgeschichliche
Denkmäler.* Budapest,
1896. pp 807–810

**112. The Master Book of
the Chimneysweeps' Guild
of Pest-Buda**
Inv. No.:
Udgy.1972.53.1–3
1828–1850s, Pest
Leather binding, with
a painted tin case with
leather covering made
in 1835
Box: length: 46 cm, height:
8.5 cm, width: 33 cm
Book: 42.5 x 29 c
Ref.: Eri, I.–Nagy,
L.–Nagybákay, P. (eds.):
*A magyarországi céhes
kézművesipar
forrásanyagának katasztere*
(Survey of the Source
Material Concerning the
Hungarian Guilds in the
Handicrafts Industry).
2 vols. Budapest, 1975
Vol. 2, p. 359

**113. Freemason's
master cloth**
Inv. No.: 1981.131.651
Second half of the 18th
century
Goat-skin, with coloured
copper plate etching
Height: 28 cm,
width: 32 cm
Ref.: *Zirkel und
Winkelmass. Katalog zur
Sonderausstellung des
Historischen Museums der
Stadt Wien.* Vienna, 1984.
pp. 62–63; Nagy, Zs.:
*Szabadkőművesek*
(Freemasons). Budapest,
1988. p. 21

**114. Statue of a Freemason**
Inv. No.: 1981.131.26
19–20th century, Meissen
Porcelain
Height: 24 cm,
width: 10.5 cm
Ref.: *Österreichische
Freimaurerlogen Humanität*

*und Toleranz im 18.
Jahrhundert. Katalog
Schlossmuseum Rosenau bei
Zwettl.* Löcker Verlag.
Vienna, 1981

**115. Doll's house**
Inv. No.: 1961.44–58,
1961.1570, 1961.1659,
1961.1748–1756
1850s–1860s, Hungarian ?
Wood, paper, metal,
porcelain, textile
Height: 63 cm, width:
31 cm, depth: 27 cm

**116. Portrait of Baron
Gábor Kemény**
by Ferenc Veress
(1832–1916)
Inv. No.: 1961.1806
1870s, Kolozsvár
Diameter: 22 cm

**117. Vase**
Inv. No.: 1905.44
1872, Sevres
Porcelain, gilded,
gilded brass
Height: 68 cm
Ref.: Vámbéry, G.: "A
Magyar Nemzeti Múzeum
súlyai" (Weights in the
Hungarian National
Museum) Part I. *FM*,
10/1982. p. 120

**118. Pipe**
Inv. No.: D.1974..221
1870s, Hungarian ?
Meerschaum, silver
Length: 14 cm,
height: 19 cm

**119. Jewelry to be worn
with Hungarian dress**
Inv. No.: 1971.291–6 Belt:
7th century, the other
pieces: 19th century
Assembled around 1867
Gold, citrine, gilded silver,
pearl
Belt: length: 83 cm,
width: 5.5 cm
Chain for fastening the
*mente*: length: 65 cm,
width: 5 cm
Plumes of aigrette: length:
15 cm, width: 7.5 cm
Buttons: diameter:
1.5–2 cm
Ref.: about the clasp
dating from the age of the
Hungarian Conquest:
Garam, É.: "VII. századi
ékszerek a Magyar
Nemzeti Múzeumban"
(Seventh-century Jewelry in
the Hungarian National
Museum). *FA*, 31/1980.
pp. 157–174; *MNM*, 1977.
pp. 214–215

**120. Ornate attire to be
worn during the Coronation
ceremony**
Inv. No.: 196.543.1–5
1867–1916, Göttmann and
Mérő; Monaszterly and
Descendants of Kuzmik
White silk and crimson
velvet, white tulle, with
golden strands and laces,

embroidery in gold
Girth: 76 cm, length of
back: 336 cm, length of
skirt: 320 cm (at the back),
length of apron: 106 cm,
length of veil: 304 cm,
length of *mente*: 90 cm
Ref.: *Hungarian Costume;
The Imperial Style*

**121a) Hungarian-style
lady's dress**
Inv. No.: 1953.653.1–2
Around 1938, Budapest,
Salon Pántlika
Royal blue silk-satin, pink
broadcloth, gold
passemente, white and blue
silk embroidery
Length of dress: 149 cm,
length of cloak: 51 cm

**b) Hungarian-style
gentleman's suit**
Inv. No.: T.1973.175.1–2
1933, Budapest,
Pál Mohácsy
Length of back: 77 cm,
length of trousers: 112 cm
Ref.: *Hungarian Costume*

**c) Gentleman's belt**
Inv. No.: T.1973.177
Black silk cord
Width: 3 cm

**d) Neck-tie**
Inv. No.: T.1973.178
1933, Budapest
Black silk, gold tassel
Length: 93 cm

## Department of Coins and Medals

**122. Tetradrachma.
Imitation of the Philippos II
Tetradrachma.
Mászlony-puszta type**
(Tolna county)
Inv. No.: 82/1899
2nd century, B.C., Celtic
Silver
12.17 grams
Ref.: Gohl, O.: "A
szalacskai kelta pénzverő
és bronzöntő műhely" (The
Minting and Bronze
Casting Workshop at
Szalacska). *NK*, 6/1907.60

**123. Late third-century
engraving die of the reverse
of an Antoninianus**
Inv. No.: 3A/1973
284–294, Antioch
Bronze
83.07 grams
Ref.: Alföldi, M.: "Római
verőtő a Magyar Történeti
Múzeum új szerzeményei
között" (An Engraving Die
Among the New
Acquisitions of the
Hungarian Historical
Museum). *AÉ*, 76/1949.
pp. 37–38

**124. Maximianus Herculius. Medallion**
Inv. No.: 67A/1905
286–305 Gold
21.55 grams
Site: Szár, Fejér county
Ref.: Gohl, O.:
"Maximianus Herculius arany medaillonja" (Gold Medallion of Maximianus Herculius). *NK*, 4/1905. p. 85; *RIC*, 1

**125. Half Aureus of Maximianus Herculius. Subaeratus imitation**
Inv. No.: 16A/1986
286–305
Bronze, gilt, moulded
Ref.: *RIC*, 30; Alföldi, A.: "Anyaggyűjtés a római pénzek Magyarországon készült egykorú utánzatainak osztályozásához" (Collection of Data to Be Used in the Classification of the Contemporary Imitations of Roman Coins in Hungary). *NK*, 26–27/1927–28. p. 59

**126. Anastasius I. Medallion**
Inv. No.: 146/1972
491–518
Silver
13.04 grams
Ref.: Bíró Sey, K.: "Silver Medal of Anastasius I in the Numismatic Collection of the Hungarian National Museum." *FA*, 27/1976. pp. 121–127

**127. Die of Solomon's denarius number CNH.I.19**
Inv. No.: 16-B/1981–1
1063–1074
Iron
Length: 3.5 cm, diameter: 2.2 cm
Ref.: Gedai, I.: "A Magyar Nemzeti Múzeum verőszerszám-gyűjteménye" (The Collection of Dies and Minting Tools in the Hungarian National Museum). *NK*, 84–85/1985–86. p. 48

**128. Wladislas II, king of Hungary and Bohemia. Gold coin**
Inv. No.: N.II.1840
1499
Gold
14.14 grams
Ref.: CNH II, p. 266

**129. Fifty-ducat piece of Mihály Apafi, prince of Transylvania**
Inv. No.: 75/1977
1677
Gold
172.67 grams
Ref.: Gedai, I.: "Apafi Mihály 50 dukátos verete" (A Fifty-ducat Coin of Mihály Apafi). *FA*, 30/1979. pp. 257–261

**130. Lajos Kossuth credit note issued during his emigration in London**
Inv. No.: 41/1933
1860–1861
Paper
12 x 9.8 cm
Ref.: Halász, G.: "A magyar papírpénzekről" (On Hungarian Notes). *NK*, 4/1905 p.66

**131. Medallion with the portraits of Louis II and Queen Mary**
Inv. No.: N.III.1743
Around 1526–1532, Körmöcbánya, Christoph Fuessl (active: 1546–1561)
Gold, beaten
Diameter: 43.5 cm, weight: 50.95 grams
Ref.: Weszerle, B. XVI. Plate 2.; Huszár-Procopius, p. 15

**132. Holy Trinity medal**
Inv. No.: Ebenhöch 3909
1544, Hans Reinhart (active: 1535–1568)
Silver, cast
Diameter: 10.3 cm
Ref.: Habich, II. 1. 1962; Domanig, 758; *MNM*, 1977. pp. 284–285

**133. Biblical medal**
Inv. No.: N.III.371
1537, Joachimstal, Hieronimus Magdeburger (active: 1530–1548)
Silver, gilt, beaten
Diameter: 4.6 cm
Ref.: Katz, p. 106

**134. Chain and emblem of the English Order of the Bath**
Inv. No.: 15.C./986–4-5
1835
Gold, jewel, enamel
Ref.: Gritzner, pp. 95–96, Figures 128–129

**135. Cross of the Russian Order of St. Anne, Third Class**
Inv. No.: 15.C./983–3
1856
Gold, diamond, enamel
Ref.: Gritzner, p. 429, Figure 486

## Historical Gallery

**136. Portrait of the Lord Chief Justice, Count Ferenc Nádasdy**
by Benjamin Block (1631–1690)
1656
Inv. No.: 2321
Oil on canvas
182 × 120 cm
Ref.: Rózsa, 1977. No. 5; *MNM*, 1977. pp. 298–299; Cennerné Wilhelmb, Gizella: *Stilprobleme der ungarischen provinziellen Porträt-Mahler im 17. Jahrhundert.* vol 2. Krakow, 1985. pp. 106–107

**137. Kuruc–Labanc Battle Scene**
Painter unknown (early 18th century)
Around 1700
Inv. No.: T.6920
Gouache on paper
15.9 x 21.5 cm
Ref.: Cennerné, pp. 192–193; *MNM*, 1977. pp. 302–303

**138. Portrait of Count Dénes Bánffy**
by Martin van Meytens (1695–1770)
c. 1760
Inv. No.: 54.13
Oil on canvas
207 x 116 cm
Ref.: Rózsa, 1977. No. 19; *Főúri ősgalériák, családi arcképek a Magyar Történelmi Képcsarnokból* (Ancestral Galleries of the Aristocracy and Family Portraits in the Historical Gallery). Budapest, 1988. c. No. 2

**139. Dwellings in the Tihany Caves**
by Joseph Fischer (1769–1822)
Around 1800
Inv. No.: 36/1952.R
Water-colour on paper
27,6 x 40 cm
Ref.: Rózsa, Gy.: "Die ungarische Landschaft im Werk Josef Fischers." *Mitteilungen der Österreichischen Galerie* 26–27/1982–83. pp. 166–168

**140. Portrait of Gustav Hadik as a Child**
by Vinzenz Georg Kininger (1767–1851)
1806
Inv. No.: 53.41
Tempera on paper
43.2 x 32.3 cm
Ref.: *Művészet, 1780–1830.* No. 103

**141. Portrait of János Batsányi**
by Friedrich Heinrich Füger (1751–1818)
1808
Inv. No.: 95
Oil on canvas
68 x 51 cm
Ref.: Rózsa, 1977. No. 31

**142. View of Buda and Pest from the Gellért Hill**
by Antal Fülöp Richter (active between 1804–1829) after a drawing by András Petrich (1768–1842)
1819
Inv. No.: T.1169
Coloured etching on paper
40.5 x 57.4 cm
Ref.: *Művészet, 1780–1830.* No. 23

**143. Peasant Women from Veszprém County**
by Franz Jaschke
(1775–1842)
1821
Inv. No.: T.5028
Coloured aquatint on paper
39.7 x 32.5 cm
Ref.: Kresz, M.: *Magyar parasztviselet* (Hungarian Peasants' Costume). Budapest, 1956. pp. 40, 109, Plate 25

**144. Portrait of Ferenc Bene**
by Vilmos Egger (1792–1830)
1825
Inv. No.: 128
Oil on canvas
74 × 59.5
Ref.: *Művészet, 1780–1830.* No. 117

**145. Portrait of Kázmér Batthyány**
by Miklós Barabás (1810–1898)
1847
Inv. No.: 21/1951.R
Water-colour on ivory plate
17 x 12.8 cm
Ref.: *Barabás Miklós önéletrajza* (The Autobiography of Miklós Barabás). Budapest, 1944. p. 260, No. 1190; Szvoboda, G.: *Barabás Miklós.* Budapest, 1983. pp. 58, 91, Illustration 32

**146. Portrait of Ferenc Pulszky**
by Wolfgang Böhm (middle of the 19th century)
1849
Inv. No.: 1552
Oil on canvas
91,5 x 72,5 cm
Ref.: Rózsa, 1977. No. 43

**147. Electioneering in front of the National Museum**
by Ferenc Weiss (middle of the 19th century)
1847
Inv. No.: 71.69
Colour lithograph on paper
32,2 x 44.3 cm
Ref.: Fejős, I.: "A Nemzeti Múzeum ábrázolásai" (Portraits and Representations in the National Museum). *FA,* 7/1955. p. 215, 219, No. 18; Cennerné, p. 294

**148. View of Visegrád**
by Károly Klette (1793–1874)
Middle of the 19th century
Inv. No.: T.6978
Water-colour on paper
28.3 x 40.3
Ref.: *Pest megye műemlékei* (Monuments of Pest County). vol 2. Budapest, 1958. p. 410, No. 42

**149. Battle of Nagysalló, 1849**
by Mór Than (1828–1899)
Early 1850s
Inv. No.: T.6690
Water-colour on paper
37 x 51.6 cm
Ref.: *A szabadságharc kilenc nagy csatája* (Nine Great Battles of the War of Liberation in 1848–1849). Budapest, 1978. pp. 52–53 (Bárcy, Z.), pp. 110–111

**150. Portrait of Ágoston Kubinyi**
by Frigyes Lieder (1780–1859)
1852
Inv. No.: 149
Oil on canvas
114 x 89.5 cm
Ref.: Rózsa, 1977. No. 41

**151. Portrait of Bertalan Szemere**
by Sándor Kozina (1808–1873)
1851
Inv. No.: 1554
Oil on canvas
96 x 70.5 cm
Ref.: *Művészet, 1830–1870.* No. 343

**152. Pécs Cathedral**
by Ludwig Rohbock (middle of the 19th century)
1850s
Inv. No.: T.691
Water-colour on paper
19.5 x 26.5 cm Ref.: Rózsa, 1986

**153. Royal Hunt**
by Wilhelm Richter (1824–1892)
1872
Inv. No.: 1897
Oil on canvas
141.5 x 254 cm
Ref.: *Das Zeitalter Kaiser Franz Josephs.* Vienna, 1984. No. 18.1

**154. Portrait of Pál Rosty**
by Bertalan Székely (1835–1910)
Around 1874
Ref. No.: 68.17
Oil on canvas
132 x 106 cm
Ref.: *Művészet, 1830–1870.* No. 363

**155. Self-portrait**
by István Réti (1872–1945)
1898
Inv. No.: 1433
Oil on canvas
76,5 x 52 cm
Ref.: Aradi, N.: *Réti István.* Budapest, 1960. p. 80, No. 27

# Catalogue. Black-and-white Illustrations

## Department of Archaeology

**1. Spearhead**
Inv. No.: Pb.82
Palaeolithic Age, 30th millennium B.C.
Quartz porphyry, knapped
Length: 10.8 cm
Site: Miskolc-Szeleta Cave, Borsod-Abaúj-Zemplén county
Ref.: Vértes, L.: "Paläolithikum (Altsteinzeit)" In: Thoman, E. (ed.): *Archäologische Funde in Ungarn.* Budapest, 1956. p. 31; *Az őskor és átmeneti kőkor emlékei Magyarországon* (Archaeological Finds in Hungary from the Palaeolithic and Mesolithic Ages). Budapest, 1965. Plate 21

**2. Spearhead**
Inv. No.: Pb.916.6
Palaeolithic Age, 30th millennium B.C.
Black flint, knapped
Length: 23.8 cm
Site: Miskolc-Bársony House, Borsod-Abaúj-Zemplén county
Ref.: Vértes, L.: "Paläolithikum (Altsteinzeit)" In: Thoman, E. (ed.): *Archäologische Funde in Ungarn.* Budapest, 1956. p. 21; *Az őskor és átmeneti kőkor emlékei Magyarországon* (Archaeological Finds in Hungary from the Palaeolithic and Mesolithic Ages). Budapest, 1965. Plate 8

**3. Bomb-shaped bowl**
Inv. No.: 8/1924.117
Second half of 5th millennium B.C.
Clay
Height: 18.5 cm
Site: Bodrogkeresztúr, Borsod-Abaúj-Zemplén county
Ref.: Tompa, F.: *A szalagdíszes agyagművesség kultúrája Magyarországon–Die Bandkeramik in Ungarn.* Budapest, 1929. Plate 14, p. 4

**4. Sacrificial vessel with human figure**
Inv. No.: 26/1950.8
Second half of 2nd millenium B.C.
Clay, shaped by hand
Height: 10 cm
Site: Szelevény-Vadas, Szolnok county
Ref.: Kalicz, Illustrations 28 and 29

**5. Painted bowl**
Inv. No.: 55.32.256
First half of 4th millennium B.C.
Clay, shaped by hand
Height: 18 cm
Site: Berettyóújfalu, Hajdú-Bihar county

**6. Libation table**
Inv. No.: 41/1935.1
First half of 4th millennium B.C.
Clay, shaped by hand
Height: 11 cm
Site: Szeged area, Csongrád county
Ref.: Kalicz, Illustration 41

**7. Bowl with hollow pedestral**
Inv. No.: 74.29.57
Clay, shaped by hand
Height: 43.2 cm
Site: Tiszavalk-Tetes, Borsod-Abaúj-Zemplén county
Ref.: Patay, P.: "A Tiszavalk-tetesi temető és telep–Kupferzeitliches Gräberfeld und Siedlung von Tiszavalk-Tetes". *FA/29/1978.* p. 35, Illustration 16, 6

**8. Lid with zoomorphic handle**
Inv. No.: 53.1.601
First half of 3rd millennium B.C.
Clay
Height: 12.9 cm
Site: Polgár, Hajdú-Bihar county
Ref.: Bognár-Kutzián, I.: *The Copper Age Cemetery of Tiszapolgár-Basatanya.* Budapest, 1963. Plate 84, 1

**9. Statue of a goddess**
Inv. No.: 70.31.82
Clay
Height: 9.6 cm
Site: Tiszafüred, Szolnok county
Ref.: Kalicz, N.: "Újabb adatok a rézkori hunyadi-halmi csoport időrendjéhez–Neue Beiträge zur Chronologie der Kupferzeitlichen Hunyadihalom-Gruppe". *Szolnok Megyei Múzeumok Évkönyve 1979–1980.* pp. 54–54, Illustrations 6–7

**10. Libation vessel**
Inv. No.: 80.11.100
Middle of the 3rd millennium B.C.
Clay, shaped by hand
Height: 10.9 cm
Site: Tiszalúc-Sarkad, Borsod-Abaúj-Zemplén county
Ref.: Patay, P.: "A Tiszalúc-sarkadi rézkori telep ásatásának eddigi eredményei–Bisherige Ergebnisse der Ausgrabung in der kupferzeitlicher Siedlung von Tiszalúc-Sarkad". *FA 38/1987.* p. 107, Illustration 22

**11. Clay model of a wagon with solid wheels**
Inv. No.: 72.19.1
Second half of 3rd millennium B.C.
Clay, shaped by hand
Height: 8.2 cm
Site: Szigetszentmárton, Pest county
Ref.: Kalicz, N.: "Ein neues kupferzeitliches Wagon-Modell aus der Umgebung von Budapest". *Festschrift R. Pittioni* vol. 1. Wien, 1976. p. 188; *MNM,* 1977. pp. 34–35

**12. Suspension vessel**
Inv. No.: 20/1931.1
18th century B.C.
Clay, shaped by hand
Height: 13.5 cm
Site: Nagyrév, Szolnok county
Ref.: Patay, P.: *Korai bronzkori kultúrák Magyarországon–Früh-bronzezeitliche Kulturen in Ungarn.* Budapest, 1938. Plate 5, 4

**13. Bird-shaped vessel**
Inv. No.: 75/1881.52
17th century B.C.
Clay, shaped by hand
Height: 20.5 cm
Site: Mindszent, Csongrád county
Ref.: Kalicz, N.: *Die Frühbronzezeit in Nordostungarn.* Budapest, 1968. Plate 114, 1

**14. Bowl**
Inv. No.: 5/1949.31
15th century B.C.
Clay, shaped by hand
Site: Megyaszó, Borsod-Abaúj-Zemplén county
Height: 8.5 cm
Ref.: Bóna, I.: *Die mittlere Bronzezeit Ungarns und ihre südöstlichen Beziehungen.* Budapest, 1975. Plate 177, 1

**15. Disk-shaped pectoral**
Inv. No.: 100/1903
16th century B.C.
Gold plate
Diameter: 13.5 cm, weight: 83.31 g
Site: Ottlaka
Ref.: Mozsolics, A.: "Die Goldfunde des Depotfund horizontes von Hajdúsámson". *Bericht der Römisch-Germanischen Komission, Mainz,* 46–47/1965–1966. p. 49, Plate 23, 2

**16. Bracelet ornamented with a bull's head**
Inv. No.: 58/1902 16th century B.C.
Gold, cast
Diameter: 10.8 cm, weight: 611.84 gr
Site: Transylvania
Ref.: Kovács, 1977. Illustrations 32–33

**17. Bird-shaped vessel with human face**
Inv. No.: 72.4.125
14th century B.C.
Clay, shaped by hand
Height: 14 cm
Site: Tiszafüred, Szolnok county
Ref.: Kovács, 1977. Illustrations 45–46

**18. Vessel shaped like a human being with a dagger**
14th century B.C.
Clay, shaped by hand
Height: 64 cm
Site: Mende-Leányvár, Pest county
Ref.: Kovács, T.: "Representations of Weapons on Bronze Age Pottery". *FA 24/1973.* pp. 8–9, Illustrations 1–2

**19. Swords**
Inv. No.: 66/1929.1–2
14th century B.C.
Bronze, cast
Length: 71.9 and 63.6 and 58.2 cm
Site: Zajta, Szabolcs-Szatmár county
Ref.: Mozsolics, A.: *Bronzfunde des Karpatenbeckens.* Budapest, 1967. Plates 64–65

**20. Diadem**
Inv. No.: 164/1872.1
12th century B.C.
Bronze, cast
Diameter: 23.5 cm
Site: Vácszentlászló, Pest county
Ref.: Mozsolics, A.: *Die Bronze- und Goldfunde des Karpatenbeckens.* Budapest 1973, Plate 24, 1

**21. Spiral-shaped armrings**
Inv. No.: 120/1901.57, 59
11th century B.C.
Sheet bronze
Length: 34 and 39 cm
Site: Pécska
Ref.: Kemennli, T.: "Der Bronzefund von Pecice/Péska". *FolArch,* 42, 1991. Plate 1

**22. Bird-shaped vessels**
Inv. No.: 63/1905, 60/1951.16
11th century B.C.
Bronze, cast
Height: 14.5 and 11.4 cm
Site: Csicser and an unknown place in Hungary
Ref.: Kovács, 1977. Illustrations 69–70

**23. Fibula with stylized bird figures**
Inv. No.: 57.77.1
10th century B.C.
Sheet bronze and wire
Length: 39.4 cm
Site: Medvese
Ref.: Kovács, 1977. Illustration 75

**24. Bronze bucket**
Inv. No.: 33/1858.1
9th century B.C.
Sheet bronze
Height: 31.5 cm
Site: Hajdúböszörmény, Hajdú-Bihar county
Ref.: Patay, P.: "Der Bronzefund von Mezőkövesd". *Acta ArchHung,* 21/1969. p. 176, Plate 46, 2

**25. Sceptre with a horse's head**
Inv. No.: 6/1850.1
8th century B.C.
Cast bronze
Length: 12.1 cm
Site: Sárvíz Canal, Fejér county
Ref.: Gallus, S.–Horváth, T.: *A legrégibb lovasnép Magyarországon–Un peuple cavalier préscythique en Hongrie.* Budapest, 1939. Plate 44, 1

**26. Cauldrons and cup**
Inv. No.: 60.1.1–3
8th century B.C.
Sheet gold
Height: 9.1 and 8.5 and 4.7 cm; weight: 247.8 and 243.1 and 193.1 g
Site: Budapest–Angyalföld
Ref.: Tompa, F.: "Az angyalföldi kincslelet"

(Gold Finds in Angyalföld). *AÉ*, 42/1928. p. 54, Plate 1

**27. Urn**
Inv. No.: 72.7.73
7th century B.C.
Clay, shaped by hand
Height: 75 cm
Site: Nagyberki-Szalacska, Somogy county
Ref.: Kemenczei, T.: "Ujabb leletek a Nagyberki-szalacskai halomsírokból–Neue Funde aus den früheisenzeitlichen Hügelgräbern von Nagyberki-Szalacska". *AÉ,* 101/1974. p. 11, Illustration 8

**28. Statue of a deity**
Inv. No.: 55.52.1 6th century B.C.
Cast bronze
Height: 13 cm
Site: Nyergesújfalu, Komárom-Esztergom county Ref.: Szabó, M.: "Rapports entre le Picénum et l'Europe extra-méditerranéenne a l'age du fer". *Savaria*, 16/1982. pp. 230–231, Illustrations 12–16

**29. Hydria from Sparta**
Inv. No.: 60.3.11
First half of 6th century B.C., Scythian Age
Sheet bronze
Height: 43.4 cm
Site: Ártánd, Hajdú-Bihar county
Ref.: Párducz, M.: "Graves from the Scythian Age at Ártánd". *Acta ArchHung*, 17/1965. p. 149, Plates 1–3

**30. Mirror**
Inv. No.: 68.7.1
Second half of 6th century B.C.
Cast bronze
Length: 32.1 cm
Site: Szécsény, Nógrád county
Ref.: Párduc, M.: "Scythian Mirrors in the Carpathian Basin". *Swiatowit*, 23/1960

**31. Quiver mounting**
Inv. No.: 35/1931.1
Second half of 6th century B.C., Scythian Age
Cast bronze
Length: 11.4 cm
Site: Mátraterenye, Nógrád county
Ref.: Kemenczei, T.: "Mitteleisenzeitliche Köcherbeschläge aus dem Alföld". *FA* 37/1986. p. 120, Illustration 3

**32. Stag-shaped shield ornament**
Inv. No.: 97/1923.1
Second half of 6th century, Scythian Age

Sheet
Length: 22.7 cm
Site: Tápiószentmárton, Pest county
Fettich, N.: "A tápiószentmártoni aranyszarvas–Der Goldhirsch von Tápiószentmárton". *AÉ*, 41/1927. p. 138

**33. Vessel with handles ending in the head of a bull or a ram**
Inv. No.: 46/1951.409
3rd century B.C., Celtic Age
Clay, made on a potter's wheel
Height: 18.3 cm
Site: Kósd, Pest county
Ref.: Márton, p. 20, Plate 7

**34. Jar with a handle in the shape of a female figure**
Inv. No.: 46/1951.446
3rd century B.C., Celtic Age
Clay, made on a potter's wheel
Height: 12.5 cm
Site: Kósd, Pest county
Ref.: Márton, p. 20, Plate 2

**35. Jug with a handle surmounted by plastically rendered head**
Inv. No.: 46/1951.740
3rd century B.C., Celtic Age
Clay, made on a potter's wheel
Height: 18.5 cm
Site: Kósd, Pest county
Ref.: Szabó, M.: *A kelták nyomában Magyarországon* (The Celtic Heritage in Hungary). Budapest, 1971. Illustrations 34–35

**36. Torques with rich plastic decoration**
Inv. No.: 98/1902
3rd century B.C., Celtic Age
Sheet gold
Diameter: 32 cm
Site: Hercegmárok
Ref.: Hunyady, p. 91, Plate 26, 2

**37. Anthropomorphic knife-handle**
Inv. No.: 15/1906.1
3rd century B.C., Celtic Age
Cast bronze
Length: 12 cm
Site: Dinnyés, Fejér county
Ref.: Hunyady, Plate 47, 3

**38. Scabbard engraved with dragon figures**
Inv. No.: 46.1951.140
2nd century B.C., Celtic
Iron, wrought
Length: 72 cm
Site: Kósd, Pest county
Ref.: Szabó, M.: *A kelták nyomában Magyarországon* (The Celtic Heritage in

Hungary). Budapest, 1971. Illustration 39

**39. Bracelet**
Inv. No.: 3/1931
2nd century B.C., Celtic Age
Glass
Diameter: 6.8 cm
Site: Érsekújvár
Ref.: Hunyady, Plate 32, 5

**40. Belt chain with zoomorphic clasp**
Inv. No.: 106/1886.6 2nd century B.C., Celtic Age
Bronze and enamel
Length: 104 cm
Site: Tolna county
Ref.: Hunyady, Plate 34, 8

**41. Bronze lamp**
Inv. No.: 78/1913
First decades of the Roman period, Italian workshop
Cast bronze
Site: Mór, Fejér county
Ref.: Supka, G.: "Bericht vom Jahre 1913 über die Erwerbungen des Ungarischen Nationalmuseums (Archäologische Abteilung)".
In: *Miteilungen des Archäologischen Instituts der ungarischen Akademie der Wissenschaften, 1915*. p. 24

**42. Plated ornamental dagger**
Inv. No.: 72.3.1
Second half of 1st century, central army workshop
Iron, plated, enamel inlay
Dagger: length: 32.6 cm, width: 6.1 cm
Sheet: length: 28.4 cm, width: 7.3 cm
Site: Dunaföldvár (from the Danube), Tolna county
Ref.: Thomas, E.B.: *Helme, Schilde, Dolche. Studien über römisch-pannonische Waffenfunde*. Budapest, 1971. p. 47

**43. Military diploma**
Inv No.: 10/1951.45
74 A.D.
Bronze, engraved
Height: 18.6 cm,
Width: 14.6 cm
Site: Sikátor, Veszprém county
Ref.: Mócsy, A.: *Die Bevölkerung von Pannonien bis zu den Markomannenkriegen*. Budapest, 1959. p. 244, 162/1

**44. Statuette of Victory**
Inv. No.: 65.4.1
1st century
Cast bronze, chiselled
Height: 18.6 cm
Site: Akasztó-Döbrögec puszta, Bács-Kiskun county
Ref.: B. Bónis, É.–Soproni,

S.–Tóth, E.: *Római kor. Magyarország népeinek története az őskortól a honfoglalásig* (The Roman Period. A History of the Peoples of Hungary from Ancient Times Until the Conquest). Budapest, 1971. pp. 57–58

**45. Glazed vessel**
Inv. No.: 30/1912
1st century A.D., Pannonia
Clay with green lead glaze
Height: 12.2 cm
Site: Kiskőszeg
Ref.: Paulovics, I.: "Római kori gyűjtemény" (Roman Period Collection). *Magyar Nemzeti Múzeum–Országos Magyar Történeti Múzeum. Vezető a régészeti gyűjteményben.* Budapest, 1938. p. 105

**46. Gravestone of a native**
Inv. No.: 104/1901
End of 1st century–early 2nd century A.D., northeast Pannonia
Limestone
Height: 120 cm, width: 59 cm, depth: 12 cm
Site: Csobánka, Pest county
Ref.: Barkóczi, L.–Soproni, S.: *Die römischen Inschriften Ungarns 3*. Budapest, 1981. pp. 282, 942

**47. Pair of fibulas with openwork decoration**
Inv. No.: 50/1879, 4.1884
First half of 2nd century A.D., southwest Pannonia
Silver, with reticulated decoration, sheet gold with filigree work; inlaid with cornelian
Height: 15.4 cm
Site: Pátka, Fejér county
Ref.: Tóth, E.: *Római gyűrűk és fibulák. Évezredek, évszázadok kincsei 3.* (Roman Rings and Fibulae. Treasures From Down the Ages). Budapest, 1985. p. 54

**48. Waxed tablet**
Inv. No.: R-D.591
March 17, 130 A.D.
Wooden tablet, waxed
Height: 16 cm,
Width: 14.3 cm
Site: Verespatak
Ref.: Pólay, E.: A dáciai viaszostáblák szerződései (Contracts Written on Waxed Tablets in Dacia). Budapest, 1972. p. 277; Russu, I.I.: *Inscriptiile Daciei Romane 1.* (Inscriptions from Roman Dacia 1). Bucuresti, 1975. p. 212, 36

**49. Chariot ornament**
(Dionysos)
Inv. No.: 91/1885.1
Middle of the 2nd century A.D., chariot burial,

probably Balkan
Cast bronze, chiselled
Height: 28.5 cm
Site: Somodor, Komárom-Esztergom county
Ref.: Gaul, K.: "Ókori kocsi helyreállítása a somodori sírlelet alapján" (The Restoration of an Ancient Cart Based on the Finds in the Somodor Graves). *AÉ*, 9/1889. pp. 193–205

**50. Chariot ornament**
(Head of a satyr)
Inv. No.: 78/1888.1
Middle of the 2nd century A.D., chariot burial, probably Balkan
Cast bronze, chiselled
Diameter: 18.6 cm, Height: 11 cm
Cf. No. 49.

**51. Wheel-disk with the head of a swan**
Inv. No.: 78/1888.4
Middle of the 2nd century A.D., chariot burial, probably Balkan
Cast bronze, chiselled
Height: 20 cm
Ref.: Alföldi, A.: "Állatdíszes kerékvető-fejek kelta-római kocsikról" (Wheel-disk Heads with Animal Ornamentation on Celtic-Roman Carts). *AÉ*, 48/1935. pp. 190–213, 263–270

**52. Decorated helmet**
Inv. No.: 2/1942.2
2nd century, central weapon manufacturing workshop of the Danubian provinces
Sheet bronze, chased and engraved
Height: 29 cm
Site: Szőny, Komárom-Esztergom county
Ref.: Barkóczi, L.: Római díszsisak Szőnyből (A Roman Decorated Helmet from Szőny). *FA*, 6/1954. pp. 45–48

**53. Statue of Liber Pater**
Inv. No.: 20/1907.21
2nd century A.D.
Cast bronze, chiselled
Height: 19.5 cm
Site: Tatabánya, Komárom-Esztergom county
Ref.: *Römerzeit. Die Geschichte der Völker Ungarns bis Ende des 9. Jahrhunderts. Führer durch die Ausstellung.* Budapest, 1967. 60

**54. Emblem of a native official**
Inv. No.: 123/1884.26
Second half of 2nd century A.D.
Bronze
Height: 28.8 cm
Site: Sárszentmiklós,

Fejér county
Ref.: Mócsy, A: "Hivatali
elvény a sárszentmiklósi
kocsisírban" (An Official's
Emblem from the Chariot
Grave in Sárszentmiklós).
FA, 14/1962. pp. 35–39

**55. Head of Hygieia**
Inv. No.: 116/1887.2
2nd century A.D., copy of
a Hellenistic original
Marble
Height: 22 cm
Site: Budapest, found in
the Danube near the
Parliament building
Ref.: Hekler, A.:
"Márványfej és
bronzmaszk a Nemzeti
Múzeumban" (The Marble
Head and Bronze Mask in
the Hungarian National
Museum). AÉ, 28/1908. pp.
231–238

**56. Relief of Athene**
Inv. No.: 62.84.1
2nd century A.D.
Limestone, fragment of
a sawn up sarcophagus
Height: 72 cm,
Width: 97 cm, depth: 16 cm;
Site: Pécs–Aranyhegy,
Baranya county
Ref.: Sz. Burger, A.:
"Római szarkofág a pécsi
Aranyhegyről" (A Roman
Sarcophagus from
Pécs's Aranyhegy). AÉ,
100/1973. pp. 42-49

**57. Leda and the Swan**
Inv. No.: 62.85.2
2nd century A.D.
Limestone, fragment of
a sawn up sarcophagus
Height: 72 cm, width: 38
cm, depth: 19 cm;
Site: Pécs-Aranyhegy,
Baranya county
Ref.: Sz. Burger, A.:
"Római szarkofág a pécsi
Aranyhegyről" (A Roman
Sarcophagus from
Pécs's Aranyhegy). AÉ,
100/1973. pp. 42-49

**58. Relief depicting the
myth of Ganymede**
Inv. No.: 62.85.1
2nd century A.D.
Limestone, fragment of
a sawn up sarcophagus
Height: 60 cm, width: 38
cm, depth: 17 cm;
Site: Pécs-Aranyhegy,
Baranya county
Ref.: Sz. Burger, A.:
"Római szarkofág a pécsi
Aranyhegyről" (A Roman
Sarcophagus from
Pécs's Aranyhegy). AÉ,
100/1973. pp. 42-49

**59. Relief of Iphigenia**
Inv. No.: 62.84.2
2nd century A.D.
Limestone, fragment of
a sawn up sarcophagus
Height: 72 cm, width: 99
cm, depth: 15 cm;
Site: Pécs - Aranyhegy,

Baranya county
Ref.: Sz. Burger, A.:
"Római szarkofág a pécsi
Aranyhegyről" (A Roman
Sarcophagus from
Pécs's Aranyhegy). AÉ,
100/1973. pp. 42-49

**60. Heracles and Alcestis**
Inv. No.: 100.1912.128
Second half of the 2nd
century–first third of the
3rd century A.D.,
Pannonia
Limestone, coloured
Height: 120 cm,
Width: 90 cm, depth: 25 cm
Site: Dunapentele
(Intercisa), Fejér county
Ref.: Erdélyi, G.:
"Kőemlékek. Intercisa
(Dunapentele–Sztálinváros)
története a római korban
I." (The History of
Intercisa
[Dunapentele–Sztálinváros]
in the Roman Period. Part
I). ArchHung, 3/1954.
p. 177, 180; Erdélyi,
G.–Fülep, F.: op. cit. 257,
192

**61. Orpheus among animals**
Inv. No.: 22/1905.28
Second half of the 2nd
century–first third of the
3rd century A.D.,
Pannonia
Limestone
Height: 118 cm,
Width: 89 cm, depth: 23 cm
Site: Dunapentele
(Intercisa), Fejér county
Ref.: Erdélyi, G.:
"Kőemlékek. Intercisa /
Dunapentele–Sztálinváros)
története a római korban I.
(The History of Intercisa
[Dunapentele–Sztálinváros]
in the Roman Period. Part
I). ArchHung, 3/1954. p.
178, 182

**62. Baking mould with the
figure of Victory**
Inv. No.: 10.1951.22
2nd–3rd century A.D.
Clay, fired
Diameter: 17.2 cm
Site: Szombathely, Vas
county
Ref.: Alföldi, A.:
"Tonmodel und
Reliefmedaillons aus den
Donauländern". Laureae
Aquincenses 1. DissPan
Ser.II:10. Budapest, 1938.
p. 337

**63. Sarcophagus**
Inv. No.: 23.1849.1
First half of 3rd century,
was used again for burial
around the beginning of
the 4th centuries; probably
from the stone carving
workshop of Viminacium
(Moesia Superior)
Height: 148 cm,
Width: 218 cm, Depth:
110; the present cover was
probably added at the time
of the second utilization

Site: Szekszárd, Tolna
county
Ref.: Nagy, L.: "Pannonia
sacra". In: Emlékkönyv
Szent István király
halálának kilencszázadik
évfordulóján (Memorial
Volume Published on the
Occasion of the
Ninehundredth
Anniversary of St.
Stephen's Death)
Budapest, 1938. pp. 48–51

**64. Milestone**
Inv. No.: 10.1951.203
229, Pannonia Inferior
Limestone
Height: 165 cm, diameter:
35 cm
Site: Szentendre, Pest
county
Ref.: Corpus Inscriptionum
Latinarum. Berlin,
1873–1902. No. 3738

**65. Bust of Trebonianus
Gallus**
Inv. No.: 2.1942.1
Middle of the 3rd century
A.D. Made in
a state-owned
weapon-manufacturing
workshop in the Danube
region
Sheet silver, chased and
engraved
Height: 26 cm
Site: Szőny,
Komárom-Esztergom
county
Ref.: Radnóti, A.:
"Trebonianus Gallus
ezüstlemez mellképe" (The
Sheet-silver Bust of
Trebonianus Gallus). FA,
6/1954. pp. 49–61;
201–204

**66. Necklace** Inv. No.:
54.67.1–9
Part of treasure hidden in
the spring of 260 A.D.
Gold, emerald
Site: Rábakovácsi, Vas
county
Ref.: R. Alföldi, M.: „A
rábakovácsi római
ékszerlelet" (Roman
Jewelry Found in
Rábakovácsi). FA, 6/1954.
pp. 62–73; 204–205

**67. Mithras tablet**
Inv. No.: 6.1943.1
3rd century A.D. Made in
a state-owned
weapon-manufacturing
workshop in the Danube
region
Sheet bronze, chased and
engraved
Height: 32.7 cm,
Width: 30.1 cm, thickness:
less than 1 mm
Site: Szőny,
Komárom-Esztergom
county
Ref.: Radnóti, A.: "Bronz
Mithras tablet
Brigetióból–Le bas-relief
mithriaque de bronze de
Brigetio". AÉ, III.

7–9/1946–1948. pp.
137–155

**68. Table with a rescript**
Inv. No.: 4.1944
The law was codified in
Serdica on July 9, 311
A.D.
Cast bronze, chiselled
Height: 78.5 cm, width:
68 cm, depth: 3–5 mm
Site: Szőny,
Komárom-Esztergom
county
Ref.: Paulovics, I.: "A
szőnyi törvénytábla–La
table de privileges de
Brigetio". ArchHung,
20/1936

**69. Bronze casket
mountings**
Inv. No.: 14.1927.1–2
4th century A.D.
Sheet bronze, chased
Height: 9 cm, length:
32.5 cm
Site: Kisárpás,
Győr-Moson-Sopron
county
Ref.: Gáspár, D.:
"Römische Kästchen aus
Pannonien. Antaeus".
Mitteilungen des
Archäologischen Instituts
der ungarischen Akademie
der Wissenschaften,
15/1986. Budapest, 1986. p.
218, Nos. 837–838

**70. Tripus**
Inv. No.: 54.1878
4th century A.D., made in
one of the more
noteworthy workshops in
a province of the Roman
Empire
Cast silver, chiselled
Height: 113–114 cm
Site: Polgárdi, Fejér county
Ref.: Erdélyi, G.: "A
polgárdi ezüst tripus" (The
Silver Tripus from
Polgárdi). AÉ, 45/1931. pp.
1–28; 291–299.

**71. Moesian plates**
Inv. No.: 71.1908.2–3
4th century A.D.
Silver, chiselled
Diameter: 41.5 and
43.5 cm
Ref.: Lenkei, M.: "Három
későrómai, ún. moesiai
ezüsttál a Nemzeti
Múzeumban–Three Silver
Dishes from Moesia in the
Hungarian National
Museum". FA, 7/1955.
pp. 97–109; 238–239

**72. Engraved glass**
Inv. No.: 108.1912.4
End of 4th–early 5th
century A.D.
Glass
Height: 16.3 cm
Site: Pécs, Baranya county
Ref.: Barkóczi. L.:
"Pannonische Glassfunde
in Ungarn". Studia
Archaeologica, 9/1988.
p. 104, No. 165

**73. Christ monogram**
Inv. No.: 1.1903
4th century A.D.
Bronze Diameter: 23.3 cm
Site: Bonyhád, Tolna
county
Ref.: Nagy, L.: "Pannonia
sacra". In: Emlékkönyv
Szent István király
halálának kilencszázadik
évfordulóján (Memorial
Volume Published on the
Occasion of the Nine
Hundredth Anniversary of
the Death of St. Stephen).
Budapest, 1938. vol. 1.
p. 47

**74. Inscription on
a sepulchral monument**
Inv. No.: R-D.175
End of 4th–early 5th
century A.D.
Limestone, painted
Height: 58 cm, length:
238 cm
Site: Óbuda, Budapest
Ref.: Corpus Inscriptionum
Latinarum. Berlin,
1873–1902. No. 3576;
Rómer F.–Desjardins, E.:
"A Magyar Nemzeti
Múzeum feliratos emlékei"
(Inscribed Monuments in
the Hungarian National
Museum). Acta Nova
Musei Nationalis
Hungarici. Budapest, 1873.
No. 175.

**75. Cauldron**
Inv. No.: 22/1869.1
5th centuryA.D., Hunnish
age
Cast bronze Height: 85 cm
Site: Törtel, Pest county
Ref.: Fettich, 1953. Plate
XXXVI, 1; Kovrig, I.:
"Hunnischer Kessel aus der
Umgebung von
Várpalota". FA, 23/1972.
pp. 95–121,
Illustration 13, 1

**76. Cicada pair of fibulas**
Orn. Jank. 47–48
First half of the 5th
century A.D.
Cast silver, pressed gold,
with garnet inlays
Length: 6.3 cm
Site: Györköny, Tolna
county
Ref.: Hampel, 1905. Plate
9, 1; Fettich, 1953. Plate
XL/4–5; Die Geschichte der
Völker Ungarns bis Ende
des 9. Jahrhunderts.
Budapest, 1963.
Illustration 31

**77. Electron cup**
Inv. No.: 81.1.1
First half of the 5th
century A.D., Hunnish age
Sheet gold, hammered,
silvered, on the body there
used to be glass inlays
Diameter: 11.1 cm
Site: Szeged-Nagyszéksós,
Csongrád county
Ref.: Fettich, 1953.
Plate XVII, 1

**78. Shield mounting**
Inv. No.: 97/1878
5th century A.D., Hunnish age
Gold plate, precious stone inlays
Width: 6 cm
Site: river Sárvíz area, Somogy county
Ref.: Hampel, Plate 39; Kiss, A.: *Der goldene Schildrahmen von Sárvíz aus dem 5. Jahrhundert und der Skirenkönig Edica. Alba Regia.* Under publication.

**79. Buckle**
Inv. No.: 51/1895.318
First half of the 5th century A.D., Hunnish age
Silver, with solid ring; sheet gold ornamented with garnet inlays
Length: 6 cm
Site: Murga, Tolna county
Ref.: Alföldi, A.: "Leletek a hun korszakból és ethnikai szétválasztásuk–Funde aus der Hunnenzeit und ihre ethnische Sonderung". *ArchHung*, 9/1932. Plate XXVI. 2–3

**80. Heart-shaped pommel**
Inv. No.: 52.66.2
Second half of the 5th ícentury A.D., Hunnish age
Gold with garnet inlays
Length: 6 cm Site: Oros, Borsod-Abaúj-Zemplén county
Ref.: Kovrig, I.: "Nouvelles trouvailles du Ve siecle découvertes en Hongrie". *Acta ArchHung*, 10/1959. pp. 209–225

**81. Necklace**
Inv. No.: 19/1860.2
5th century A.D., Germanic
Gold with red garnet
Length: 36.5 cm
Site: Dunapataj-Bakodpuszta, Bács-Kiskun county
Ref.: Hampel, Plate 2; Fettich, N.: "Régészeti tanulmányok a késői hun fémművesség történetéhez–Archäologische Studien zur Geschichte der späthunnischen Metallkunst". *ArchHung*, 31/1951. Plate XI, 4; Kiss, pp. 95–131; Illustration 4, 4

**82. Glass cup**
Inv. No.: 77/1897.5
Second half of the 5th century A.D., Hunnish age; from a Gepid grave
Green glass
Height: 15 cm
Site: Barabás, Szabolcs-Szatmár county
Ref.: Hampel, pp. 51–53, Plate 4; Kovrig, Illustration 37; Bóna, I.: "Szabolcs-Szatmár megye régészeti emlékei" (Archaeological Finds in Szabolcs-Szatmár county). In: *Szabolcs-Szatmár-Bereg műemlékei* (The Monuments of Szabolcs-Szatmár-Bereg County). Budapest, 1986. pp. 71–72. Illustration 22

**83. Belt buckle**
Inv. No.: 119/1907.1
Second half of the 5th century
Cast silver, gilded
Length: 15 cm
Site: Bácsordas
Ref.: Kovrig, Illustration 38 b; Kiss, pp. 95–131, Illustrations 9, 11

**84. Fibula**
Inv. No.: 54.3.1
Second half of the 5th century A.D., Germanic
Cast silver, gilded
Length: 27 cm
Site: Répcelak, Vas county
Ref.: Kovrig, Illustration 39a

**85. Eagle-shaped fibula**
Inv. No.: 69/1906.5
Second half of the 5th century A.D., Gepid
Gold with almadine inlays
Length: 3.6 cm
Site: Tiszavid, Szabolcs-Szatmár-Bereg county
Ref.: Csallány, D.: "Archäologische Denkmäler der Gepiden im Mitteldonaubecken". *ArchHung*, 38/1961. p. 220, No. 177; Bóna, 1974. p. 100, Illustration 3; Bóna, 1986. p. 74, Illustration 24

**86. Belt buckle**
Inv. No.: 61.95.1
End of the 5th century A.D.
Gilded silver, with niello decoration and almadine inlays
Length: 19.3 cm
Site: Hungary
Ref.: Bóna, 1974. p. 48, Illustrations 39–40

**87. Pair of fibulas**
Inv. No.: 61.96.1
Second half of the 5th century A.D., Eastern Germanic–Gepid
Gilded silver
Length: 16.7 cm
Site: allegedly Transylvania
Ref.: Bóna, 1974. p. 48, Illustration 1; Bóna: "Dáciától", pp. 146–149, Colour Illustration 6

**88. Pendant**
Inv. No.: 27/1891.1
Second half of the 5th century A.D., from a Gepid royal grave
Gold, almadine inlays
Length: 15 cm
Site: Apahida

Ref.: Fettich, 1953. Plate XXI, 3; Bóna: "Dáciától", pp. 146–149, Colour Illustration 6

**89. Torque**
Inv. No.: 101/1902
4th–5th century A.D.
Solid gold
Diameter: 18 x 14.7 cm
Site: Szamosújlak, Szabolcs-Szatmár-Bereg county
Ref.: Hampel, J.: "A Nemzeti Múzeum Régiségtár gyarapodása 1902-ben" (New Acquisitions of the Archaeology Department of the Hungarian National Museum in 1902). *AÉ*, 22/1902. pp. 419–448; Bóna: "Dáciától", Illustration 15, 1

**90. Pair of fibulas with lions**
Inv. No.: 122/1895.5 From Gepid royal treasure hidden around 420 A.D.
Pure gold
Length: 15.3 cm
Site: Szilágysomlyó
Ref.: Fettich, 1932. Plates II-III

**91. Pair of disk-shaped fibulas**
Inv. No.: 122/1985.8
From Gepid royal treasure hidden around 420 A.D.
Gold, semi-precious stones
Length: 10.7 cm
Site: Szilágysomlyó
Ref.: Fettich, 1932. Plates V-VI

**92. Pair of fibulas**
Inv. No.: 122/1895.3–3a
From Gepid royal treasure hidden around 420 A.D.
Silver, plated with gold, precious stone inlays
Length: 24.8 cm
Site: Szilágysomlyó
Ref.: Fettich, 1932. Plates XXIII-XXIV

**93. Scabbard mounting**
Inv. No.: 42/1902.250
End of the 5th century A.D.
Gilded with silver mounting at the opening
Width: 6.6 cm Site: Felpéc, Győr-Sopron-Moson county
Ref.: Fettich, N.: *Győr története a népvándorláskorban* (The History of Győr in the Age of the Great Migrations). Győr, 1943. vol 2, Plate 2; Bóna, 1974. p. 54, Illustration 41

**94. S-shaped fibulas**
Inv. No.: 65.9.2
First half of the 6th century, Lombard
Silver
Height: 3 cm
Site: Kápolnásnyék, Fejér county

Ref.: Bóna, 1974. p. 54, Illustration 47

**95. Pair of stirrups**
Inv. No.: 8/1938.5
End of the 6th century, Avar
Wrought iron
Length: 12 cm
Site: Csengőd, Bács-Kiskun county
Ref.: Lengyelné–Kovrig, I.: "Avar lószerszámveretek Csengődről (Pest megye)–Ferrure de harnais avare de Csengőd (Comitat de Pest)". *Magyar Múzeum*, October 1945, pp. 10–13, 48–49

**96. Bit**
Inv. No.: 4/1894.130
Around the beginning of the 7th century; from an early Avar age horse grave
Iron
Length: 26.8 cm
Site: Cikó, Tolna county
Ref.: Wosinszky, M.: "A cikói népvándorláskori sírmező" (Graves in Cikó from the Age of the Great Migrations). *ArchKözl*, 17/1894. pp. 35–101; Somogyi, P.: *A cikói temető–Das Gräberfeld von Cikó.* DissPann Ser. III. 2. Budapest, 1984. pp. 33–101

**97. Arrow heads**
Inv. No.: 64.20.248
6th–7th century, early Avar age
Wrought iron
Length: 6.5 and 10.5 cm
Site: Halimba, Veszprém county

**98. Handle of a sword and scabbard mounting**
Inv. No.: 6/1937.1–2
First half of 7th century, early Avar age
Sheet gold
Width: 5.7 and 7 cm
Site: Kecel, Bács-Kiskun county
Ref.: László, pp. 232–239, Plates LI-LIII

**99. Necklace**
Inv. No.: 69.1.90, 69.1.269
6th–7th century, woman's grave from the early Avar age
Glass paste
Diameter: 1.2 and 1.5 cm
Site: Környe, Komárom-Esztergom county
Ref.: Salamon, A.–Erdélyi, I.: "Das völkerwanderungszeitliche Gräberfeld von Környe". *Studia Archaeologica*, 5/1971. Plate XIV

**100. Pressing moulds**
Inv. No.: 72/1899.1–28
End of the 6th century–first half of the 7th century, from the grave of

an Avar-age silversmith
Bronze
Length: 1.2–7.6 cm
Site: Fönlak
Ref.: Dömötör, L.: "A fönlaki korakőzépkori préselőmintákról" (On the Early Middle Ages Pressing Moulds at Fönlak). *AÉ*, 10/1900. pp. 117–123; Fettich, N.: "Az avarkori műipar Magyarországon–Das Kunstgewerbe der Awarenzeit in Ungarn". *ArchHung*, 1/1926. 15, 32–33; Bóna: "Dáciától", pp. 166–168, Illustration 31

**101. Basket-shaped earrings**
Inv. No.: 100/1891.2–3
8th century
Sheet bronze and filigree wire
Diameter: 9.5 cm
Site: Raposka, Veszprém county
Ref.: Hampel, Plate 167

**102. Head-dress**
Inv. No.: 5/1937.1
End of the 7th century
Mountings pressed from sheet gold
Length: 6 cm
Site: Cibakháza, Jász-Nagykun-Szolnok county
Ref.: László, pp. 239–252, Plates LIV-LV

**103. Belt ornaments**
Inv. No.: 275/1871.56
End of the 7th century, from a royal grave
Sheet gold, pressed
Length: 9 and 6 and 3 cm
Site: Ozora-Tótipuszta, Tolna county
Ref.: Rómer, pp. 292–293; Hampel, Plates 267-268; László pp. 256–258, Plate LIX; Bóna, 1982–83. pp. 104–114, Illustration 9

**104. Earring**
Inv. No.: 275/1871.12
End of the 7th century, from a royal grave
Gold with cornelian pendants
Length: 5.5 cm
Site: Ozora-Tótipuszta, Tolna county
Ref.: Hampel, Plate 267; László pp. 256–258; Bóna, 1982–83. pp. 104–114

**105. Finger ring**
Inv. No.: 279/1871.10
End of the 7th century, from a royal grave
Gold, with almadine
Diameter: 1.9 cm
Site: Ozora-Tótipuszta, Tolna county
Ref.: Hampel, Plate 266; László pp. 256–258; Bóna, 1982–83. pp. 104–114, Illustration 8

**106. Belt mounting**
Inv. No.: 55.16.1
8th century, from a late
Avar man's grave
Cast bronze
Length: 7.5 cm
Site: Csuny
Ref.: Garam, É: "Die
Awaren". In. Roth, H.:
*Kunst der
Völkerwanderungszeit.
Propyläen Kunstgeschichte
Supplementband IV.*
Frankfurt/Main–Berlin–
Wien, 1979. Illustration
108a

**107. Large strap-end**
Inv. No.: 8/1921.1
First half of the 8th
century
Cast bronze
Length: 12.2 cm
Site: Zilah
Ref.: *Magyarország
népeinek története az
őskortól a honfoglaláskorig*
(The History of the
Peoples of Hungary from
Earliest Times until the
Conquest). Budapest, 1976.
p. 96, Illustration 22

**108. Large strap-end**
Inv. No.: 26/1935.558
Second half of the 8th
century, late Avar age
Cast bronze
Length: 15.6 cm
Site: Szebény, Baranya
county
Ref.: Garam, É.: "The
Szebény Cemetery". In:
*Avar Finds in the
Hungarian National
Museum.* Budapest, 1975.
Plate XII, 3

**109. Strap-end shaped like
a boar's head**
Inv. No.: 161/1885.1
End of the 8th century,
late Avar age
Cast bronze
Length: 9.7 cm
Site: Nemesvölgy
Ref.: Hampel, Plate 105,
12–13; Garam, É.: "A
bőcsi késő avarkori lelet és
köre" (The Late Avar
Finds in Bőcs and Other
Related Finds). *AÉ,*
108/1981. pp. 34–50,
Illustrations 7, 9

**110. Disk**
Inv. No.: 31/1931.10
8th century, late Avar
woman's grave
Cast bronze
Diameter: 5.7 cm
Site: Tiszaderzs, Szolnok
county
Ref.: Kovrig, I.: "The
Tiszaderzs Cemetery". In:
*Avar Finds in the
Hungarian National
Museum.* Budapest, 1975.
pp. 209–233,
Plate XXIX, 6

**111. Pair of stirrups**
Inv. No.: 89/1902. 35–36

End of the 7th century
Iron, plated with silver
Length: 18.2 cm
Site: Vörösmart
Ref.: Hampel, Plate 499;
Garam, É.: "Der Fund
von Vörösmart im
archäologischen Nachlass
der Awarenzeit". *FA,*
33/1982. pp. 187–213,
Illustration 4

**112. Phalera**
Inv. No.: 21/1936. 114.a-b
End of the 8th century
Sheet bronze, engraved,
blanched, punched
Diameter: 11.4 cm
Site: Szob,
Komárom-Esztergom
county
Ref.: Kovrig, I.: "The
Szob Cemetery". In: *Avar
Finds in the Hungarian
National Museum.*
Budapest, 1975. pp.
157–208, Plate XXVII

**113. Phalera**
Inv. No.: 61.31.1
Second half of the 8th
century, late Avar age
Cast bronze
Length: 6 cm
Site: Bőcs,
Borsod-Abaúj-Zemplén
county
Ref.: Garam, É.: "A bőcsi
késő avarkori lelet és köre"
(The Late Avar Finds in
Bőcs and Other Related
Finds). *AÉ,* 108/1981. pp.
34–51, Illustration 1, 7

**114. Jar with a spout**
Inv. No.: 21/1936.69 8th
century, late Avar age
Clay, made on a potter's
wheel
Height: 15 cm
Site: Szob,
Komárom-Esztergom
county
Ref.: Kovrig, I.: "The
Szebény Cemetery". In:
*Avar Finds in the
Hungarian National
Museum.* Budapest, 1975.
pp. 157–208, Plate XXV, 7

## Medieval Department

**115. Corpus**
Inv. No.: 1864.29
Second third of the 11th
century
Cast gold, beaten,
engraved; used to belong
to a cross adorned with
precious stones
Height: 7.1 cm, width:
6.6 cm
Site: Újszász, Pest county
Ref.: Kovács, 1974. 11–12

**116. Summoning sigil of the
Veszprém Collegiate
Church**
Inv. No.: 1890.127.10
11th century, Hungarian
Cast bronze, traces of
gold-plating

Diameter: 6.7 cm
Ref.: Gerevich, T.:
*Magyarország románkori
emlékei* (Romanesque
Monuments in Hungary).
Budapest, 1938.
Plate CCXXIX, 7

**117. Aspersorium**
Inv. No.: 1903.15
First half of the 12th
century, Byzantine
Cast silver, beaten,
engraved, gold-plated
Height: 22.1 cm
Site: Beszterec,
Szabolcs-Szatmár-Bereg
county
Ref.: Hampel, J.: "A M.N.
Múzeumi régiségosztály
gyarapodása az 1903.-ik
évben" (New Acquisitions
in the Antiquities
Department of the
Hungarian National
Museum in 1903). *AÉ,*
23/1903. pp. 436–438;
Fettich, N.: "A besztereci
aspersorium". In:
*A Nyíregyházi Jósa András
Múzeum Évkönyve* (The
Beszterec Aspersorium.
The Yearbook of the
András Jósa Museum,
Nyíregyháza).
Nyíregyháza, 1959. pp.
33–50

**118. Head of a crosier**
Inv. No.: 60.4.B
12th century
Antler, carved
Length: 11.3 cm, largest
diameter: 7.9 cm
Site: Feldebrő, Heves
county
Ref.: Kempis, A.: "A
feldebrői pásztorbot" (The
Feldebrő Crosier). *AÉ,*
88/1961. pp. 109–114,
Illustrations 3–4

**119. Ring**
Inv. No.: 58.68.B
12th century, Hungarian?
Cast gold, beaten, with
cloisonné enamel
Diameter: 2.3 cm
Ref.: Rosenberg, M.:
*Zellenschmelz.*
Frankfurt/Main, 1922. p.
14; Hlatky, pp. 12–13;
Deér, p. 60

**120. Aquamanile decorated
with a female head**
Inv. No.: 1852.5.51
1160s, Rhone-Maas region
Brass, engraved, cast,
enchased
Height: 28.2 cm
Ref.: Lovag, Zs.: "Das
Frauenkopf-Aquamanile
des Ungarischen
Nationalmuseums". *Acta
HistArt,* 22/1976. pp. 53–71

**121. Aquamanile decorated
with a riding scene**
Inv. No.: 1885.99
Second half of the 12th
century, Hungarian
Cast bronze, enchased

Height: 26 cm,
Length: 30 cm
Site: Büngösdpuszta, Békés
county
Ref.: Lovag, Zs.:
*Aquamanilék*
(Aquamaniles). Budapest,
1984. pp. 25–33,
Illustrations 14–15; *MNM,*
1977. pp. 116–117

**122. Base of a cross**
Inv. No.: 1870.25.2
Second half of the 12th
century, Rhone-Maas
region
Cast bronze, gilt, engraved
Height: 15.1 cm Site:
Dunaszentmiklós,
Komárom-Esztergom
county
Ref.: Lovag, 16; *MNM,*
1977. pp. 120–121

**123. Reliquary in the form
of a patriarchal cross**
Inv. No.: 1883.137.1
Second half of the 12th
century, Hungarian
Gold, embossed, with
filigree decoration
Height: 6.7 cm,
Width: 5 cm
Ref.: Kovács, 1974. 14

**124. Processional crucifix**
Inv. No.: 1904.79
Second half of the 12th
century, Hungarian
Bronze, gilt, engraved, cast
Height: 15.4 cm, width:
11.1 cm
Site: Cegléd, Pest county
Ref.: Lovag, 13; *MNM,*
1977. pp. 122–123

**125. Censer**
Inv. No.: 1879.117
Second half of the 12th
century, Hungarian or
German
Height: 21.5 cm
Ref.: Lovag, 19–20

**126. Candlestick in the
form of a siren**
Inv. No.: 1892.105
Second half of the 12th
century, Rhone region
Cast bronze, engraved
Height: 20.5 cm
Site: Hajdúhadház, on the
site of a ruinous village
church, Hajdú-Bihar
county
Ref.: Lovag, 17; *MNM,*
1977. pp. 118–119

**127. Funerary crown of
Béla III**
Inv. No.: 1848.64.2.b
1196
Silver, beaten, traces of
gold-plating
Height: 10 cm,
diameter: 18 cm
Site: Székesfehérvár,
Cathedral, Fejér county
Ref.: Czobor, B.: III. Béla
és hitvese halotti ékszerei
(The Funerary Jewelry of
Béla III and his Queen).
In: Forster, Gy.: III. Béla

magyar király emlékezete
(In Memory of King Béla
III of Hungary). Budapest,
1900. pp. 207–230; Kovács,
1969. pp. 17–18,
Illustrations 13–14; *MNM,*
1977. pp. 124–125

**128. Funerary Crown of
Anne of Antioch**
Inv. No.: 1848.64.1
See inv. No. 127
Silver, gilt, beaten
Height: 7.7 cm, diameter:
19.7 cm

**129. Funerary sceptre and
sword of Béla III**
Inv. No.: 1848.64.2.h,i
See inv. No. 127
Silver, beaten
Length of sceptre: 50.8 cm,
length of sword: 53 cm

**130. Bracelet and pair of
spurs of Béla III**
Inv. No.: 1848.64.2.e,k
See Inv. No. 127
Silver, beaten, cast
Diameter of bracelet:
8.4 cm, length of spurs:
10.3 cm

**131. Enkolpion from the
grave of Béla III**
Inv. No.: 1848.64.2.c,d
See Inv. No. 127
Second half of the 12th
century, Byzantine
Silver, beaten, cast, with
cloisonné enamel plaques
Diameter: 6.4 cm

**132. Processional cross
from the grave of Béla III**
Inv. No.: 1848.64.2.f
See Inv. No. 127
Middle of the 12th century,
Hungarian
Bronze, gilt, beaten, cast
Height: 22.3 cm,
Width: 10.3 cm

**133. Rings of Béla III and
Anne of Antioch**
Inv. No.: 1848.61.2,
1848.64.2.g
See Inv. No. 127
Second half of the 12th
century
Cast gold, beaten,
engraved, with granite and
almandine
Diameter: 2.8 and 2 cm

**134. Gold lacework from
the grave of Anne of
Antioch**
Inv. No.: 61.2026
See Inv. No. 127
Second half of the 12th
century
Silk, golden thread, woven,
openwork. (Only fragments
have survived; they
belonged to a veil and
a kerchief)

**135. Cup**
Inv. No.: 1871.141.1
12th-13th centuries,
Hungarian
Silver, beaten, stamped

Ref.: Vattai, E.: "Die Agnus Dei-Schale des Ungarischen Nationalmuseums". *Acta HistArt*, 12/1966. pp. 41–59

**136. The Golden Bull of Béla IV**
Inv. No.: 1881.26
Between 1235–1270, Hungarian, (13 copies are known)
Gold, impression
Diameter: 6.8 cm
Ref.: Bartoniek, E.: "Az Árpádok Ércpecsétei" (Metal Seals of the Arpadian Kings). *Turul*, 38/1924. pp. 20–25

**137. Clasp (Fürspan)**
Inv. No.: 1878.115
Middle of the 14th century, Hungarian, royal goldsmiths' workshop of Béla IV
Cast gold, engraved
Height: 3.8 cm, width: 3.2 cm
Site: Tömörd, Komárom-Esztergom county
Kovács, É.: "Uber einige Probleme des krakauer Kronenkreuzes". *Acta HistArt*, 17/1971. p. 240

**138. Clasp**
Inv. No.: 61.64.1.C
Around 1260
Gold, with niello decoration, engraved, cast
Size: 10 x 4.4 cm
Site: Kígyóspuszta (close to Kiskunmajsa), Bács-Kiskun county
Ref.: Tóth, Z.: "La bouche de Kígyóspuszta". *AÉ*, 63/1943. pp. 174–184; H. Kolba, J.: "Epigráfiai adatok a kígyóspusztai öv kormeghatározásához" (Epigraphical Data Concerning the Age of the Kígyóspuszta Belt). *FA*, 15/1963. pp. 77–85

**139. Earthenware cauldron**
Inv. No.: 58.102.77.B
11th–13th centuries
Clay, made on a Potter's wheel by hand, fired, dark-brown, traces of red paint
Height: 20.5 cm, diameter at the mouth: 27.3 cm
Site: Kardoskút-Hatablak, Békés county
Ref.: Méri, I.: *Árpád-kori népi építkezésünk feltárt emlékei Oroszháza határában* (Finds Relating to Hungarian Peasant Architecture in the Oroszháza Region). RégFüz Ser. II:12. Budapest, 1964. pp. 45–46, Plate IX, 1; Takács, M.: *Die arpadenzeitlichen Tonkessel im Karpatenbecken*. Varia Archaeologica Hungarica. Budapest, 1986

**140. Earthenware pot**
Inv. No.: 30/1931.3
13th century
Clay, made on a potter's wheel, fired, yellowish-white
Height: 16 cm, diameter at the mouth: 13.4 cm
Site: Budapest, Vármegyeház utca 7.
Ref.: Parádi, N.: "A balatonfenyvesi agyagpalack" (An Earthenware Bottle from Balatonfenyves). *FA*, 7/1955. p. 144, Plate XXXV, 4; Holl, I.: "Középkori cserépedények a budai várpalotából" (Medieval Earthenware Vessels from Buda Castle). *BudRég*, 20/1963. pp. 335–340, Illustrations 1–2, 66

**141. Bowl from the Körmend Find**
Inv. No.: Cim. Sec. II.V.7
Middle of the 14th century
Silver, partially gilded, embossed, stamped
Diameter: 18 cm
Site: Körmend, Vas county
Ref.: Vattai, E.: "A körmendi lelet" (The Körmend Find). *AÉ*, 83/1956. p. 71, Plate XIII 5, 2

**142. Engraving die**
Inv. No.: 58.205.C
Middle of the 15th century
Cast bronze
Size: 13.5 x 4.5 cm
Ref.: *Művészet I Lajos király korában. 1342-1382* (Art in the Age of King Louis I of Hungary, 1342–1382). Budapest, 1982. p. 303, No. 157

**143. Reliquary from Trencsény**
Inv. No.: Cim.Sec. II.IX.1
Around 1370
Copper, gilt, engraved, embossed, stamped
Length: 53,3 cm, height: 37.7 cm
Ref.: *Művészet I. Lajos király korában. 1342-1382* (Art in the Age of King Louis I of Hungary, 1342–1382). Budapest, 1982. p. 309, No. 164

**144. The Sigismund Crown**
Inv. No.: 1934.415.a
Late 14th century
Silver, gilt, with rubin and emerald
Height: 8 cm, diameter: 15.6 cm
Ref.: Kovács, É.: "Magyarország. Anjou-koronák" (Hungary. Anjou Crowns). *ArsHung*, 4/1976. pp. 7–19

**145. Baptismal font**
Inv. No.: 1914.132
Second half of the 14th century, Igló

Cast bronze, engraved
Height: 89 cm
Place of origin: The church of Liptótepla
Ref.: *Művészet, 1300–1470*, pp. 251–261

**146. Gravestone of Zsuzsanna Kompolthy**
Inv. No.: 60.286.C
Late 14th century
Length: 159 cm, width: 55 cm
Site: Budapest, Margaret Island ?
Ref.: Magyar Művelődéstörténet I.(Hungarian Cultural History). Budapest, n. d. vol 1. pp. 413, 629; *Művészet, 1300–1470*, p. 586, Fig. 2

**147. Stove tile**
Inv. No.: 60.8.359.C
Clay, fired, yellowish-brown, brown glaze
Height: 18.2 cm, width: 19.2 cm
Site: Pomáz-Klissza, Pest county
Ref.: Holl, I.: "Középkori kályhacsempék Magyarországon. I." (Medieval Stove Tiles in Hungary. Part I). *BudRég*, 18/1958. 224

**148. Trough pan**
Inv. No.: 36/1916.3
14th century
Borov pine, carved from a tree-trunk, iron fittings
Length: 285 cm, height: 47 cm, width: 55–65 cm
Place of origin: Szepesbéla

**149. Iron tools**

**a) Anvil**

Inv. No.: 69.52.C
15th century
Iron, forged
Height: 21.5 cm, top slab: 19 x 9 cm, base slab: 13 x 6.7 cm
Site: Gerjen, Tolna county

**b) Ploughshare, coulter, hatchet**
Inv. No.: 604.1–3.C
14th century
Iron, forged
Ploughshare: length: 31 cm, width: 17.5 cm, length of coulter: 47.5 cm, width of blade: 7.8 cm, length of hatchet: 22.3 cm, width of blade: 12.8 cm
Site: Máriabesnyő, Pest county

**c) Broad axe**
Inv. No.: HN. 14/1912.4
15th century
Iron, forged
Length: 19 cm, width of blade: 11.5 cm
Site: Zsámbék, Pest county
Ref.: *MNM*, 1977. pp. 156–157

**150. Bell**
Inv. No.: 260/1873
1468
Cast bronze
Height: 90 cm, diameter at the rim: 72 cm
Place of origin: Bulcs, among the ruins of the monastery
Ref.: Patay, P.: *Régi harangok* (Old Bells). Budapest, 1977. pp. 11–12, Illustrations 8–9

**151. Monstrance**
Inv. No.: 4/1937
Early 15th century, Hungarian
Cast silver, gilt, engraved, some enamel
Height: 65 cm
Place of origin: The Catholic church at Szendrő
Ref.: *Művészet Zsigmond király korában 1387-1437* (Art in the Age of King Sigismund of Hungary, 1387–1437). Budapest, 1987. p. 415, No. 0.8

**152. Belt**
Inv. No.: 1900.79.1
Gilt, partially silver, engraved
Size: 7.8 x 7 cm
Place of origin: Nagytállya, Heves county
Ref.: Szendrei, J.: "Régi övek a Magyar Nemzeti Múzeumban" (Old Belts in the Hungarian National Museum). *AÉ*, 23/1903. pp. 1–11; *Művészet Zsigmond király korában 1387-1437* (Art in the Age of King Sigismund of Hungary, 1387–1437). Budapest, 1987. p. 415, No. 0.8

**153. The Matthias Glass Goblet**
Inv. No.: 1929.9
Second half of the 15th century, Venice
Glass, base: silver-gilt, with engraved inscriptions
Height: 43 cm, diameter at the rim: 27.5 cm
Ref.: Balogh, J.: *A művészet Mátyás király korában* (Art in the Age of King Matthias Corvinus). 2 vols. Budapest, 1966. vol. I. p. 440; *Corvinus Matthias und die Renaissance in Ungarn*. Wien, 1982. pp. 496–497, No. 514

**154. Waffle-iron**
Inv. No.: 84.43.C.a-b
1497
Iron, forged, engraved
Diameter: 16.7 cm
Site: Northern Hungary ?
Ref.: Nagybákay, P.: "Címeres ostyasütő vasak a Magyar Nemzeti Múzeumban" (Waffle-irons with Seals in the Hungarian National Museum). *FA*, 39/1988. pp. 195–224

**155. Easter candlestick**
Inv. No.: 20/1919
15th century, Transylvania
Iron, forged
Height: 131.5 cm, diameter: 27 cm

**156. Earthenware drinking cup**
Inv. No.: 60.10.4.C
Second half of the 15th century
Clay, made on a potter's wheel, fired, green glaze
Height: 12 cm, diameter at the rim: 10.8 cm
Site: Pomáz-Klissza, Pest county
Ref.: Holl, I.: "Középkori cserépedények a budai várpalotából" (Medieval Earthenware Vessels from Buda Castle). (13th–15th centuries). *BudRég*, 20/1963. p. 362, Illustration 60

**157. Chalice**
Inv. No.: 55.12.C
Cast silver, silver gilt, with filigree work, engraved
Height: 219 cm
Ref.: *Régi egyházművészet országos kiállítása* (National Exhibition of Old Ecclesiastic Art). Budapest, 1930. pp. 45–46, No. 223

**158. Ciborium**
Inv. No.: 90/1902.4
Late 15th century
Silver, gilt, cast, embossed
Height: 27 cm
Place of origin: Radna, R.
Ref.: Mihalik, S.: "The Hungarian Cup of the Kremlin". *Acta HistArt*, 6/1959. pp. 342–343; *Corvinus Matthias und die Renaissance in Ungarn*. p. 492, No. 509

**159. Reliquary of Balázs Besztercei**
Inv. No.: 1879.114.14
1500, Hungarian
Cast silver, gilt, engraved, carved mother-of-pearl
Height: 33 cm
Ref.: Kohlhaussen, H.: *Nürnberger Goldschmiedskunst des Mittelalters und der Dürerzeit, 1240 bis 1540*. Berlin, 1968. No. 330, Illustration 374

**160. Section of a Gothic iron door**
Inv. No.: 89/1915
Around 1480
Iron, wrought, with cast bronze door knob
Height (of the whole door): 181.5 cm, width: 74 cm
Place of origin: Bártfa, St. Egidius's Church
Ref.: Kovalovszky, p. 10, Illustrations 15–16

**161. Capital**
Inv. No.: 282/1875 Last

third of the 15th century
Marble, carved, red
Height: 54 cm, width: 50 cm
Site: Budapest, the area of the Buda Town Hall (Szentháromság utca 2)
Ref.: *MNM*, 1977. pp. 154–155

**162. Bookstand**
Inv. No.: 163/1934
15th century
Larchwood, carved
Height: 23 cm, width: 45 cm
Place of origin: Nagybobróc
Ref.: Éber, L.: "A bútorművesség emlékei Magyarországon". (The Art of Furniture-making in Hungary. In: *Az iparművészet könyve* (The Book of the Applied Arts). 2 vols. Budapest, 1905. vol 2. p. 455. (Ed.: Ráth, Gy.)

**163. Book binding from the former library of St. Egidius's Church, Bártfa**
Inv. No.: 63.18.C
Late 15th century–early 16th century, Upper Hungary ?, Bártfa ?
Leather binding reinforced by wooden boards, with blind-stamped decoration, embossed, repoussé mounts
Length: 32.6 cm, width: 23.5, thickness: 9.5 cm
Place of origin: Bártfa
Ref.: Abel, Dr. J.: *A bártfai Sz. Egyed templom könytárának története* (The History of the Library of St. Egidius's Church, Bártfa). Budapest, 1885. p. 151

**164. Stove tile**
Inv. No.: 58/1894.1
Late 15th century
Clay, fired, light brownish-yellow
Height: 35.3 cm, Width: 25 cm
Site: Besztercebánya (Alsó utca 49)
Ref.: Hampel, J.: "A N. Múzeumi Régiségtár gyarapodása 1894 április-májusban" (New Acquisitions by the Department of Antiquities in the Hungarian National Museum, April-May, 1894). *AÉ*, 14/1894. p. 268, 270; Parádi, N.: "Későközépkori kályhacsempe negatívok" (Late Medieval Stove Tile Moulds). *FA*, 9/1957. p. 180–181, Plate XXX, 2–3

**165. Iron door**
Inv. No.: 166/1909
16th century
Iron, wrought
Height: 178.5 cm, width: 101 cm
Place of origin: Körmöcbánya

**166. Choirstalls (two seats)**
Inv. No.: 86/1915.1
Early 16th century
Larchwood, ash wood panelling, marquetry made of different kinds of wood
Height: 321 cm, Width: 137 cm
Place of origin: Bártfa, St. Egidius's Church
Ref.: Zlinszky-Sternegg, M.: *Marqueterie renaissance dans l'ancienne Hongrie*. Budapest, 1966. pp. 21–22, Illustrations 4–6

**167. Trousseau locker**
Inv. No.: 42/1929
Pine, ash wood panelling, marquetry made of different kinds of wood
Length: 162 cm, height: 103 cm, width: 76 cm
Place of origin: Késmárk
Ref.: Zlinszky-Sternegg, M.: *Marqueterie renaissance dans l'ancienne Hongrie*. Budapest, 1966. p. 43, Illustration 33

**168. Earthenware jug**
Inv. No.: 75.75.50.C
Second half of the 15th century–first half of the 16th century
Clay, made on a potter's wheel, fired, red
Height: 32.5 cm, Diameter at the rim: 10 cm
Site: Sümeg-Sarvaly, Veszprém county
Ref.: Holl–Parádi, pp. 99–101, Plate 161, 8

**169. Earthenware drinking cup**
Inv. No.: 75.68.6.C
Second half of the 15th century–first half of the 16th century
Clay, made on a potter's wheel, fired, some greyish-brown colouring
Height: 11.3 cm, diameter at the mouth: 6.8 cm
Site: Sümeg-Sarvaly, Veszprém county
Ref.: Holl–Parádi, pp. 101–103, Plate 161, 8

**170. Stove tile**
Inv. No.: 75.82.147.C
Second half of the 15th century–first half of the 16th century
Clay, fired, red
Height: 17.5 cm, width: 17.5 cm
Site: Sümeg-Sarvaly, Veszprém county
Ref.: Holl–Parádi, p. 108, Plate 167, 4

**171. Crest-tile of a stove**
Inv. No.: 89/1912
Late 15th century–16th century
Clay, fired, yellowish-red
Height: 26.5 cm, width: 14.5 cm
Site: Bácstóváros-Nagy-báncsa dűlő

Ref.: Szabó, K.: *Az alföldi magyar nép művelődestörténeti emlékei* (Historical Relics of the Hungarians Living on the Great Plain) Bibliotheca Humanitatis Historica 3. Budapest, 1938. p. 96, Illustrations 450–454

**172. Corner tile**
Inv. No.: 56.20.401.C
Late 15th century–16th century
Clay, fired, red
Height: 28.8 cm, width: 12.2 cm
Site: Túrkeve-Móric, Szolnok county
Ref.: Méri, I.: "Beszámoló a tiszalök-rázompusztai és túrkeve-mórici ásatások eredményeiről II." (Report on the Findings of the Excavations at Tiszalök-Rázompuszta and Túrkeve-Móric. Part II). *AÉ*, 81/1954. p. 148, Plate XXXVII, 3

**173. Crest-tile of a stove**
Inv. No.: 93/1880.2
16th century
Clay, fired, red
Height: 22 cm, width: 18.5 cm
Site: Nadab Castle
Ref.: Méri, I.: "A nadabi kályhacsempék" (Stove Tiles from Nadab). *AÉ*, 84/1957, pp. 187–202, Plate XLIV, 1

**174. Cup**
Inv. No.: 17/1887.5
16th century
Silver, engraved, embossed
Height: 3.3 cm, diameter: 12.6 cm
Site: Keresztúri puszta
Ref.: Fehér, G.: "A Magyar Nemzeti Múzeum lelőhellyel jelölt hódoltságkori ezüst csészéi" (Silver Cups with the Designation of the Site of Discovery from the Age of Ottoman Rule in the Hungarian National Museum). *FA*, 15/1963, pp. 88, 93–94, Plate 2, Fig. 32

**175. Guild badge from Brass**
Inv. No.: 1887.67
1556
Silver, engraved, embossed
Height: 16 cm
Place of origin: Brassó
Ref.: Resch, A.: "A brassói ötvösség bemondó táblája 1556-ból" (Guild badge of the Brassó Goldsmiths from 1556). *AÉ*, 7/1887. pp. 287–293; *MNM*, 1977. pp. 166–167

**176. Queen Mary's ring**
Inv. No.: Ann.Jank.300
Middle of the 16th century, Hungarian ?
Gold, enamelled, with diamonds

Diameter: 2.2 cm
Ref.: Hlatky, p. 79, Plate VII, Illustration 69; Radvánszky, B: *A magyar családélet és háztartás* (Family Life and Households in Hungary). vol 1. p. 348, No. 188

**177. Flagon**
Inv. No.: 1934.334
1563 and 1654, Transylvania
Partially gilded silver, engraved
Height: 26 cm
Place of origin: Csenger, The Calvinist Church, Szabolcs-Szatmár-Bereg county
Ref.: Radvánszky, B.: *A magyar családélet és háztartás* (Family Life and Households in Hungary). vol. 1. p. 351, No. 219

**178. Beaker with standard**
Inv. No.: 55.175.C
Late 16th century, Nagyszeben, Georgius Sturm (active: 1589–1609)
Silver, gilt, engraved, embossed, with antique coins
Height: 22.2 cm
Ref.: *Tresors de l'orfevrerie hongroise du Xe au XIXe siecle*. Bruxelles, 1970. No. 76

**179. The Barcsay Plate**
Inv. No.: 59.285.C
Around 1602, and 1658–1661, Nagyszeben, Andreas Eckhardt
Silver, gilt, engraved, embossed, the coat-of-arms in the centre was engraved later
Diameter: 24.5 cm
Ref.: *Erdély régi művészeti emlékeinek kiállítása* (Exhibition of Old Transylvanian Art). Budapest, 1931. p. 45, No. 219

**180. Spice-container with mine scenes**
Inv. No.: 60.71.C
1629
Partially gilded silver, engraved
Height: 20.3 cm
Ref.: Cennerné, p. 206

**181. Can**
Inv. No.: 90/1912
16th–17th centuries
Copper with engraved decoration
Height: 28.5 cm, diameter at the rim: 5 cm
Ref.: Fehér, pp. 14, 35, 69, Illustration 70

**182. Candlestick**
Inv. No.: 23/1917.b
16th–17th centuries
Copper, top is cast, engraved on the base
Height: 28 cm, diameter at the base: 14.5 cm

Ref.: Fehér, pp. 24, 35–36, Illustrations 72–73

**183. Pair of slippers**
Inv. No.: 260/1871
17th century
Light brown leather, outside: embellishment woven of silver thread, inside: on gilded base openwork decoration cut out of cordovan
Length: 22 cm, Width: 8.5 cm
Ref.: Fehér, pp. 13, 30, Illustration 11

**184. Scales weight**
Inv. No.: 57/1903.2
Second half of the 17th century, Turkish
Cast bronze, with faded stamp
Height: 6.4 cm, Width: 3.9 cm
Site: Buda
Ref.: Báránné Oberschall, M.: "Iparművesség Budán a török korban" (Artisanship in Buda During the Period of Turkish Rule). In: *Budapest története* (A History of Budapest). vol 3. Budapest, 1944. pp. 363–364

**185. Turkish memorial stone slab**
Inv. No.: 62.15.C
1668–1669
Marble, carved, yellowish-grey
Height: 68 cm, Width: 68 cm
Site: Buda ?
Ref.: Feridoun, Omer: "Budai török emlékek" (Turkish Relics in Buda). *AÉ*, 33/1913. pp. 411–414

**186. Mehmed Ali's ring**
Inv. No.: 59.5.C
Cast gold; on the head–which contains a cornelian stone–and on the inside of the ring are inscriptions engraved in Arabic letters; on the outside of the ring inscriptions in Gothic letters
Length of the head of the ring: 2.2 cm, diameter of the ring: 1.8 cm
Ref.: Fehér, G.: "Les cachets et anneaux sigillaires à inscription turque du Musée National Hongrois". *FA*, 11/1959. p. 195, Plate XXVI, 12, Fig. 36, 24

**187. Goblet belonging to a guild**
Inv. No.: 1949.77
1699, Paulus Karsai (mentioned: 1648–1674)
Partially gilded silver, engraved
Height: 12 cm

## Department of Modern Times

**188. Helmet (Hundsgugel)**
Inv. No.: 58.7631
14th century, West
European
Wrought iron
Height: 28.5 cm
Ref.: Kalmár, J.:
"A Történeti Múzeum
fegyvertárának középkori
sisakjai" (Medieval
Helmets in the Arms and
Armour Department at the
Historical Museum). *AÉ,*
85/1958. pp. 191-195

**189. Seal of the Rudabánya
mining town**
Inv. No.: P.1961.58.c
14th century
Silver, engraved
Diameter: 7.2 cm
Legend: SIGILLUM
CIVITATIS RUDE
Ref.: *Művészet, 1300–1470.*
p. 164

**190. Seal of the Ujbánya
mining town**
Inv. No.: Cim.Sec. I. V.4
Silver, engraved
Diameter: 5.3 x 6.1 cm
Legend: + SIGILLUM
CIVITATIS DE MONTE
REGIS; above the
kneeling king:
LVDOWICuS
Ref.: *Cimeliotheca Musei
Nationalis Hungarici.* Buda,
1825. pp. 10–11; *MNM,*
1977. 264–265; *Művészet,
1300–1470,* p. 163

**191. Saddle**
Inv. No.: 53.3117
Early 15th century, West
European
Bone, wood, carved
Length: 54 cm,
width: 42 cm
Ref.: Kárász, L.:
"Elefánt-csont nyergek
a N. Múzeumban (Ivory
Saddles in the Hungarian
National Museum). *AÉ,*
14/1894. pp. 53–59; Eisler,
J.: "Zu den Fragen der
Beinsättel des Ungarischen
Nationalmuseums I".
*FA,* 28/1977. pp. 189–209; II.
*FA* 30/1979. pp. 205–248

**192. Shield**
Inv. No.: 55.3264
Second half of the 15th
century, Hungarian
Wood, engraved
Height: 119 cm,
Width: 59 cm
Ref.: Kalmár, J.: "Mátyás
király hadtörténelmi
emléktárgyai" (War
History Relics of King
Matthias Corvinus).
*Hadtörténeti Közlemények,*
22/1975. pp. 530-552;
*Arms and Armour,* p. 63,
Illustration 9

**193. Pair of spurs**
Inv. No.: 55.3217.1–2

Late 15th century,
Hungarian
Iron, brass, gold-plated,
engraved
Length: 22 cm, diameter of
the rowel: 4 cm
Ref.: Kalmár, p. 362;
Zschille, R.–Forrer, R.:
*Die Steigbügel.* Berlin,
1896. p. 14

**194. Shield**
Inv. No.: 55.3226
Around the beginning of
the 16th century,
Hungarian
Iron, gold-plated, engraved
Height: 72 cm,
Width: 39.2 cm
Ref.: *A bécsi
gyűjteményekből,* p. 49;
*Arms and Armour,* p. 64

**195. Tournament armour**
Inv. No.: 55.3267
Around the beginning of
the 16th century, West
European
Steel, forged
Height: 115 cm
Ref.: *A bécsi
gyűjteményekből,* pp.
51–53; *Waffenschätze,*
pp. 63–64

**196. Suit of armour**
Inv. No.: 55.3277
Early 16th century, West
European Steel, forged
Height: 176 cm
Ref.: *A bécsi
gyűjteményekből,* p. 49;
Kalmár, p. 295;
*Waffenschätze,* p. 64

**197. Powder-horn**
Inv. No.: 56.5801
Early 16th century,
West-European
Wood, silver, embossed
Height: 25.3 cm,
Width: 20 cm
Ref.: Kalmár, pp. 229–236

**198. Dagger**
Inv. No.: 55.3237
1543, Hungarian
Steel, silver, gilt, embossed
Length: 482 cm
Ref.: *A bécsi
gyűjteményekből,* p. 39;
Boeheim, W.:
*Waffenkunde.* Leipzig,
1890. p. 298

**199. Can of the
Shoemakers' guild at
Gölnicbánya**
Inv. No.: 1877.119.45.c
1524, Kassa
Tin, engraved, cast
Height: 54 cm
Ref.: Hintze, E.: *Die
deutschen Zinngiesser und
ihre Marken.* Leipzig, 1931.
vol. 7. No.: 2604; Németh,
pp. 15–18, 38–39;
Toranova, E.: *Cinarstvo na
Slovensku* (Tinsmith's
Work in Slovakia).
Bratislava, 1980. p. 143;
Weiner, P.:
*Zinngiessermarken in*

*Ungarn 16–19.
Jahrhunderts.* Budapest,
1978. p. 56
(Earlier the can was
incorrectly thought to have
belonged to the
Bootmakers' Guild.)

**200. Can of an unknown
Blacksmiths' Guild**
Inv. No.: 1889.18.2
1558, Nagyszeben
Tin, engraved, cast, the
iron handle used to be
gold-plated
Height: 44.5 cm
Ref.: Németh, pp. 18,
39–40

**201. Lace**
Inv. No.: 1954.629
White linen thread, sewn,
flower and figure patterns
made by punto in aria
technique
Length: 48.5 cm,
Width: 3.3 cm
Ref.: Ember, 1980. p. 53,
Illustrations 65-66; V.
Ember, M.: "Reneszánsz
csipkék" (Renaissance
Lacework). *FA,* 7/1955. pp.
175-181

**202. Homespun material**
Inv. No.: 1915.87.4
Blue and white cotton,
woven in zones of zig-zag
and bird and figures
Length: 151 cm,
width: 67 cm
Place of origin: Bártfa,
Roman Catholic Church
Ref.: Bobrovszky, I.:
*Középkori és reneszánsz
szövőművészet
Magyarországon* (Medieval
and Renaissance Weaving
in Hungary). Budapest,
1972; *idem:
Spätmittelalterliche
Leinentücher mit
Baumwollmerkung.*
Budapest, 1970. p. 250

**203. Pistol**
Inv. No.: 55.3244
Late 16th century, West
European
Steel, wood, bronze, bone,
gilded, inlay technique
Length: 54 cm,
calibre: 1.1 cm
Ref.: Temesváry, F.:
*Pisztolyok. A Magyar
Nemzeti Múzeum
tűzifegyver-gyűjteménye I.*
(Pistols. The Firearms
Collection of the
Hungarian National
Museum. Part I.).
Budapest, 1988. Kat. 4;
*idem: Pistolen.* Budapest,
1988. Kat. 4

**204. György Thurzó's
helmet**
Inv. No.: 55.3400 Late
16th century,
West European
Steel, engraved, gilt
Height: 260 cm
Ref.: Kalmár, J.: "A

Történelmi Múzeum
fegyvertárának középkori
sisakjai" (Helmets in the
Medieval Arms and
Armour Department of the
Historical Museum). *AÉ,*
85/1958. pp. 191-195; *Arms
and Armour,* p. 67

**205. Sand-clock**
Inv. No.: 1961.3411
Around 1600
Engraved, mother-of-pearl
and ivory stand
Height: 7.2 cm,
Diameter: 3.5 cm
Ref.: *Az idömérés története,*
p. 17

**206. István Thököli's
harpsicord**
Inv. No.: 30/1876
Around 1600, Italian;
reconstructed and painted
in the 17th century, Upper
Hungary
Cypress wood, marbled
painting
Length: 173 cm, height:
19 cm (the stand is lost),
Width: 72 cm
Ref.: Gábry, p. 10, 33,
Illustration 2

**207. The Szapárys'
letters-patent from
Ferdinand II**
Inv. No.: Udgy. 1972.5
Vienna, July 6, 1620
Parchment, with painted
coat-of-arms, reinforced
with a suspended seal
Size: 73 x 34.4 cm

**208. Platter with engraved
decoration**
Inv. No.: 1905.39
1631, with the hallmark of
Beszterce, and with the
mastermark: H K G (?)
Tin, engraved, cast
Diameter: 42 cm
Ref.: Hintze. E.: *Die
Deutsche Zinngiesser und
ihre Marken.* vol 7. No.:
2591; Németh, p. 48

**209. Wall-clock**
Inv. No.: 1967.53
Around 1640
Bronze, gilt
Length: 40 cm,
Width: 35 cm
Ref.: *Az idömérés története,*
p. 35

**210. Seal of Ferdinand II**
Inv. No.: P.1960.182
First half of the 17th
century
Gold, cast, double-faced
Diameter: 9 x 9.3 cm
Legend: FERDINANDUS
II.
D.G.EL.RO.IMP.SE.A-
UG. GERMA
: HUNGARIAE.
BOHEMIAE. DAL.
CROA. SCLA. TEC REX.

**211. Ship's cannon**
Inv. No.: 55.3288
1637, West European

Iron, engraved, cast
Length of barrel: 90 cm

**212. Embroidered table-
cloth**
Inv. No.: 1932.121
Second half of the 17ht
century, Transylvania,
embroidered by Zsuzsanna
Lorántffy
Red and green silk feather
shag, worked in satin stich
with silver and gold thread
Length: 200 cm,
Width: 182 cm
Ref.: Ember, 1980, p. 52,
Illustrations VII-VIII;
Ember, 1981, pp. 95–96,
Illustration 119;
Varjú-Ember, M.: *Alte
ungarische Stickerei.*
Budapest, 1963. pp. 34, 43,
Illustrations 13, 31

**213. Saddle cloth**
Inv. No.: 1958.26
Middle of the 17th century,
Transylvania
Green broad-cloth,
embroidered in satin stich
with silver-gilt flower
pattern
Length: 119 cm,
Width: 114 cm
Ref.: Ember, 1980. p. 53,
Illustrations 61-62; Ember,
1981. p. 120,
Illustration 232

**214. A fragment of
a cannon of György
Rákóczi I.**
Inv. No.: 57.6517
17th century, Transylvania
Cast bronze
Length: 39 cm
Ref.: Bujdosó, V.: "I.
Rákóczi György és Bánffy
Dénes ágyúi" (Cannons of
György Rákóczi I and
Dénes Bánffy). *Századok,*
9/1875. pp. 347–348;
Kalmár, p. 168; *Arms and
Armour,* pp. 67–68,
Illustration 31

**215. György Rákóczi's
chain-mail shirt**
Inv. No.: 55.3539
17th century, Transylvania
Silver, woven, gilt
Height: 75 cm
Ref.: *Kalauz
a Régiségtárban* (Guide to
the Antiquities
Department). Budapest,
1912. p. 195; *Arms and
Armour,* p. 59, Plate XVI

**216. Quiver**
Inv. No.: 55.3842
17th century, Turkish
Leather, silk, embroidered
Height: 42.5 cm
Ref.: Kalmár, p. 135

**217. Stirrup**
Inv. No.: 55.3320
17th century, Turkish
Silver with gems
Height: 19 cm,
Width: 18.5 cm
Ref.: Temesváry, F.:

*Fegyverkincsek–Díszfegyverek* (Ornate Arms and Armour). Budapest, 1982 p. 49; *Waffenschätze*, p. 58

**218. Deer antler powder-horn with the Telekis' coat-of-arms**
Inv. No.: 73.9640
17th century, Hungarian
Horn, carved
Height: 36.5 cm,
Width: 27 cm
Ref.: Boross, B.: *Alte Jagdpulver Hörner.* Budapest, 1982. pp. 83–84

**219. Pistols of King Matthias Corvinus**
Inv. No.: 55.3860
17th century, German
Height: 57 cm, calibre: 12 mm
Ref.: *Kalauz a Régiségtárban*, p. 182; Stöcklein, H.: *Meister des Eisenschnittes.* Esslingen, 1922. pp. 75–85

**220. Cloth for Communion-table**
Inv. No.: 1922.55
1660, Hungarian
Openwork in white linen thread, decorated with figures
Length of mesh: 150 cm, width of mesh: 72 cm
Ref.: Ember, 1980. p. 52, Illustration 74

**221. Chasuble**
Inv. No.: 1935.42.a.b
1670, Hungarian
Red atlas silk, worked in satin stitching with undulating gold and silver floral motifs
Length: 128 cm,
Width: 84 cm
Ref.: B. Oberschall, M.: *Magyarországi miseruhák* (Chasubles in Hungary). Budapest, 1937; Bárány-Oberschall, M.: *Ungarische Mengewänder.* Budapest, 1938. p. 22, Illustration 27; Varjú-Ember, M.: *Hungarian Domestic Embroidery.* Budapest, 1963. p. 40; Csernyászky, M.: "Magyar úrihímzésű miseruhák" (Hungarian Embroidered Chasubles). In: *Gerevich Emlékkönyv*, pp. 139–151, Illustrations 20, 27; Ember, 1980. p. 52, Plate VI, Illustrations 52–56; Ember, 1981. p. 115, Illustration 124; V. Ember, M.: *Alte Textilien.* Budapest, 1982. p. 62, Plate VI, Illustrations 55–56

**222. Beaker with István Apor's coat-of-arms**
Inv. No.: ö.II.76.3
1648–1708, Brassó, Thomas Klosch
Silver, gilt
Height: 29 cm, diameter at

the rim: 15 cm
Ref.: Bíróné, Sey, K.–T. Németh, A.: *Pogány pénzes edények. Évezredek, évszázadok kincsei* (Pagan Money Containers. Treasures From Down the Ages). Budapest, 1989. 6.

**223. Tankard with a merchant scene**
Inv. No.: 73.33
Around 1670, Besztercebánya, Michael Allert
Silver, gilt
Height: 26 cm, diameter at the base: 13.2 cm

**224. Seal of the Rimaszombat Guild of Merchants**
Inv. No.: P.1955.354.c
1683
Silver, engraved
Diameter: 3.6 cm
Legend: SIGILLUM CEHAE MERCATORIUM OPPIDI R. SZOMB.
Inscription: LAKATOS ISTVAN BIROSAGABAN 1683 LOPOTSI ISTVAN ES MESTER ANDRAS POLGAR

**225. Princely seal of Ferenc Rákóczi II**
Inv No.: P.1873.206
Late 17th century, Daniel Warou, Swedish-born engraver from Körmöcbánya or Dániel Ocsovay, engraver from Nagybánya
Silver, engraved
Diameter: 6.3 cm
Legend: FRANCISCUS DEI GRATIA PRINC: RAKOCZI.COMES DE SAAROS.DVX MVNKACSIE:ET MAKOVICSIE:DOMI-NUS:DE PERPETVVS SAAROS PATAK.TOKAI. REGECZ.ECSED.SOMLI-O.LEDNITZE.SZEREN-CS.ONOD

**226. Pocket-watch of Ferenc Pápai Páriz**
Inv. No.: Jank.86
Turn of the 17th and 18th centuries, Elias Breitt Mayr
Silver, engraved, repoussé
Diameter: 6.2 cm
Ref.: *Az időmérés története.* pp. 36–37

**227. Long-case clock**
Inv. No.: 1865.93
Around 1700, London, Daniel Quare (1648–1724)
Wood, marquetry, in a case
Height: 204 cm, width: 35 cm, depth: 25 cm
Ref.: *Az időmérés története.* p. 34

**228. Can of the Érsekújvár Butchers' Guild**
Inv. No.: 1982.51
1718, Franz Ignaz Biernpäck (Biernpeckh, Birnbeckl), a can maker from Pozsony
Tin, with cast and engraved ornaments
Height: 55 cm
Ref.: Németh, A.–Németh, G.: "Az érsekújvári mészárosréh emlékei a Magyar Nemzeti Múzeumban" (Relics of the Érsekújvár Butchers' Guild in the Hungarian National Museum). *FH*, 13/1984. pp. 59–60; Toranova, E.: *Cinarstvo na Slovensku* (Tinsmith's Work in Slovakia). p. 114, 161

**229. Privileges of the Debrecen Guild of Merchants**
Inv. No.: Udgy.1967.21
1712–1713, Debrecen
Book format, paper, leather binding made in Debrecen
Size: 31 x 20 cm

**230. The armchair of Ferenc Rákóczi II**
Inv. No.: 1967.89
Between 1720 and 1735, carved by Ferenc Rákóczi during his exile in Rodostó
Limewood, carved, painted
Height: 121 cm, width: 78.5 cm, depth: 45 cm
Oberschall, p. 25, Illustration 32; Voit, P.: *Régi magyar otthonok* (Old Hungarian Homes). Budapest, 1943. p. 194; *MNM*, 1977. pp. 234-235

**231. Strip of lace**
Inv. No.: 1955.574
Early 18th century, Hungarian
Bobbin lace of white linen, with so-called quipure base flower patterns
Length: 13.7 cm,
Width: 23 cm
Ref.: Ember, 1980. p. 54, Illustration 70; V. Ember, M.: *Alte textilien.* Budapest, 1982. p. 65, Illustration 70

**232. Covered beaker**
Inv. No.: 1961.1189.a-b
1727, Brassó, Michael May II
Silver, gilt
Height: 28 cm

**233. Bottle with a screw-in cork**
Inv. No.: 1867.58.41
Early 18th century, Nagyszeben
Cast tin
Height: 16.6 cm
Ref.: Németh, pp. 22, 42

**234. Haban plate**
Inv. No.: 1954.340

1734, Upper Hungary
Faience, tin glaze
Diameter: 29 cm

**235. Lock and key**
Inv. No.: 1932.42
1747
Wrought iron
Length: 50 cm,
Width: 31.5 cm

**236. Table ornament from the Esterházy Castle at Tata**
Inv. No.: 1954.202
18th century
Copper, embossed
Height: 31 cm, diameter at the mouth: 52 cm

**237. Table sundial**
Inv. No.: 1910.54.1
Middle of the 18th century, Buday L. Platzer
Copper, gilded
Length: 11 cm,
Width: 11 cm

**238. Mulled wine decanter with the Torockai coat-of-arms**
Inv. No.; 1946.6
Around 1750, Transylvania, undecipherable mastermark
Silver, partially gilded
Height: 31.5 cm, diameter at the base: 9.8 cm

**239. Certificate of the Diószeg Guild of Tailors**
Inv. No.: Udgy. 1961.7.c
Drawn up for György Faragó on August 24, 1754
Paper, with painted decoration, traces of the guild's seal
Size: 31 x 46 cm

**240. Mozart's Clavichord**
Inv. No.: 1965.42
1762, Augsburg, Johann Andreas Stein (1728–1792)
Walnut, varnished
Length: 99 cm, height: 11 cm, width: 35 cm
Ref.: Gábry, Gy.: *W.A. Mozart úti clavichordja* (W.A. Mozart's Travelling Clavichord). *FA* 19/1968. pp. 191–201

**241. Gala suit for a young Hungarian man**
Inv. No.: 1954.667
Around 1745, Hungarian
Pale blue repp silk, with tiny woven flowers and silver passementerie
Length of dolman: 43 cm, length of mente: 63.5 cm, length of trousers: 46 cm, height of tall fur hat: 32 cm

**242. Lady's gala dress with apron**
Inv. No.: 1935.109, 1935.133
Middle of the 18th century, material from Lyon, Hungarian
Blue lampas, the flower

pattern woven in silver and coloured silk, white Malines-type bone-lace
Waist: 61 cm, length of skirt: 106 cm, width of apron: 106 cm, length of apron: 48 cm
Ref.: Höllrigl, J.: *Régi magyar ruhák* (Old Hungarian Costumes). Budapest, 1938. p. 21, Illustration 25

**243. Hungarian gentleman's gala suit and shoes**
Inv. No.: 1928.3, 1954.618
Around 1770, Hungarian, bequeathed by Sámuel Teleki, Chancellor of Transylvania
Crimson silk, golden soutache, decorated with butterflies and embroidery, later with fur; shoes are made of dark red leather and decorated with embroidery in gold
Length of mente: 93 cm, length of dolman: 79 cm, length of trousers: 102 cm, length of shoes: 27 cm
Ref.: *Hungarian Costume; The Imperial Style*

**244. Aigrette**
Inv. No.: 1956.281
Middle of the 18th century and middle of the 19th century, Hungarian ?
Gold, rubin, almandine
Height: 19.5 cm, width: 5.5 cm

**245. Lady's belt**
Inv. No.: 1949.303
Second half of the 18th century, Hungarian ?
Silver, diamond
Length: 77 cm, width: 4 cm

**246. Aigrette**
Inv. No.: Ö.II.84.2
Second half of the 18th century, Hungarian ?
Silver, gold plates, with diamond
Height: 10.5 cm

**247. Chalice**
Inv. No.: 1901.46.1
Around 1770, Pest, Josephus Schätzl
Silver, gilded
Height: 27.5 cm, diameter at the base: 17 cm

**248. Haban pitcher**
Inv. No.: 1961.2048
1782, Hungarian
Clay, tin glaze
Height: 27 cm

**249. Falconer's tote**
Inv. No.: 55/3838
1781, West European
Leather, silk, embroidered
Height: 48 cm, width: 47.5 cm
Ref.: Temesváry, F.: *Vezető a Magyar Nemzeti Múzeum Vadászfegyverek című kiállításához* (Sporting

Weapons. Guide to the Exhibition in the Hungarian National Museum). Budapest, 1982. p. 21; Neuhaus, A.: *Deutsche Jagdaltertümer.* Nürnberg, 1935. p. 10

**250. Grain measure**
Inv. No.: 1961.2140
1785, Buda
Copper, with seal of certificate
Height: 28 cm, diameter: 54.5 cm

**251. Trumpet**
Inv. No.: 1967.8520
1789, Vienna, Ignaz Kerner
Copper, silver- and gold-plated
Length: 58.5 cm

**252. Trade-sign**
Inv. No.: 1875.263.1
1798, Jolsva
Wood, marquetry
Height: 25 cm, width: 18 cm

**253. A meeting of freemasons for the admission of new members**
Inv. No.: 1981.131.520
18th century, French
Copperplate engraving
Length: 39 cm, width: 27 cm
Ref.: *Österreichische Freimauerlogen Humanität und Toleranz im 18. Jahrhundert*, No. 79

**254. Palatine Joseph's armchair**
Inv. No.: 1869.27.1
Late 18th century
Wood, gilded, painted, with leather upholstery
Height: 90.5 cm, Width: 67 cm, depth: 60 cm

**255. Saxon jug**
Inv. No.: 1952.173
1801, Transylvania, Lutz workshop
Earthenware, blue glaze with sgraffito decoration
Height: 20 cm

**256. Oil and vinegar bottles**
Inv. No.: 1961. 1676
First half of the 19th century, Kassa
Faience, tin glaze, with tiny blue pattern
Height: 22 cm

**257. Necklace**
Inv. No.: Ö.II.82.105
Early 19th century, Italian?
Gold with scarabaeus
Weight: 92.40 grams

**258. Mente belt**
Around 1810, Pest, Franciscus Máthé
Silver, gilded, with onyx cameo
Length: 65 cm

**259. Coffee pot**
Inv. No.: 1965.8

1811–1816, Losonc, Josephus Szentpétery (1781–1862)
Silver
Height: 28 cm, diameter at the base: 8.6 cm
Ref.: Kolba, J.–Németh, A.: *Ötvösművek* (Silversmiths' Work) p. 29

**260. Covered pan for hot milk**
Inv. No.: 1965.11
1818, Pest, Aloisius Giergl (active: 1817–1850)
Silver
Height: 17.5 cm, diameter: 17.5 cm

**261. Piano that belonged to Beethoven and then to Liszt**
Inv. No.: 1887.41.29
1817, London, John Broadwood (1732–1812) and Sons
Mahogany, varnished
Length: 247 cm, height: 92 cm, width: 115 cm
Ref.: Gábry, pp. 15, 35, Illustration 12

**262. Chest of a Pest guild of masons**
Inv. No.: 1950.5
First half of the 19th century
Maple wood, with poplar root marquetry
Length: 64.5 cm, height: 54 cm, width: 41 cm
Ref.: *MNM*, 1977, pp. 236–237

**263. Medal and coin cabinet of Count Ferenc Széchényi**
Inv. No.: 1954.485.1
Early 19th century
Palisander and maple marquetry
Height: 76 cm, width: 70 cm, depth: 36 cm
Ref.: *Magyarország története*, p. 79; *Három nemzedék*, p. 77

**264. The first seal of the Hungarian National Museum**
Inv. No.: P.1961.2891
First half of the 19th century
Bronze, engraved
Diameter: 4.5 cm
Ref.: Németh, A.: "A Nemzeti Múzeum első pecsétje" (The First Seal of the National Museum). *FA*, 16/1964. pp. 251–255

**265. Bowl**
Inv. No.: 1954.326
1819, Transylvania
Earthenware, tin glaze, view of Nagyvárad encircled by a legend
Diameter: 19 cm

**266. Sugar bowl**
Inv. No.: 1971.44
1822, Pest, Aloisus Giergl
Silver
Height: 18.5 cm, diameter: 21 x 12.5 cm

**267. Glass**
Inv. No.: 1968.87
1830s, Pest ?
Glass, Kothgasser-style, gilded, painted
Height: 11.5 cm

**268. Meerschaum pipe**
Inv. No.: D. 1974.108
First half of the 19th century
Meerschaum, ember, silver
Height: 10 cm

**269. Gentleman's Hungarian gala suit and boots**
Inv. No.: 53.52–54, 1928.5/, 1957.124.2
1838, Hungarian
Mente: black velvet and imitation black Persian lamb, gold and silver soutache; dolman: crimson velvet with similar soutache, silver buttons with pearls and almandines; black trousers, black leather boots embroidered in gold
Length of mente: 74 cm, length of dolman: 61 cm, length of trousers: 101 cm, size of boots: 44 cm
Ref.: *Hungarian Costume*, p. 24; *The Imperial Style*, p. 86, Illustration 56

**270. Imre Madách's desk**
Inv. No.: 1935.84
Walnut, varnished, marquetry
Height: 79 + 23.5 cm, width: 125 cm, depth: 70.5 cm
Ref.: *Kiegyezés*, p. 13; *Három nemzedék*, p. 142

**271. Desk**
Inv. No.: 1959.278
Middle of the 19th century, inscription: "Lajos Kossuth's director's desk at the Industrial Association"
Walnut, veneered, the engraved inscription is on a copper plate
Height: 99 cm, width: 115 cm, depth: 67 cm
Ref.: *Magyarország története*, p. 81; *Három nemzedék*, p. 63

**272. Seal of the National League**
Inv. No.: P.1870.86
1845
Brass, engraved
Diameter: 3.5 x 3 cm
Legend: EGYESÜLT, HOGY EGYESITSEN NEMZETI KÖR 1845 (United in Order to Unite. National League 1845)

**273. Prime Ministerial seal from the time of the first responsible Hungarian government**
Inv. No.: P.1870.86
1848
Diameter: 4 cm

Legend: MINISTERELNÖK PECSÉTJE 1848 (Seal of the Prime Minister, 1848)

**274. Count Lajos Batthyány's prime-ministerial chair**
Inv. No.: 1959.316
1830s–1840s
Wood, velvet upholstery on a wooden frame
Height: 120 cm, width: 70 cm, depth: 64 cm
Ref.: Jókai, M. (ed.): *Az 1848–49-iki magyar szabadságharc története képekben* (History of the 1948–1949 Hungarian War of Independence in Pictures). Budapest, 1898. p. 9; *1848. A MNM 1848–49-es centenáriumi kiállítása katalógusa* (1848. Catalogue of the Centennial Exhibition in the HNM). Budapest, 1948. p. 44; *Három nemzedék*, p. 38

**275. Teapot**
Inv. No.: 1953.540.1
1846, Herend
Porcelain, painted with the Dubarry design
Height: 16 cm

**276. Glass**
Inv. No.: 1976.120
1840–1870,
Upper Hungary, from the glass-works on the Pálffy estate ?
Glass, between the double layer silver-gilt foil on the front the coat-of-arms of the Pálffys

**277. Plate**
Inv. No.: 1963.108
1840s, Hungarian ?
The "wharf-market" and the now-demolished Lloyd Building are depicted in a transfer picture
Diameter: 22 cm

**278. Bottle**
Inv. No.: 1987.31
1858, Hungarian
Glass, blown, rubin coloured, with a genre scene ground on
Height: 35.5 cm

**279. Glass commemorating Pál Almásy's imprisonment at Olmütz**
Inv. No.: 1981.131.20
After 1865
Glass
Height: 16 cm, diameter: 9.8 cm

**280. Platter**
1850–1870, Tata
Faience, with painted Chinese scene
Diameter: 31.5 cm

**281. Episcopal pectoral cross**
Inv. No.: 1959.323

Middle of the 19th century, Hungarian ?
Gold, amethyst, with diamond
Height: 11.6 cm, width: 6.7 cm

**282. Armchair from the Upper House of Parliament**
Inv. No.: 1961.1461
Around 1860
Cast iron, with velvet upholstery Height: 145.5 cm, width: 66 cm, depth: 60 cm
Ref.: Lechner, Dr. J.: *A Magyar Nemzeti Múzeum épülete 1836–1926* (The Building of the Hungarian National Museum, 1836–1926). Pécs, 1927. p. 58 (on the picture a similar armchair is shown from Borsod county)

**283. The chairman's seat from the last dietal session in Transylvania**
Inv. No.: B.1974.9
1861
Walnut, lathe-turned, carved, with velvet upholstery
Height: 180 cm, width: 75 cm, depth: 70 cm
Ref.: *Kiegyezés*, 22

**284. Guitar of Kornelia Lotz**
Inv. No.: 1953.361
Late 19th century, Orense, Jose Fernandes Silva, painting by Károly Lotz (1833–1904)
Length: 71 cm, height: 8 cm, width: 23,5 cm
Ref.: Gábry, p. 20, Plate 24

**285. Freemason's watch pendant**
Inv. No.: 1981.131.1233
Late 19th century
Silver skull fastened by a ring, openable enamelled bijou with a medal set in a frame
No reference material

**286. Portraits of Mór Fischer and his wife**
Inv. No.: 1948.4–5
1898, Herend, Veszprém county
Porcelain
Height: 27 cm, width: 22.5 cm
Ref.: Veres, L.: "Festett herendi porcelánportrék a Magyar Nemzeti Múzeumban" (Painted Porcelain Portraits from Herend in the Hungarian National Museum). *FH*, 14/1988 pp. 51–66

**287. Pipe**
Inv. No.: D.1974.112
1896, Budapest, Adler
Meerschaum, silver
Length: 18 cm

**288. Seal of Franz Joseph I**
Inv. No.: 59.552
Second half of the 19th
century
Silver, engraved
Legend: Iö FERENCZ
JÓZSEF
I.K.AUST:CSASZAR.-
MAGYAR·
CSEH.DALM·HORV·
TOT·HOL·ES
LOD·ORSZ·AP·KIRA-
LYA·
AUS·FOHER·SAT

**289. Bodice formerly belonging to Queen Elizabeth of Hungary**
Inv. No.: 1956.530 1898
Black taffeta silk, black
maschine-made lace, and
Waist: 52 cm, length of
back: 32.5 cm
Ref.: *Erzsébet királyné
emlékmúzeum* (The Queen
Elizabeth Museum).
Budapest, 1908

**290. Armchair from Queen Elizabeth of Hungary's sitting-room furniture**
Inv. No.: 1959.288.1
Second half of the 19th
century
Walnut, carved, with atlas
silk upholstery
Height: 100 cm, width:
59 cm, depth: 65 cm
Ref.: *Három nemzedék*

**291. Chandelier from the former Royal Palace**
Inv. No.: 1961.287
Late 19th century,
Hungarian
Copper, gilded
Height: 46 cm

**292. Chalice**
Inv. No.: 1953.616
Late 19th century,
Budapest
Silver gilt, with basse-taille
enamels
Height: 26 cm, diameter at
the base: 16 cm

**293. Beaker with lid commemorating Lajos Kossuth**
Inv. No.: 1961.1809
1903, Budapest, designed
by Károly Csányi
(1873–1955), made by
Samu Hibán (1864–1919)
Silver, gilt, decorated with
filigree enamel and
precious stones
Height: 42 cm, diameter at
the base: 16 cm

**294. Broach**
Inv. No.: Ö.II.86.2
Around 1900, Vienna,
Gustav Nauthe
Gold, with pique d'ajour
enamel and pearl
Height: 4.5 cm

**295. Necklace**
Inv. No.: Ö.II.85.10
1902–1910, Budapest,
Wintermantel and

Szombathy
White gold, with cut
diamond and pearl
Length: 19 cm

**296. The flag of the "Progressio" masonic lodge**
Inv. No.: 1981.131.702
1911, Budapest
Length: 100 cm, width:
69 cm

**297. Freemason's watch**
Inv. No.: 1981.131.1236
Early 20th century, Swiss
hallmark
Silver, in a case
Diameter: 5 cm

**298. Model of a spring hammer** Inv. No.:
1961.2184
1910, Budapest, Ajax
Factory, today steelworks
Copper on marble base,
steel
Length of base: 20 cm,
width of base: 11 cm,
height: 18.5 cm

**299. Beaker of the "Világ" masonic lodge**
Inv. No.: 1981.131.1
1917
Metal, gilded, silver plated

**300. Beaker commemorating Imre Steindl**
Inv. No.: 1961.1370
1913, Budapest, Károly
Brachruch
Silver, with cloisonné
enamel and precious stones
Height: 33.5 cm, diameter
at the base: 17 cm

**301. Field marshal's baton**
Inv. No.: 57.6796
1917, Berlin
Silver, gilded, engraved,
velvet
Length: 49.5 cm

**302. Memorial bayonet**
Inv. No.: 57.6795
1918, Hungarian
Iron, engraved
Length: 36.2 cm

**303. Necklace**
Inv. No.: Ö.II.1985.2
1920, Budapest, Tivadar
Hirschmann
Gold, painted porcelain,
synthetic blue sapphire
Height: 38.5 cm

**304. Fashion design**
Inv. No.: T.1973.138
1933, Nagyajtai Teréz,
a design submitted for the
"Hungarian-style fashion"
tender
Aquarelle
Size: 30 x 44 cm

# Department of Coins and Medals

**305. Leontino. Tetradrachma**
Inv. No.: 7.A/1985–2
Around 440 B.C., Sicily
Silver
Weight: 17.30 grams
Ref.: Rizzo, Plate XXIV, 4

**306. Syracuse. Decadrachma**
Inv. No.: Delhaes 100
425–400 B.C., Sicily
Silver
Weight: 43.08 grams
Ref.: *SNG Copp.*, 690

**307. Tetradrachma. Sikelo-pun**
Inv. No.: 7.A/1985–1
Late 4th century B.C.,
Sicily
Silver
Weight: 16.63 grams
Ref.: *SNG Copp.*, 56.1977,
Plate 21, 261

**308. Thasos. Tetradrachma**
Inv. No.: 186/1936
2nd century B.C., Thrace
Silver
Weight: 16.97 grams Ref.:
*SNG Copp.*, 1038

**309. Croisos. Stater**
Inv. No.: 8.A/1912–1
561–546 B.C., Lydia
Gold
Weight: 8.05 grams
Ref.: *BMC*, 32

**310. Artaxerxes I. Dareikos**
Inv. No.: Kiss 412
465–425 B.C., Persian
Gold
Weight: 8.15 grams
Ref.: *BMC*, 48, Plate 24,
26

**311. Tetradrachma. Zichy-Újfalusi type**
Inv. No.: Dess.343
2nd century B.C., Celtic
Silver
Weight: 13.15 grams
Ref.: Dessewffy, 343

**312. Tetradrachma. Regöly type**
Inv. No.: R.I. 6097
1st century B.C., Celtic
Silver
Weight: 12.83 grams
Ref.: Dessewffy, 238

**313. Tetradrachma. Audoleon type**
Inv. No.: Dess. 380
2nd century B.C., Celtic,
Countermark on reverse
Silver
Weight: 13.09 grams
Ref.: Dessewffy, 380

**314. Tetradrachma. Noricum type**
Inv. No.: N.I. 4661
2nd–1st centuries B.C.,
Celtic
Silver

Weight: 9.52 grams
Ref.: Dessewffy, 160

**315. Tetradrachma with Apollon's portrait. Fertőrákos type**
Inv. No.: N.I. 4708
2nd-1st centuries B.C.,
Celtic
Silver
Weight: 12.25 grams
Ref.: Dessewffy, 105

**316. Tetradrachma. Alexandros type**
Inv. No.: Dess.316
3rd-2nd centuries B.C.,
Celtic
Silver
Weight: 16.34 grams
Ref.: Dessewffy, 316

**317. Barbarian tetradrachma. The so-called Transylvanian sciphatus (bowl-shaped type)**
Inv. No.: N.I. 5174
2nd-1st centuries B.C.
Silver
Weight: 11.55 grams
Ref.: Dessewffy, 820

**318. Barbarian tetradrachma. Thasostype**
Inv. No.: Dess. 404
1st century B.C.
Silver
Weight: 15.81 grams
Ref.: Dessewffy, 404

**319. Boi tetradrachma with the inscription BVSV**
Inv. No.: N.I. 4557
1st century B.C., Celtic
Silver
Weight: 17.04 grams
Ref.: Paulsen, 786

**320. Boi drachma. Tótfalusi type**
Inv. No.: N.I. 4585
1st century B.C., Celtic
Silver
Weight: 2.51 grams
Ref.: Paulsen, Plate C, 46

**321. Eraviskus denarius**
Inv. No.: 39/1967.59
1st century B.C., Celtic
Silver
Weight: 3.20 grams
Ref.: see Neudeck:
A quádok pénzei (Quad
Coins). *AÉ* 3/1883. 97, 23

**322. Tiberius. As**
Inv. No.: Weszerle 153
14–37
Bronze
Weight: 10.57 grams
Ref.: Cohen, 23

**323. Vitellius and Son. Denarius**
Inv. No.: N.I. 276
69
Silver
Weight: 3.43 grams
Ref.: see Cohen, 4, de
H./LIBERI IMP GERM
*AG*

**324. Faustina II. Sestertius**
Inv. No.: 46/1952.46
161–180
Bronze
Weight: 27.28 grams
Site: Zalahosszúfalu, Zala
county
Ref.: Cohen, 173

**325. Septimus Severus. Quinar**
Inv. No.: N.I. 894
193–211
Silver
Weight: 1.56 g, hybrid
Ref.: see Cohen, 612;
*BMC*, p. 180, "h"

**326. Clodius Albinus. As**
Inv. No.: N.I. 934
196–197
Bronze
Weight: 9.84 grams
Ref.: see Cohen, 18

**327. Plautilla. Denarius**
Inv. No.: Kiss 72
198–217
Silver
Weight: 3.17 grams
Ref.: Cohen, 10

**328. Paulina. Denarius**
Inv. No.: Delhaes 2122
235–238
Silver
Weight: 3.11 grams
Ref.: Cohen, 2

**329. Pacatianus. Antoninianus**
Inv. No.: 282/1872.40
248
Silver
Weight: 4.62 grams
Ref.: Cohen, 4

**330. Laelianus. Antoninianus**
Inv. No.: Delhaes 1230-VI
268
Bronze
Weight: 4.29 grams
Ref.: *RIC*, 9 (F)
Moguntiacum

**331. Magnia Urbica and Carinus quinarius**
Inv. No.: N.I. 1720
283–285
Bronze
Weight: 1.39 grams
Ref.: Cohen, 1

**332. Diocletianus. Denarius argenteus**
Inv. No.: Delhaes 1408-VI
284–305
Silver
Weight: 3.14 grams
Ref.: *RIC* 16 a, Aquileia

**333. Reduced follis. Alexander Tyrannis**
Inv. No.: 1A/1987.5
308–311, African
Bronze
Weight: 4.43 grams
Ref.: see *RIC*, 70

**334. Constantinus II. Medallion**
Inv. No.: 10A/1987

337–340
Bronze
Weight: 30.8 grams
Ref.: *RIC*, 344, Rome

**335. Valens. Centenionalis**
Inv. No.: 6A/1987
364–378
Bronze
Weight: 2.36 grams
Ref.: Cohen, 47

**336. Byzantine coin weight. Eighteen solidus**
Inv. No.: 67/1899
402–565
Bronze with silver inlay
Weight: 71.95 grams
Site: Fejér county
Ref.: Gohl, O.: "Bizánci súlyok" (Byzantine Weights). *NK*, 12/1913. p. 57, 2; Gohl, O.: "A Magyar Nemzeti Múzeum bizánci súlyai (Byzantine Weights in the Hungarian National Museum). *AÉ*, 21/1901. p. 195

**337. Contemporary imitation of an Antoninus Pius denarius**
Inv. No.: 51/1951.3
2nd century
Silver
Weight: 2.98 grams
Ref.: *AECO*, 1.5, 13

**338. Contemporary imitation of a fourth-century follis**
Inv. No.: R.I. 6769
Bronze
Weight: 10.48 grams

**339. Avar imitation of a Byzantine silver coin. Constans II**
Inv. No.: 6/1970
661–648
Silver
Weight: 3.75 grams
Site: Endrőd-Öregszőlő, Békés county
Ref.: Bíróné Sey, K.: "Újabb avar utánzatú ezüst-pénz a *MNM* éremgyűjteményében" (A New Avar Imitation of a Silver Coin in the Coin and Medal Collection of the Hungarian National Museum). *NK*, 76–77/1977–1978. Plate I, 1

**340. King Stephen denarius**
1010–1020, Esztergom (Székesfehérvár ?)
Silver
Weight: 1.09 grams
Ref.: *CNE*, vol. I, 7; Gedai, I.: *A magyar pénzverés kezdete* (The Beginning of Minting Money in Hungary). Budapest, 1986. pp. 96–98

**341. Imitation of a King Andrew I denarius**
Inv. No.: N. II. 44
Second half of the 11th century, North European
Silver

Weight: 0.56 grams
Ref.: Gedai, I.: "I. András király denárának utánverete" (Imitation of King Andrew I's Denarius). *NK*, 78–79/1979–1980. pp. 41–42

**342. Three-ducat gold coin issued by Ladislas V**
Inv. No.: 10 B/1928
1453–1457, Körmöcbánya (mint mark: K-A)
Gold
Weight: 11.7 grams
Ref.: *CNH*, vol. 2, 169

**343. Gold groat coin issued by Matthias I**
Inv. No.: 75/1933
1479–1485, Körmöcbánya (mint mark: K-B)
Gold
Weight: 42.23 grams
Ref.: *CNH*, vol. 2, 267A

**344. Guldiner coin issued by Ladislas II**
Inv. No.: Sz.I. 100.14
1500, Körmöcbánya
Gold
Weight: 42.23 grams
Ref.: *CNH*, vol. 2, 267A

**345. Essay plate of a Ferdinand I denarius**
Inv. No.: 16-B/1981–26
1526–1564, Körmöcbánya (mint mark: K-B)
Lead
Size: 20 x 14 cm
Ref.: Gedai, I.: "A Magyar Nemzeti Múzeum verőszerszám-gyűjteménye" (The Collection of Dies and Minting Tools in the Hungarian National Museum). *NK*, 84–85/1985–86. 49

**346. Three-ducat coin issued by Rudolph**
Inv. No.: 55B/1904–2
1580, Körmöcbánya (mint mark: K-B)
Gold Weight: 10.41 grams
Ref.: Huszár, 999

**347. Three-thaler coin issued by Matthias II**
Inv. No.: 6/1948–6
1611, Körmöcbánya (mint mark: K-B)
Silver
Weight: 85.28 grams
Ref.: Huszár, 1101

**348. Five-thaler coin issued by Ferdinand III**
Inv. No.: R.II.1210
1651, Körmöcbánya (mint mark: K-B)
Silver
Weight: 143.73 grams
Ref.: Huszár, 1231

**349. Three-ducat coin issued by Leopold I.**
Inv. No.: Sz.I.237–1
1661, Körmöcbánya (mint mark: K-B)
Gold

Weight: 14.4 grams
Ref.: Huszár, 1310

**350. Two-ducat coin issued by Leopold I.**
Inv. No.: P. 919
1684, Körmöcbánya (mint mark: K-B)
Gold
Weight: 6.88 grams
Ref.: Huszár, 1315

**351. Maria Theresa fifteen-kreutzer gold coin**
Inv. No.: 64/1937–26
1743, Nagybánya (mint mark: N-B)
Gold
Weight: 13.05 grams
Ref.: Huszár, 1647

**352. 10,000 crown weight**
Inv. No.: 9-B/1981
1902
Nickel
Weight: 3387.33 grams

**353. Design of the ten-crown coin of the Hungarian Republic of Councils**
Inv. No.: 69/1935
1919
Weight: 31.42 grams
Ref.: g-n: "A magyarországi Tanácsköztársaság 10 koronás pénzei" (Ten-crown Coins of the Hungarian Republic of Councils). *NK*, 21-22/1922–23. p. 39

**354. Two-pengő gold coin to commemorate Péter Pázmány**
Inv. No.: 67/1963
1935, Budapest, (mint mark: BP)
Gold
Weight: 19 grams
Ref.: Huszár, 2290/a

**355. Ten-ducat coin showing Count Miklós Esterházy**
Inv. No.: N.II.1852
1770, Vienna
Gold
Weight: 34.77 grams

**356. Ten-ducat coin issued by John Szapolyai**
Inv. No.: R.IV. 497
1540, Nagyszeben
Gold
Weight: 35.2 grams
Ref.: Resch, 33

**357. Double thaler issued by John Szapolyai**
Inv. No.: 26/1979
1565, Nagyszeben
Silver
Weight: 57.36 grams
Ref.: Resch, 50. variation

**358. Five-ducat coin issued by Zsigmond Báthori**
Inv. No.: 31/1896–62
1590, Nagyszeben
Gold Weight: 1753 grams
Ref.: Resch, 48

**359. Szeben ten-ducat coin**
Inv. No: R.IV. 498
1605, Nagyszeben
Gold
Weight: 32.4 grams
Ref.: Resch, 2a

**360. Ten-ducat coin issued by Mózes Székely**
Inv. No.: Sz.II. 21.1
1603, Negyszeben
Gold
Weight: 35.14 grams
Ref.: Resch, 1

**361. Six-ducat coin issued by Gábor Báthory**
Inv. No.: 31/1896–15
1613, Nagybánya (mint mark: N-B)
Gold
Weight: 20.48 grams
Ref.: Resch, 185

**362. Two-ducat coin issued by György Rákóczi I**
Inv. No.: 75B/1907–23
1632, Kolozsvár
Gold
Weight: 6.88 grams
Ref.: Resch, 7a

**363. Essay plates of a György Rákóczi thaler and denarius**
Inv. No.: 3B/1903–420
1653 and 1658, Nagybánya (mint mark: N-B)
Silver
Weight: 140 grams
Ref.: Resch, 125

**364. Crescent-shaped ten-ducat coin issued by Leopold I**
Inv. No.: 3B/1903–437
1694, Kolozsvár (mint mark: C-V)
Gold
Weight: 34.4 grams
Ref.: Resch, 5

**365. Ducat issued by Ferenc Rákóczi II**
Inv. No.: 50B/1917–108
1707, Kolozsvár (mint mark: K-V)
Gold
Weight: 3.46 grams
Ref.: Resch, 4

**366. Denarius of Bernhard, duke of Carinthia**
Inv. No.: L. 6/1974–249
First quarter of the 13th century, Landstrass
Silver
Weight: 0.98 grams
Site: Szigetcsép, Pest county
Ref.: Gedai, I.: "A szigetcsépi friesachi denárlelet" (The Friesach Denarius Hoard at Szigetcsép). *NK*, 74–75/1975–1976 p. 31

**367. Real issued by Maximilian I**
Inv. No.: Delhaes II. 91
1487, Vienna
Gold
Weight: 14.74 grams

**368. Three-ducat coin issued by Ladislas II**
Inv. No.: 3B/1903–116
Early 16th century, Bohemia
Gold
Weight: 10.24 grams
Ref.: CNH II. 285

**369. Hundred-ducat coin issued by Ferdinand III**
Inv. No.: 24/1962–26
1629, Bohemia
Gold
Weight: 350.5 grams
Ref.: Domanig, 550

**370. Hundred-ducat coin issued by Sigismund III, king of Poland**
Inv. No.: 24/1962–57 1621, Polish
Gold
Weight: 348.8 grams
Ref.: Hutten–Czapski, 1414

**371. Fifteen-ducat coin issued by Sigismund III, king of Poland**
Inv. No.: 7-B/1987–2
1614, Danzig (Gdansk, Poland)
Gold
Weight: 51.35 grams
Ref.: Hutten–Czapski, variation 1308

**372. Denarius issued by Juga, prince of Moldavia**
Inv. No.: 105/1887.I.1
1374, Moldavia
Silver
Weight: 1.15 grams

**373. Ducat issued by Heraclius, prince of Moldavia**
Inv. No.: 105/1887.I.195
1563, Suceava, Moldavia
Gold
Weight: 3.52 grams
Ref.: Luchian, O.–Buzdugan, G.–Oprescu, C.: *Monede si bancnote romanesti* (Romanian Coins and Banknotes). Bucureşti, 1977. No. 797

**374. The Wass-Molitor Company's fifty-dollar coin**
Inv. No.: 11/1856
1855, San Francisco
Gold
Weight: 83.56 grams
Ref.: Friedberg, R.: *Gold Coins of the World*. New York, 1958. No. 190

**375. The marriage of Maximilian I and Mary of Burgundy. Medallion**
Inv. No.: Delhaes XI. 7
1479, Gianmarco Cavallo (after 1454-before 1511)
Silver, beaten
Diameter: 42 mm
Ref.: Stpl I. 1

**376. Piefort of Maximilian I. Medallion.**
Inv. No.: Delhaes 9
1519, Hall
Silver, beaten
Diameter: 46 mm
Ref.: Domanig, II. Plate 13

**377. Portrait issued by Tamás Bakócz. Medallion**
Inv. No.: 17/880
No date, (around 1512), Italian
Cast bronze
Diameter: 65 mm
Ref.: Hill:
*A Corpus of Italian Medals of the Renaissance before Cellini*. London, 1930. p. 857

**378. Portrait of Martin Luther. Medallion**
Inv. No.: 26A/914–42
1521, monogram: HG
Silver, cast
2Diameter: 59 mm
Ref.: Habich I. 1, 721

**379. Louis II. Relief**
Inv. No.: 27C/1980–1
1526, school of Hans Daucher (around 1485–1538)
Alabaster
Diameter: 61 mm
Ref.: Habich I. 1, 97

**380. Queen Mary of Hungary. Relief**
Inv. No.: 27.C/1980–2
1526, school of Hans Daucher
Alabaster
Diameter: 61.5 mm
Ref.: Habich, I. 1, 97

**381. Biblical medal from Joachimstal. Last Supper-Last Judgement**
Inv. No.: N. III. 463
1546, Nickel Milicz (active: 1539–1575)
Silver, beaten
Diameter: 55 mm
Ref.: Katz, 346, Plate XLVIII, 6

**382. Biblical medal from Joachimstal. The Temptation–The Expulsion**
Inv. No.: Ebenhöch 4461
1549, Nickel Milicz
Silver, beaten
Diameter: 62 mm
Ref.: Katz, 355

**383. Portrait of Gianbattista Castaldo. Medallion**
Inv. No.: 39/880
No date, Cesare da Bagno
Bronze, cast
Diameter: 74 mm
Ref.: Resch, 217, Plate 10

**384. Biblical medal from Körmöcbánya. The Temptation–The Expulsion-The Adoration of the Shepherds**
Inv. No.: Delhaes I. 41
1565, Lucas Richter
Silver, beaten

Diameter: 61 mm
Ref.: Huszár–Procopius, 47

**385. Portrait of Maximilian II. Medallion**
Inv. No.: 133/874–3
1566, Jakob Stampfer (1505–1579)
Silver, beaten
Diameter: 51 mm
Ref.: Stpl. I. 55

**386. Portraits of Ferdinand I, Maximilian II and Mary. Medallion**
Inv. No.: Sz. I. 132. 3
1577, Lucas Richter
Silver, beaten
Diameter: 35 mm
Ref.: Huszár–Procopius, 59

**387. Portraits of Rudolph II and Prince Ernst. Medallion**
Inv. No.: Weszerle 89
No date, Antonio Abondio (1538–1591
Silver, cast
Diameter: 35 mm
Ref.: Habich, II. 2. 3418

**388. Portrait of Rudolf II. Medallion**
Inv. No.: Delhaes 96
No date (around 1582), Antonio Abondio
Silver, cast
Diameter: 47 mm
Ref.: Habich, II 2. 3419

**389. Portrait of David Hohenberger. Medallion**
Inv. No.: 266/881–4
1593, Joachim Elsholtz (active: 1579–1602)
Silver, beaten
Diameter: 37 mm
Ref.: Huszár–Procopius, 84

**390. Portrait of Georg Basta. Medallion**
Inv. No.: Sz. II. 233
1605, Master NW
Silver, beaten
Size: 35 x 41 mm
Ref.: Huszár–Procopius, 84

**391. Matthias II riding a horse. Medallion**
Inv. No.: R. III. 142
No date, (around 1612), Christian Maler (1578–1652)
Silver, beaten
Diameter: 51.5 mm
Ref.: Forrer, III. 541

**392. Portrait of Catherine of Brandenburg. Medallion**
Inv. No.: N. III. 1749
No date
Gold, cast
Size: 44x 42 cm
Ref.: Resch, 226.77. 66T 77

**393. The Peace of Westfalia. Medallion**
Inv. No: R. III. 484
1649, Sebastian Dadler (1586–1657)
Silver, beaten
Diameter: 78 mm
Ref.: Forrer, I. 321

**394. Death of Ferdinand III. Medallion**
Inv. No.: Delhaes 160
1657
Silver, beaten
Diameter: 45 mm

**395. Coronation ceremony of Joseph I, king of Hungary. Medallion**
Inv No.: Delhaes XI. 334
1687, Martin Brunner (1659–1725)
Silver, beaten
Diameter: 74 mm
Ref.: Gohl, 8. 3

**396. Homage paid by Transylvania at the coronation ceremony of Maria Theresa. Medallion**
3.A./1904–1
1741, Joseph Wellisch (1718–1761)
Silver, beaten
Diameter: 70 mm
Ref.: Probst, 32. XXV

**397. Maria Theresa's medal issued on the occasion of founding the Royal Hungarian Order of St. Stephen**
Inv. No.: Sz. I. 374.125
1764, Aloisius Wideman (1724–1792)
Silver, beaten
Diameter: 40.5 mm
Ref.: Stpl, II. 888

**398. Cross of the Royal Hungarian Order of St Stephen**
Inv. No.: 14/951–130
First half of the 19th century
Gold, silver, enamel
Ref.: Kassics, III. Plate IV

**399. Chain of the Order of Leopold**
Inv No.: 40. C/986
Late 19th century
Gold, silver, enamel
Ref.: Kassics, Plate V

**400. Coronation ceremony of Queen Elizabeth of Hungary. Medallion**
Inv. No.: Delhaes I 436
1867, Joseph Tautenhayn (1837–1911)
Silver, beaten
Diameter: 49 mm
Ref.: Stpl, II. 2445

**401. Medallion issued in commemoration of the death of Hans von Bülow**
Inv. No.: 46/961–5
1894, Anton Scharff (1845–1903)
Silver, beaten
Diameter: 59 mm
Ref.: Forrer, V. 369

**402. Kelemen Mikes. Medallion**
Inv. No.: 27 A/912–3
No date (1908), Fülöp Ö. Beck (1873–1945)
Silver, beaten
Diameter: 60 mm

Ref.: Huszár–Procopius, 859

**403. Sándor Körösi Csoma. Medallion**
Inv. No.: 20A/1910
No date (1909), Lajos Beran (1882–1943)
Silver, beaten
Diameter: 60 mm
Ref.: Huszár–Procopius, 1117

**404. Portrait of Konrad Röntgen. Medallion**
Inv. No.: 45.A/923
1923, Erzsébet Esseö (1883–1954)
Cast bronze
Diameter: 82 mm

## Historical Gallery

**405. View of Buda from the Shedel Chronicle**
1492
Inv. No.: 57.88
Woodcut on paper
24.2 x 53 cm
Ref.: Rózsa, 1963. No. 86

**406. View of Esztergom**
by an unknown master, after a drawing by Jakob Hoefnagel (1575–1630)
1590s
Ref. No.: 53.855
Etching on paper
35 x 52 cm
Ref.: Leopold, A.:
*Esztergom régi látképei* (Old Views of Esztergom). Budapest, 1944. No. 19; *MNM*, 1977. pp. 296–297

**407. Portrait of István Báthory**
by Jobst Amman (1539–1591)
1576
Inv. No.: 9792
18.2 x 12.9 (cut around the edges)
Ref.: Komornicki, E. S.:
*Essai d'une iconographie du roi Etienne Báthory Roi de Pologne, Prince de Transsylvanie.* Cracovie, 1935. p. 428, 433

**408. The Recapture of Győr, 1598**
by Franz Hogenberg (before 1540–1590)
1590s
Ref. No.: 81.185
Etching on paper
20 x 27.1 cm (cut around the edges)
Ref.: *W. Drugulin's Historischer Bilderatlas.* Leipzig, 1867. No. 76

**409. Footsoldiers' Attack in Tolna, 1599**
by Johann Sibmacher (+1611)
1600
Inv. No.: T.974
Etching on paper
26.5 x 32 cm (cut around

the edges)
Ref.: Cennerné, p. 111

**410. View of Buda from the North**
by Wilhelm Dilich (1571/1572–1650)
1600
Inv. No.: 71.30
Etching on paper
10 x 19.9 cm
Ref.: Rózsa, 1963. No. 40

**411. Portrait of Miklós Zrinyi, the Hero of Szigetvár**
by Domanicus Custos (after 1550–1612), after a drawing by Giovanni Battista Fontana (after 1524–1587)
1601
Inv. No.: 9421
Engraving on paper
42.5 x 29.1
Ref.: Cenner-Wilhelmb, G.: "Der Augsburger Kupferstecher Dominicus Custos und Ungarn". *FA* 18/1966–1967. pp. 243–245

**412. View of Győr**
by an unknown master, after a drawing by Nicole Aginelli (second half of the 16th century)
1590s
Inv. No.: T.5571
Etching on paper
37 x 52.5 cm
Ref.: Bachmann, p. 202, No. 1731

**413. View of Kassa**
by an unknown master, after a drawing by Agid de Rye (d. 1605)
1617
Inv. No.: T.5883
Etching on paper
30.5 x 54 cm (cut around the edges)
Ref.: Bachmann, p. 78, No. 0397

**414. View of Eger**
by an unknown master (early 17th century)
1617
Inv. No.: T.2085
Etching on paper
32.5 x 45 cm
Ref.: Bachmann, p. 110, No. 0744

**415. Portrait of Gábor Bethlen**
by Egidius Sadeler (1570–1629)
1620
Inv. No.: 776
Engraving on paper
28 x 18 cm
Ref.: Rózsa, Gy.: "Ein unbekanntes Werk von Egidius Sadeler". *FA* 21/1970. pp. 169–176

183

**416. Portrait of Péter Pázmány**
by György Szelepcsényi (1595–1685)
Second quarter of the 16th century
Ref. No.: 84.39
Engraving on paper
24.6 x 16.6 cm
Ref.: Vayer, L.: *Pázmány Péter ikonográfiája* (The Iconography of Péter Pázmány). Budapest, 1935. p. 23; Vayer, L.: *Szelepcsényi György, a művész* (György Szelepcsényi, the Artist). Budapest, 1937. pp. 9–11

**417. Portrait of Gáspár Lippay**
by Elias Widemann (1619–1652)
1649
Inv. No.: 2936
Engraving on paper
15.1 x 11.2 cm
Ref.: Cenner-Wilhelmb, G.: "Über die ungarischen Porträtfolgen von Elias Widemann". *Acta HistArt*, 4/1957. p. 332, 345

**418. Turkish–Hungarian combat**
by Isaac Major (c. 1576–1630)
First quarter of the 17th century
Inv. No.: 58.3846
Etching on paper
18.7 x 28.2 cm
Ref.: Rózsa, Gy.: *Magyar történetábrázolás a 17. században* (Hungarian Historical Representations in the 17th Century). Budapest, 1973. p. 117

**419. Gáspár Illésházy on his catafalque**
by an unknown master from the 17th century 1648
Inv. No.: 30
Oil on canvas
136 x 221 cm
Ref.: Pigler, A.: "Portraying the Dead". *Acta HistArt*, 4/1957, pp. 59–60, 63

**420. View of Pozsony**
by an unknown master from the 17th century
1650
Inv. No.: T.2390
Etching on paper
24.6 x 34.8 cm
Ref.: Bachmann, p. 201, No. 1714

**421. View of Tokaj**
by Kaspar Merian (1627–1686), after a drawing by Lukas Georg Saicha
Middle of the seventeenth century
Inv. No.: 961
Etching on paper
19.8 x 26.2 cm
Ref.: Fauser, A.: *Repertorium älterer*

*Topographie*. Wiesbaden, 1978. No. 14020

**422. View of Hatvan**
by Wenzel Hollar (1607–1677)
1657
Inv. No.: T.2303
Etching on paper
34.8 x 47.8 cm

**423. Portrait of Miklós Zrínyi**
by Gerard Bouttats (middle of the 17th century) after a drawing by Johannes Thomas (1617–1678)
1663–1664
Inv. No.: 9423
Engraving on paper
33 x 23.5 cm
Ref.: Cennerné Wilhelmb, G.: "Zrínyi Miklós, a költő arcképeinek ikonográfiája" (The Iconography of the Poet Miklós Zrínyi's Portraits). *FA* 16/1964. No. XIV.

**424. Portrait of Imre Thököly**
by Pieter Stevens (second half of the 17th century) after a drawing by David van der Plaas (1647–1704)
1680s
Inv. No.: 4347
Engraving on paper
37 x 27,6 cm
Ref.: Cennerné Wilhelmb, G.: "Thököly Imre és szabadságharca az egykorú grafikában" (Imre Thököly and His Fight for Freedom as Seen in the Drawings of His Time). In: Köpeczi B.: *Magyarország a kereszténység ellensége* (Hungary, the Enemy of Christianity). Budapest, 1976. p. 361, No. 25

**425. Portrait of Kristóf Batthyány**
by an unknown painter (middle of the 17th century)
Middle of the seventeenth century
Inv. No.: 570
Oil on canvas
234 x 170 cm
Ref.: Rózsa, p. 197, No. 7

**426. The Siege of Esztergom**
Justus van den Nypoort (c. 1625–c. 1694) and Johann Martin Lerch (second half of the 17th century)
1683
Inv. No.: T.1270
Etching on paper
36.3 x 50.1 cm
Ref.: Rózsa, Gy.: *Schlachtenbilder aus der Zeit der Befreiungsfeldzüge*. Budapest, 1987. p. 26

**427. Medical consultation at the bedside of the Sultan**
Caricature from the age of the freedom fights against the Ottoman Empire by

Philibert Bouttats (second half of the 17th century)
1686
Inv. No.: 4301
Etching and copperplate engraving on paper
36 x 50.5 cm (cut around the edges)
Ref.: *W. Drugulin's Historischer Bilderatlas*, No. 3198

**428. The Siege of Buda, 1686**
by an unknown master (second half of the 17th century)
1686
Inv. No.: 106
Etching on paper
18.3 x 29.7 cm
Ref.: Rózsa, 1963. No. 59

**429. Detail from the siege of Buda, 1686**
by Michel Wening (1645–1718) after a drawing by L.N. de Hallart (second half of the 17th century)
1686
Inv. No.: T.3928
Etching on paper 33 x 57 cm
Ref.: Rózsa, Gy.: *Schlachtenbilder aus der Zeit der Befreiungsfeldzüge*. Budapest, 1987. p. 22

**430. Battle of Nagyharsány. 1687**
by Romeyn de Hooghe (1645–1708)
1687
Inv. No.: T.1283
Etching and engraving on paper
44.5 x 59.8 cm
Ref.: Rózsa, Gy.: "Romeyn de Hooghe und die Türkenkriege in Ungarn". *Oud-Holland* 77/1962. p. 104, 108

**431. Allegory of the successful wars for freedom**
by Jan Onghers (1656?–c. 1735)
after 1699
Inv. No.: 11.176
Indian ink and wash on paper
60.6 x 44.2 cm
Ref.: Cennerné, pp. 178–179

**432. Portrait of Ferenc Rákóczi II**
by Ádám Mányoki (1673–1757)
1708
Inv. No.: 65.8
Oil on canvas 77 x 55 cm
Ref.: *Mányoki Ádám emlékkiállítás katalógusa* (Catalogue of the Ádám Mányoki Memorial Exhibition). Budapest, 1957. No. 9

**433. Kuruc horseman**
by Georg Philipp Rugendas the Elder

(1666–1742)
Early 18th century
Ref. No.: 56.1340
Mezzotint on paper
46.8 x 36.1 cm
Ref.: Cennerné, p. 187

**434. View of Esztergom**
by Johann Christoph Leopold (1690–1755) after a drawing by Bernhard Werner (1690–1778)
1740s
Inv. No.: T.3878
Engraving and etching on paper
20.6 x 30.2
Ref.: Rózsa, 1974. No. 18

**435. View of Sopron**
by Johann Christoph Leopold after a drawing by Bernhard Werner
1740s
Inv. No.: T.3895
Etching and engraving on paper
20.4 x 30 cm
Ref.: Rózsa, 1974. No. 15

**436. View of Székesfehérvár**
by Johann Christoph Leopold after a drawing by Bernhard Werner
1740s
Inv. No.: T.3891
Etching and engraving on paper
20.3 x 29.8 cm
Ref.: Rózsa, 1974. No. 20

**437. View of Veszprém**
by Johann Christoph Leopold after a drawing by Bernhard Werner
1740s
Inv. No.: T.1009
Etching and engraving on paper
20.3 x 30.4 cm
Ref.: Rózsa, 1974. No. 21

**438. Maria Theresa's coronation procession in Pozsony, 1740**
by Johann Daniel Herz (1693–1745)
c. 1740
Inv. No.: 2105
Engraving on paper
68.7 x 93.2 cm (cut around the edges)

**439. The wife of a hussar officer from the time of the War of Austrian Succession**
by Martin Engelbrecht (1684–1756)
1740s
Inv. No.: T.6754
Coloured engraving on paper
29 x 18.5 cm (cut around the edges)

**440. Portrait of Kristóf Migazzi**
by Franz Anton Palko (born in 1717)
second half of the 18th century
Inv. No.: 73.2
Oil on canvas

92 x 74 cm
Ref.: Pötzl-Malikova, M.: "Zum Porträtwerk Franz Anton Palkos". *Művtört.Ért.* 25/1986, p. 15, 18

**441. View of Buda from the East**
by Johann Ernst Mansfeld (1739–1796) after the work of Johann Jacob Meyer (1749–1829)
1777
Inv. No.: T.2517
Etching and engraving on paper
52.9 x 82.3 cm (cut around the edges)
Ref.: Rózsa, 1963. No. 94

**442. Allegory of the Patent issued by Joseph II**
by Johann Friedrich Beer (1740–1804)
1782
Inv. No.: 10708
Etching on paper
33.1 x 21.4 cm
Ref.: Cennerné, p. 245

**443. View of Pozsony**
by Joseph and Peter Schaffer (active 1780-1810)
1787
Inv. No.: T.53.895
Coloured etching on paper
33.4 x 44.5 cm
Ref.: Pataky, D.: *A magyar rézmetszés története* (The History of Copperplate Engraving in Hungary). Budapest, 1951. p. 216, No.2

**444. Portrait of András Hadik**
by Johann Peter Pichler (1765–1807), after a work by Georg Weikert (1745–1799)
1789
Inv. No.: 2020
Mezzotint on paper 38.5 x 27 cm
Ref.: Cennerné Wilhelmb, G.: "Hadik András ikonográfiája" (The Iconography of András Hadik). *FH* 13/1987. p. 36

**445. The inauguration of Lord Lieutenant Antal Esterházy at Esterháza, 1791**
by Berkeny János (c. 1765–1822) after a drawing by Carl Schütz (1745–1800)
1791
Inv. No.: 3/1935.Gr.
Coloured etching on paper
34,4 x 47.1 cm
Ref.: Cennerné, p. 217

**446. The execution of Martinovics and his associates on the Vérmező, 1795**
by an unknown master at the end of the 18th century
1795
Inv. No.: 59.76

Gouache on paper
49.8 x 67.5 cm
Ref.: Cennerné, p. 251

**447. The Marczibányi mansion in Tornya**
Sámuel Czetter (1765–?), after a drawing by István Marczibányi (end of the 18th century)
1787
Inv. No.: T.1120
Coloured etching on paper
26 x 32 cm
Ref.: Rózsa, 1953. No. 22

**448. Portrait of Sándor Bárótzi**
by Sámuel Czetter
1797
Inv. No.: 843
Stipple engraving on paper
19.6 x 12 cm (cut aroud the edges)
Ref.: Rózsa, 1853. No. 26

**449. Portrait of Count Ferenc Széchényi**
by Sámuel Czetter
1798
Inv. No.: 117
Stipple engraving on paper
20.5 x 13 cm
Ref.: Rózsa, 1953. No. 53

**450. The Tarpatak Falls in the Tatra Mountains**
by Johann Ziegler (c1750–1812), after a drawing by Schrött Erasmus (1755–1804)
1799
Inv. No.: 62.54 Coloured etching on paper
46.2 x 29.8 cm (cut around the edges)
Ref.: *Művészet, 1780–1843.* No. 4

**451. Portrait of Ferenc Kazinczy**
Friedrich John (1769–1843), after a work by Vinzenz Georg Kininger (1767–1851)
1804
Inv. No.: 64
Stipple engraving on paper
20.4 x 18 cm
Ref.: Rózsa, Gy.: "Kazinczy Ferenc a müvészetben" (Ferenc Kazinczy in Art). *Művtört.Ért.* 6/1957. No. 4

**452. Portrait of Mihály Csokonai Vitéz**
by Friedrich John, after the work of János Eröss (early 19th century)
After 1805
Inv. No.: 4590
Stipple engraving on paper
16.7 x 12.7 cm
Ref.: Rózsa, G.: "Friedrich John und die Schriftsteller der Aufklärung in Ungarn". *Acta HistArt* 4/1957. pp. 150–151

**453. Portrait of Count Ferenc Barkóczy**
by Peter Krafft (1780–1856) 1812
Inv. No.: 2221
Oil on canvas
180 x 127 cm
Ref.: Rózsa, 1977. No. 32

**454. View of Kecskemét on a certificate of a master**
by Ferenc Karacs (1771–1838), after a drawing by János Szokolai Hartó (1781–1853)
After 1814
Inv. No.: 56.297
Engraving on paper
39.4 x 52.5 cm
Ref.: *Művészet, 1780–1830.* No. 9

**455. Portrait of Benedek Virág**
by János Donát (1744–1830)
1815
Inv. No.: 92
Oil on canvas
59 x 49 cm
Ref.: *MTKCS Catalogue,* No. 345

**456. A peasant and a maidservant from Pest county**
by Kilian Ponheimer (1757–1828), after a drawing by Joseph Bikkessy-Heinbucher (first half of the 19th century) and János Blaschke (1770–1833)
1810s
Inv. No.: 59.217
Coloured etching on paper
25 x 19 cm
Ref.: Kresz, p. 107, Plate 2

**457. Portrait of János Bihari**
by János Donát
1820
Inv. No.: 110
Oil on canvas
57.8 x 47.5 cm
Ref.: *Művészet, 1780–1830.* No. 113

**458. Portrait of Colonel József Simonyi**
by an unknown master (early 19th century)
early 19th century
Inv. No.: 829
Oil on canvas
73 x 58 cm
Ref.: *MTKCS Catalogue,* No. 336

**459. View of Mohács**
by Adolph Kunike (1777–1838), after a drawing by Jacob Alt (1789–1872)
1820s
Inv. No.: T.2333
Lithograph on paper
37 x 49.5 cm
Ref.: Nebehay, I.–Wagner, R.: *Bibliographie alterösterreichischer*

*Ansichtenwerke aus fünf Jahrhunderten.* Graz, 1981–1985. No. 336/157

**460. Horse-racing in Pest. 1827**
by János Schmid (first half of the 19th century), after a drawing by Johann Gottlieb Prestel (1804–1885) and Sándor Clarot (1796-1842)
1827
Inv. No.: T.2204
Coloured lithograph on paper
42.3 cm x 66.4 cm
Ref.: Gerszi, T.: *A magyar kőrajzolás története a XIX. században* (The Nineteenth-Century History of Lithography in Hungary). Budapest, 1960. p. 199, No. 49

**461. Blasting at the Iron Gate**
by A. Mink (active in the 1830s), after a drawing by József Lántz (first half of the 19th century)
1833
Ref. No.: T.1470
Lithograph on paper
55 x 69 cm
Ref.: Gerszi, T.: *A magyar kőrajzolás története a XIX. században* (The Nineteenth-Century History of Lithography in Hungary). Budapest, 1960. p. 184, No. 2

**462. Kálvin Square during the flood in 1838**
by Franz Collar (first half of the 19th century)
1838
Ref. No.: 58.2864
Engraving on paper
25.4 x 34.5 cm
Ref.: *Jégszakadás és Duna kiáradása Pest-Buda, 1838* (The Bursting of the Danube's Banks and the Flood in Pest-Buda, 1838). Budapest, 1988. No. 151

**463. Portrait of András Fáy**
by Adám Ehenreich (c. 1784–1852)
1820s
Inv. No.: 6568
Engraving on paper
24.9 x 17.7 cm
Ref.: Pataky, D.: *A magyar rézmetszés története* (The History of Engraving in Hungary). Budapest, 1951. p. 111, No. 59

**464. Portrait of the Palatine Joseph**
by Anton Einsle (1801–1871)
1840
Inv. No.: 480
Oil on canvas
65 x 53 cm
Ref.: *MTKCS Catalogue,* No. 529

**465. The Vigadó building in Pest**
by Franz Xaver Sandmann (1805–1856), after a drawing by Rudolf von Alt (1812–1905)
1845
Inv. No.: T.3430
Lithograph on paper
14.7 x 19.6 cm
Ref.: Schoen, No. 219

**466. Portrait of Franz Liszt**
by Miklós Barabás (1810–1896)
1847
Inv. No.: 178
Oil on canvas
132 x 102 cm
Ref.: Rózsa, 1977. No. 39

**467. Portrait of Count István Széchényi**
by Miklós Barabás
1848
Inv. No.: 1470 Oil on canvas
66 x 52,5 cm
Ref.: Vayer, L.: "Széchényi képe" (A Picture of Széchényi). *Magyarságtudomány*, 1942. p. 107, No. 18

**468. Portrait of Sándor Petőfi**
by Miklós Barabás
1848
Inv. No.: 3652
Lithograph on paper
47 x 31.5 cm
Ref.: Rózsa, Gy.: "Petőfi Sándor képmásai" (Portraits of Sándor Petőfi). *Irodalomtörténet,* 1951. p. 213, No. 7

**469. The flight of Metternich.**
Caricature by an unknown Austrian master (middle of the 19th century)
1848
Inv. No.: 54.366
Coloured copperplate engraving on paper
25.5 x 17.8 cm

**470. The distribution of the first publications of free press in Pest. March 15, 1848**
by Vinzenz Katzler (1823–1882)
1848 Inv. No.: T.2208
Lithograph on paper
26.7 x 19.5 cm

**471. Portrait of Richárd Guyon**
by János Perger (middle of the 19th century)
1848
Inv. No.: 601
Aquarelle on paper
55.5 x 45 cm
Ref.: Rózsa - Spira, No. 577

**472. Portrait of Lajos Kossuth**
by August Prinzhofer (1817–1885)

1848
Inv. No.: 8408
Lithograph on paper
49.7 x 35.1 cm
Ref.: Rittershausen, G.: *August Prinzhofer.* Wien–Bad Bocklet–Zürich, 1962. No. 135

**473. Portrait of József Bem**
by Miklós Barabás
1849
Inv. No.: 10857
Pencil and wash on paper
28 x 24 cm
Ref.: Rózsa - Spira, No. 511

**474. Portrait of Artúr Görgey**
by Miklós Barabás
1849
Inv. No.: 10836
Pencil on paper
41.8 x 30.8 cm
Ref: Rózsa - Spira, No. 475

**475. A group of horseherds**
by an unknown master (middle of the 19th century)
1849
Inv. No.: 2/1917.R
Pencil and white lead
14.5 x 20.9 cm
Ref.: Cennerné, 315

**476. Hussars breaking out from Komárom. February 24, 1849**
by Vinzenz Katzler
1849
Inv. No.: T.440
Lithograph on paper
31 x 40 cm
Ref.: Rózsa–Spira, No. 562

**477. Battle of Szolnok. March 5, 1849**
by Miklós Szerelmey (1803–1875) after a drawing by Charles de Fer 1850
Inv. No.: T.2999
Lithograph on paper
44 x 58.5 cm
Ref.: Gosztola, A.: "Szerelmey Miklós litográfus" (Miklós Szerelmey, Lithographer). *Művtört.Ért.* 34/1985. p. 25

**478. Battle of Isaszeg. April 6, 1949**
by Mór Than (1828–1899)
early 1850s
Inv. No.: T.6684
Water-colour on paper
28 x 40 cm
Ref.: Cennerné Wilhelmb, G.: *Than Mór.* Budapest, 1982. No. 27

**479. The Recapture of Buda. May 21, 1849**
by August Pettenkofen (1822–1889)
1849
Inv. No.: T.363
Lithograph on paper
33.5 x 44 cm

Ref.: Rózsa–Spira,
No. 676

**480. Portrait of László
Józsefné de Caux Mimi**
by Miklós Barabás
1850 Inv. No.: 831
Oil on canvas
76 x 60.5 cm
Ref.: Szvoboda, G.:
*Barabás Miklós.* No. 99

**481. Self-portrait**
by Frigyes Lieder
(1780–1859)
1850
Inv. No.: 127
Oil on canvas
100 x 77 cm
Ref.: *Művészet, 1830–1870.*
No. 346

**482. Portrait of Lázár
Mészáros**
by Károly Brocky
(1807–1855)
c. 1850
Inv. No.: 431
Oil on canvas
61 x 51.5 cm
Ref.: Lajta, E.: *Brocky
Károly.* Budapest, 1984.
No. 121

**483. Portrait of Gereben
Vas**
by Agost Canzi
(1808–1866)
Around 1850
Inv. No.: 1423
Oil on canvas
90 x 70 cm
Ref.: *Művészet, 1830–1870.*
No. 311

**484. Szentháromság tér in
Buda**
by Franz Xaver
Sandmann, after a drawing
by Rudolf von Alt
1850s
Inv. No.: T.4042
Coloured lithograph on
paper
19.2 x 26.3 cm Ref.:
Schoen, No. 308

**485. Portrait of Imre
Székely**
by Bálint Kiss (1802–1868)
1851
Inv. No.: 180
Oil on canvas
98 x 77 cm
Ref.: Zádor, A.: "Kiss
Bálint". In: *A Magyar
Művészettörténeti
Munkaközösség Évkönyve.*
Budapest, 1953. p. 40

**486. Prison cell in Olmütz**
by Lénárd Berzsenyi
(middle of the 19th century)
Around 1850
Inv. No.: 53.277
Oil on cardboard
23.5 x 61 cm
Ref.: *Művészet, 1830–1870.*
No. 168

**487. The shore of the
Danube**
by Franz Xaver

Sandmann, after a drawing
by Rudolf von Alt
1850s
Inv. No.: T.4025
Coloured lithograph on
paper
18.8 x 25.6 cm
Ref.: Schoen, No. 291

**488. Shepherd from the
Great Plain**
by Théodore Valérie
(1819–1879)
1853
Inv. No.: T.6822
Etching on paper
18.3 x 13.4 cm
Ref.: Cennerné Wilhelmb,
G.: "Théodore Valérie
Magyarországon"
(Théodore Valérie in
Hungary). *FH* 6/1978. p.
55, 63

**489. Detail of Balatonfüred**
by Rudolf von Alt after
a drawing by Károly Lajos
Libay (1816–1888)
1850s
Inv. No.: T.6469
Lithograph on paper
23.1 x 30.1 cm

**490. Portrait of Ferenc
Erkel**
by Alajos Györgyi-Giergl
(1821–1863)
1855
Inv. No.: 210
Oil on canvas
132 x 98 cm
Ref.: *Művészet, 1830–1870.*
No. 317

**491. View of Miskolc**
by Johann Poppel
(1807–1882) after
a drawing by Ludwig
Rohbock (middle of the
19th century)
1850s
Inv. No.: T.3186
Steel engraving on paper
16.8 x 22.8 cm
Ref.: Rózsa, 1986

**492. Portrait of Mihály
Horváth**
by Bertalan Székely
(1835–1910)
1860s
Inv. No.: 173
Oil on canvas
27 x 20 cm
Ref.: *Magyar írók
arcképei. A Petőfi Irodalmi
Múzeum kiállítása*
(Portraits of Hungarian
Writers. Exhibition in the
Petőfi Museum of
Literature). Budapest,
1960. p. 10

**493. Portrait of Miklós Izsó**
by Bertalan Székely
1860s
Inv. No.: 825
Oil on canvas
56 x 43 cm
Ref.: *Művészet, 1830–1870.*
No. 361

**494. Portrait of Géza
Mészöly**
by Béla Pállik (1845–1908)
1872
Inv. No.: 535
Oil on canvas
79 x 67 cm
Ref.: Rózsa, 1977. No. 47

**495. Portrait of Gyula
Andrássy**
by Bertalan Székely
1872
Inv. No.: 1606
Oil on canvas
58 x 42.5 cm
Ref.: *Das Zeitalter Kaiser
Franz Josephs*, No. 21.2

**496. Portrait of Lajos
Kossuth**
by Vilma Parlaghy
(1864–1923) 1885
Inv. No.: 1222
Oil on canvas
175 x 126 cm
Ref.: Vayer, L.: "Kossuth
alakja az egykorú
müvészetben" (Kossuth as
Depicted in the Art of His
Time). In: *Emlékkönyv
Kossuth Lajos születésének
150. évfordulójára*
(Memorial Volume in
Honour of Lajos Kossuth
Published on the 150th
Anniversary of His Birth).
I-II. Budapest, 1952. vol. 2,
pp. 460–464

**497. Portrait of Queen
Elizabeth of Hungary**
by Gyula Benczur
(1844–1920)
Around 1890
Inv. No.: 1861
Oil on canvas
142 x 94.5 cm
Ref.: "Das Zeitalter Kaiser
Franz Josephs". vol. 2.
Wien, 1987. No. 13.29

**498. Rail production in the
Diósgyőr Factory**
by Árpád Feszty
(1865–1914)
1880s
Inv. No.: T.7659
Indian ink on paper
29.2 x 40.8 cm
Ref.: Cennerné Wilhelb,
G.: 'Az Osztrák-magyar
Monarchia írásban és
képben' illusztrációi és
illusztrátorai (Illustrations
and Illustrators in the
Book "Austro-Hungarian
Empire in Writing and
Pictures". Compilation).
*FH* 8/1981. p. 61, 63, 66

**499. The first May Day
Parade in Budapest. 1890**
by Károly Cserna
(1867–after 1944)
1890s
Inv. No.: 53.573
Print on paper
4.2 x 19.3 cm
Ref.: Kiss, S.:
*Magyarország történetének
képeskönyve 1849–1945*
(An Illustrated History of

Hungary, 1849–1945).
Budapest, 1969. pp. 68–69

**500. Portrait of Kálmán
Tisza**
by Lipót Horovitz
(1839–1917)
1894
Inv. No.: 847
Oil on canvas
148 x 107 cm
Ref.: *MTKCS Catalogue*,
No. 679

**501. Portrait of Mór Jókai**
by Artur Ferraris (born in
1856)
1895
Inv. No.: 846
Oil on canvas
140 x 84 cm
Ref.: *MTKCS Catalogue*,
No. 675

**502. Portrait of Madame
Révai**
by Károly Ferenczi
(1862–1917)
1897
Inv. No.: 76.22
Oil on canvas
111 x 95.5 cm
Ref.: Genthon, I.:
*Ferenczy Károly.* Budapest,
1963. p. 54, No. 90

**503. Portrait of Ödön
Lechner**
by Bertalan Pór
(1880–1964)
1903
Inv. No.: 1008
Oil on canvas
51 x 41 cm
Ref.: *Lechner Ödön
1845–1914.* Memorial
Exhibition Held on the
140th Anniversary of the
Artist's Birth. Budapest,
1985. p. 83, No. 11

**504. View of the Servite
Church from Kristóf tér in
Pest**
by István Zádor
(1882–1963)
1945
Inv. No.: 75.43
Indian ink on
tracing-paper
20.1 x 26.4 cm
Ref.: Cennerné Wilhelmb,
G.: "A Történelmi
Képcsarnok újabban
megszerzett Zádor-anyaga"
(The Recently-acquired
Zádor Collection in the
Historical Gallery).
*A Magyar
Munkásmozgalmi Múzeum
Közleményei,* 2/1978. p. 58.

**505. Dr. László Sipőcz,
Mayor of Budapest**
by an unknown
photographer
1890s
Inv. No.: None
Collodion positive on
a curved metal plate with
a varnished surface
Diameter: 12 cm

**506. Hunt in Sárpentele.
1909**
by Ferenc Czakó, teacher
Inv.: No.: None
On the left Count
Zsigmond Széchényi is
holding a gun; behind him
is his father, Count Viktor
Széchényi, in the centre
Chichette, a French
governess; on the right are
his sisters, Countesses
Sarolta and Irma. 1909,
Sárpentele, Fejér county
Dry plate and gelatine,
glass negative 9 × 12 cm

**507. An election speech
given by Count István Tisza**
by Oszkár Kallós
1910s
Inv.: No.: 81.278
Dry plate and gelatine,
glass negative 13 × 18 cm

# Abbreviations

| | |
|---|---|
| A | Austria |
| *Acta Antiqua* | *Acta Antiqua Academiae Scientiarum* |
| *Acta ArchHung* | *Acta Archaeologica Academiae Scientiarum Hungaricae* |
| *Acta HistArt* | *Acta Historiae Artium* |
| AECO | *Archivum Europae Centro-Orientalis I.* Budapest, 1935 |
| *AÉ* | *Archaeológiai Értesítő* |
| *ArchHung* | *Archaeologia Hungarica* |
| *ArchKözl* | *Archaeológiai Közlemények* |
| *Arms and Armour* | Temesváry, F.: *Arms and Armour* Budapest, 1982 |
| *ArsHung* | *Ars Hungarica* |
| *Avar Finds* | *Avar Finds in the Hungarian National Museum.* Budapest, 1975 |
| Bachmann | Bachmann, R.: *Die alten Städtebilder.* Leipzig, 1939 |
| Bárány–Oberschall | Bárány–Oberschall, M.: *Die Sankt Stephanskrone und die Insignien des Königreiches Ungarn.* Wien, 1961, 1974 |
| *A bécsi gyűjteményekből* | *A bécsi gyűjteményekből Magyarországnak jutott tárgyak kiállítása a Magyar Nemzeti Múzeumban* (Exhibition of the Objects Granted to Hungary from the Viennese Collections, Hungarian National Museum). Budapest, 1933 |
| *BMC* | *British Museum, Catalogue of the Greek Coins of Lydia.* London, 1901 |
| Bóna, 1974 | Bóna, I.: *A középkor hajnala.* (The Dawn of the Middle Ages). Budapest, 1974 |
| Bóna, 1982–83 | Bóna, I.: "A XIX. század nagy avar leletei. – Die grossen Awarenfunden des 19. Jahrhunderts." In: *Szolnok Megyei Múzeumok Évkönyve,* 1982-83. pp. 81–161 |
| Bóna, 1986 | Bóna, I.: "Szabolcs-Szatmár megye régészeti emlékei I." (Archaeological Finds in Szabolcs-Szatmár County. Part I). In: *Szabolcs-Szatmár megye műemlékei.* Budapest, 1986. pp. 15–92 |
| Bóna: "Dáciától" | Bóna, I.: "Dáciától Erdőelvéig. A népvándorlás kora Erdélyben" (From Dacia to Erdőelve. The Age of the Great Migrations in Transylvania). In: *Erdély története* (The History of Transylvania). 3 vols. Budapest, 1986. vol. 1. |
| *BudRég* | *Budapest Régiségei* (Relics and Monuments in Budapest) |
| Cennerné | Cennerné Wilhelmb, G.: *Magyarország történetének képeskönyve 896–1849* (Hungarian History in Pictures, 896–1849). Budapest, 1962 |
| *CNH* | Réthy, L.: *Corpus Nummorum Hungariae* 2 vols. Budapest, 1899, 1907 |
| Cohen | Cohen, H.: *Description historique des monnaies médailles imperiales.* 8 vols. Paris–London, 1880–1892 |
| *ComArchHung* | *Communicationes Archaeologicae Hungariae* |
| Cz | Czechoslovakia |
| Deér | Deér, J.: *A honfoglaló magyarok* (Hungarians at the Time of the Conquest). Budapest, 1972 |
| Dessewffy | *Gróf Dessewffy Miklós barbár pénzei* (Barbarian Coins of Count Miklós Dessewffy). 4 vols. Budapest, 1910–1915 |
| Dienes | Dienes, I.: *A honfoglaló magyarok* (Hungarians at the Time of the Conquest). Budapest, 1972 |
| DissPan | *Dissertationes Pannonicae* |
| Domanig | Domanig, K.: *Die Deutsche Medaille.* Wien, 1907 |
| Ember, 1980 | V. Ember, M.: *Régi textiliák* (Old Textiles). Budapest, 1980 |
| Ember, 1981 | V. Ember, M.: *Úrihímzés.* (Aristocratic Embroidery). Budapest, 1981 |
| *FA* | *Folia Archaeologica* |
| Fehér | Fehér, G.: *Török-kori iparművészeti alkotások* (Applied Art during the Time of Ottoman Rule). Budapest, 1975 |
| Fettich, 1932 | Fettich, N.: "A szilágysomlyói második kincs–Der zweite Schatz von Szilágysomlyó." *ArchHung,* 8/1932 |
| Fettich, 1937 | Fettich, N.: "A honfoglaló magyarság fémművessége–Die Metallkunst der Landnehmenden Ungarn." *ArchHung,* 21/1937 |
| Fettich, 1953 | Fettich, N.: "A Szeged-Nagyszéksósi hun fejedelmi kísérlet–La trouvaille de tombe princiere hunnique a Szeged-Nagyszéksós." *ArchHung* 32/1953 |
| *FH* | *Folia Historica* |
| Forrer | Forrer, L.: *Biographical Dictionary of Medallists, Coin, Gem and Seal-Engravers Etc. Ancient and Modern.* 6 vols. London, 1902–1916 |
| Gábry | Gábry, Gy.: *Old Musical Instruments.* Budapest, 1976 |
| Gohl | Gohl, Ö.: "A magyar királyok koronázási érmei" (Coronation Insignia of the Hungarian Kings). *NK,* 16/1917 |
| Gritzner | Gritzner, M.: *Handbuch der Ritter und Verdienstorden aller Kulturstaaten der Welt, innershalb des XIX. Jahrhunderts.* Leipzig, 1893 |
| Habich | Habich, G.: *Die deutsche Schaumünzen des XVI. Jahrhunderts.* 4 vols. München, 1929–1934 |
| Hampel | Hampel, J.: *Alterthümer des frühen Mittelalteres in Ungarn III.* Braunschweig, 1905 |
| *Három nemzedék* | *Három nemzedék ereklyetárgyai a Magyar Nemzeti Múzeumban 1823–1875* (Relics of Three Generations in the Hungarian National Museum, 1823–1875). Budapest, 1988 |
| Hlatky | Hlatky, M.: *A magyar gyűrű* (The Hungarian Ring). Budapest, 1938 |
| Holl–Parádi | Holl, I.–Parádi, N.: *Das mittelalterliche Dorf Sarvaly.* Budapest, 1982 |
| *Hungarian Costume* | *Historic Hungarian Costume from Budapest.* Manchester, 1979 |
| Hunyady | Hunyady, I.: *Kelták a Kárpát-medencében* (Celts in the Carpathian Basin) 2 vols. Budapest, 1942–44 |
| Huszár | Huszár, L.: *Münzkatalog Ungarn.* Budapest, 1979 |
| Huszár–Procopius | Huszár, L.–Procopius, B.: *Medaillen und Plakettenkunst in Ungarn.* Budapest, 1932 |
| Hutten-Czapski | Hutten-Czapski, E.: *Catalogue de la Collection des Médailles et Monnaies Polonaises.* St. Petersburg, 1871 |
| *Az időmérés története* | *Az időmérés története* (The History of Measuring Time). Exhibition Catalogue. Budapest, 1984 |
| *The Imperial Style* | *The Imperial Style. The Fashion of the Habsburg Era.* New York, 1979 |
| Inv. No. | Inventory Reference Number |
| Kalicz | Kalicz, N.: *Clay Gods.* Budapest, 1970 |
| Kalmár | Kalmár, J.: *Régi magyar fegyverek* (Old Hungarian Arms and Armour). Budapest, 1971 |
| Kassics | Kisfaludi Kassics, I.: *Érdemkoszorúk* (Wreaths of Merit). Bécs, 1840 |
| Katz | Katz, V.: *Die Erzgebirgische Prügemedaille des XVI. Jahrhunderts.* Prag, 1932 |
| *Kiegyezés* | Körmöczi, K.: *Kiegyezés 1867* (Compromise 1867). Exhibition Catalogue of the Hungarian National Museum. Budapest, 1987 |
| Kiss | Kiss, A.: "Die Skiren im Karpatenbecken, ihre Wohnsitze und ihre materielle Hinterlassenschaft." *Acta ArchHung,* 35/1983. pp. 95–131. |

Kolba H. Kolba, J.: "A Nemzeti Múzeum ötvöstárgyai a Jankovich gyűjteményből" (Jewelery Items from the Hungarian National Museum's Jankovich Collection). In: *Jankovich Miklós a gyűjtő és mecénás* (Miklós Jankovich, Collector and Patron of the Arts), (Ed.: Belitska-Scholtz, H.) Budapest, 1985

Kovalovszki Kovalovszki, J.: *Gótikus és reneszánsz bútorok* (Gothic and Renaissance Furniture). Budapest, 1980

Kovács, 1969 Kovács, É.: "Die Grabinsignien Bélae III. und Annae von Antiochie." *Acta HistArt*, 15/1969

Kovács, 1974 Kovács, É.: *Romanesque Goldsmiths' Art*. Budapest, 1974

Kovács, 1977 Kovács, T.: *The Bronze Age in Hungary*. Budapest, 1977

Kovács–Lovag Kovács, É.–Lovag, Zs.: *The Hungarian Coronation Insignia*. Budapest, 1980

Kovrig Kovrig, I.: "Die Ostgermanen im Donauraum." In: Roth, H.: *Kunst der Völkerwanderungszeit*. Propyläen Kunstgeschichte Supplementband IV. Frankfurt/Main–Berlin–Wien, 1979

Kresz Kresz, M.: *Magyar parasztviselet* (Hungarian Peasant Costume). Budapest, 1956

László László, Gy.: "Études archéologiques sur l'histoire de la société des Avars". *ArchHung* 34/1955

Lovag Lovag, Zs.: *A középkori bronzművesség emlékei Magyarországon*. Budapest, 1979

*Magyaro tört.* *Magyarország története a honfoglalástól 1849-ig* (A History of Hungary from the Time of the Conquest to 1849). Exhibition Catalogue of the Hungarian National Museum. Budapest, 1968

Márton Márton, L.: *A korai La Tene kultúra Magyarországon* (Early La Tene Culture in Hungary). Budapest 1934

*M.Műv.* *Magyar Művészet*

*MNM, 1977* *A Magyar Nemzeti Múzeum* (The Hungarian National Museum). Published on the occasion of the 175th Anniversary of the Hungarian National Museum's Foundation (Ed.: Fülep, F.). Budapest, 1977

*Művészet, 1300–1470* *Magyarországi Művészet 1300–1470 körül* (Art in Hungary from Around 1300 to 1470) (Ed.: Marosi, E.) Budapest, 1987

*Művészet, 1780–1830* *Művészet Magyarországon 1780–1830* (Art in Hungary, 1780–1830). Exhibition Catalogue. Budapest, 1980

*Művészet, 1830–1870* *Művészet Magyarországon 1830–1870* (Art in Hungary, 1830–1870). Exhibition Catalogue. Budapest, 1981

*Művtör* *Művészettörténeti Értesítő*

*MTKCS Catalogue* *Magyar Történeti Képcsarnok Katalógusa* (Catalogue of the Historical Gallery in the Hungarian National Museum). Budapest, 1922

Németh Németh, G.: *Ónedények. Évezredek, évszázadok kincsei* (Tin Vessels. Treasures from Down the Ages), vol 2. Budapest, n.d.

*NK* *Numizmatikai Közlemények*

Oberschall Bárányné Oberschall, M.: *Magyar bútorok* (Hungarian Furniture). Budapest, 1939

Paulsen Paulsen, P.: *Die Münzprägungen der Boier. Text-Tafelband*. Leipzig–Wien, 1933

Probst Probst, G.: *Corpus nummorum Hungariae*. Graz, 1958

Ref. Reference

Resch Resch, A.: *Siebenbürgische Münzen und Medaillen*. Hermannstadt, 1901

*RégFüz* *Régészeti Füzetek*

*RIC* *The Roman Imperial Coinage*. 9 vols. London, 1923–1981

Rizzo Rizzo, G.: *Monete Greche della Sicilia*. Roma, 1986

Rómer Rómer, F.: "Az ozorai kincs" (The Treasure of Ozora). *AÉ*, 5/1871. pp. 292–293

R Romania

Rózsa, 1953 Rózsa, Gy.: "Czetter Sámuel." In: *A Magyar Művészettörténeti Munkaközösség Évkönyve* (Yearbook of the Hungarian Art History Team). Budapest, 1953

Rózsa, 1963 Rózsa, Gy.: *Budapest régi látképei 1493–1800* (Old Views of Budapest 1493–1800). Budapest, 1963

Rózsa, 1974 Rózsa, Gy.: "Friedrich Bernhard Werner magyarországi vedutái" (Vedutes by Friedrich Bernhard Werner in Hungary). *Művtör*, 23/1974. pp. 28–48

Rózsa, 1977 Rózsa, Gy.: *A Történelmi Képcsarnok legszebb festményei* (The Finest Paintings in the Historical Gallery of the Hungarian National Museum). Budapest, 1977

Rózsa, 1986 Rózsa, Gy.: "Rohbock képeiről" (On Rohbock's Pictures). In: *Magyarország és Erdély eredeti képekben* (Hungary and Transylvania in Original Pictures). Text accompanying the facsimile edition. Budapest, 1986

Rózsa–Spira Rózsa, Gy.–Spira, Gy.: *Negyvennyolc a kortársak szemével* (Eighteen Forty-eight As Seen Through the Eyes of Contemporaries). Budapest, 1973

Schoen Schoen, A.: *Buda-pesti képek. Könyvek Csillag Béla gyűjteményében* (Views of Buda-Pest. Books in the Collection of Béla Csillag). Budapest, 1936

*SNG Copp.* *Sylloge Nummorum Graecorum. The Royal Collection of Coins and Medals. Danish National Museum*. Sicily Section, Copenhagen, 1942

*Stpl* *Katalog der Münzen- und Medaillen-Stempelsammlung des K.K. Hauptmünzamtes in Wien*. 4 vols. Wien, 1901–1906

U Ukraine

vers. version

*Waffenschätze* Temesváry, F.: *Waffenschätze Prunkwaffen*. Budapest, 1982

Weszerle Weszerle, J.: *Hátrahagyott érmészeti táblái*. Pest, 1873

Y Yugoslavia

# Hungarian Place-names
## as Used Today

| | | | |
|---|---|---|---|
| Apahida | Apahida, Cluj County, R. | Liptótepla | Liptovská Tepla, Cz. |
| Bácsordas | Karavukovo, Y. | Losonc | Lučenes, Cz. |
| Bácstóváros | Tovariševo, Y. | Medvedze | Medvedze nad Dravkoǔ, Cz. |
| Bártfa | Bardejov, Cz. | Nadab | Nădab, R. |
| Beregszász | Beregovo, U. | Nagybánya | Baia Mare, R. |
| Beszterce | Bistriţa, R. | Nagybobróc | Bobrovec, Cz. |
| Besztercebánya | Banská Bystrica, Cz. | Nagyszeben | Sibiu, R. |
| Bonchida | Bonţida, R. | Nagyvárad | Oradea, R. |
| Brassó | Braşov, R. | Nemesvölgy | Edelstal, A. |
| Bulcs | Bâlci, R. | Nyitraivánka | Ivanka pri Nitre, Cz. |
| Csicser | Čičarovce, Cz. | Ottlaka | Grăniceri, R. |
| Csuny | Čunovo, Cz. | Pécska | Pecica, R. |
| Érsekújvár | Nové Zámky, Cz. | Pozsony | Bratislava, Cz. |
| Fönlak | Felnac, R. | Rimaszombat | Rimavská Sobota, Cz. |
| Galgóc | Hlohovec, Cz. | Rodostó | Tekirdağ, T. |
| Hercegmárok | Gajić, Y. | Szendrő | Smederevo, Y. |
| Holics | Holič, Cz. | Szepesbéla | Spišská Bela, Cz. |
| Igló | Spišska Nová Ves, Cz. | Szepeskörtvélyes | Spišsky Hrušov, Cz. |
| Jolsva | Jelšava, Cz. | Szilágysomlyó | Simleul Silvaniei, R. |
| Kassa | Košce, Cz. | Szolyva | Szvaljava, U. |
| Keresztúri puszta | Jaša Tomič, Y. | Tarpatak | Studenỳ potok, Cz. |
| Késmárk | Kežmarok, Cz. | Memesvár | Timişoara, R. |
| Kiskőszeg | Batina, Cz. | Titel | Titel, Y |
| Kolozsvár | Cluj-Napoca, R. | Verespatak | Roşia Montană, R. |
| Kosztolác | Kostolac, Y. | Vízakna | Ocna Sibiului, R. |
| Körmöcbánya | Kremnica, Cz. | Vörösmart | Zmajevác, Y. |
| Lőcse | Levoča, Cz. | Zilah | Zalău, R. |
| Liptónádasd | Trstené, Cz. | | |

Printed in Hungary
Kossuth Printing House, Budapest